Warwickshire

Warwickshire

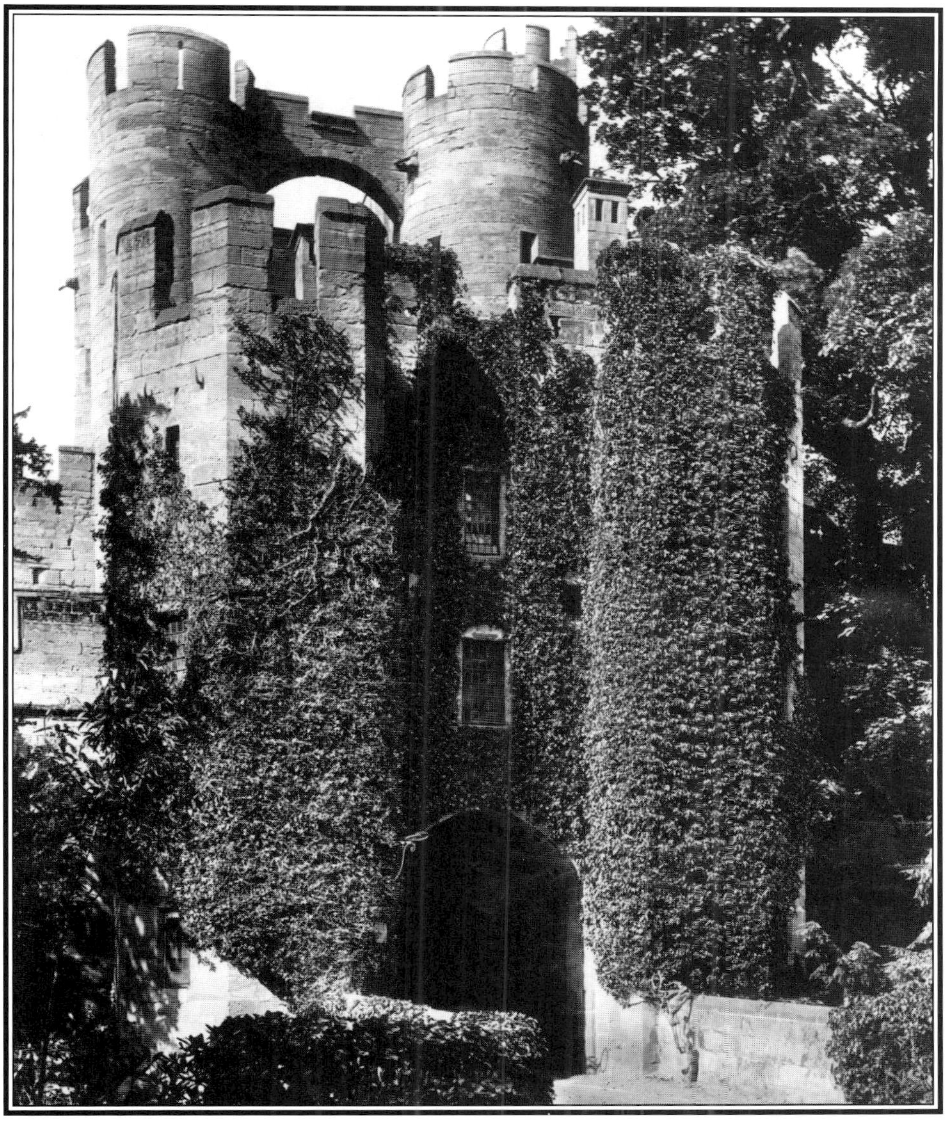

Clive Hardy

Waterton Press Limited

First published in the United Kingdom in 1999 by
Frith Publishing an imprint of Waterton Press Limited

British Library Cataloguing in Publication Data

Clive Hardy
Warwickshire

ISBN 1-84125-049-x

Reproductions of all the photographs in this book are available as framed or mounted prints. For more information please contact The Francis Frith Collection at the address below quoting the title of this book and the page number and photograph number or title.

The Francis Frith Collection,
'Friths Barn', Teffont, Salisbury, Wiltshire, SP3 5QP
Tel: 01722 716376
E mail: bookprints@francisfrith.com
Web pages: www.francisfrith.com

Typeset in Bembo Semi Bold

Printed and bound in Great Britain by
WBC Limited, Bridgend, Glamorgan.

Contents

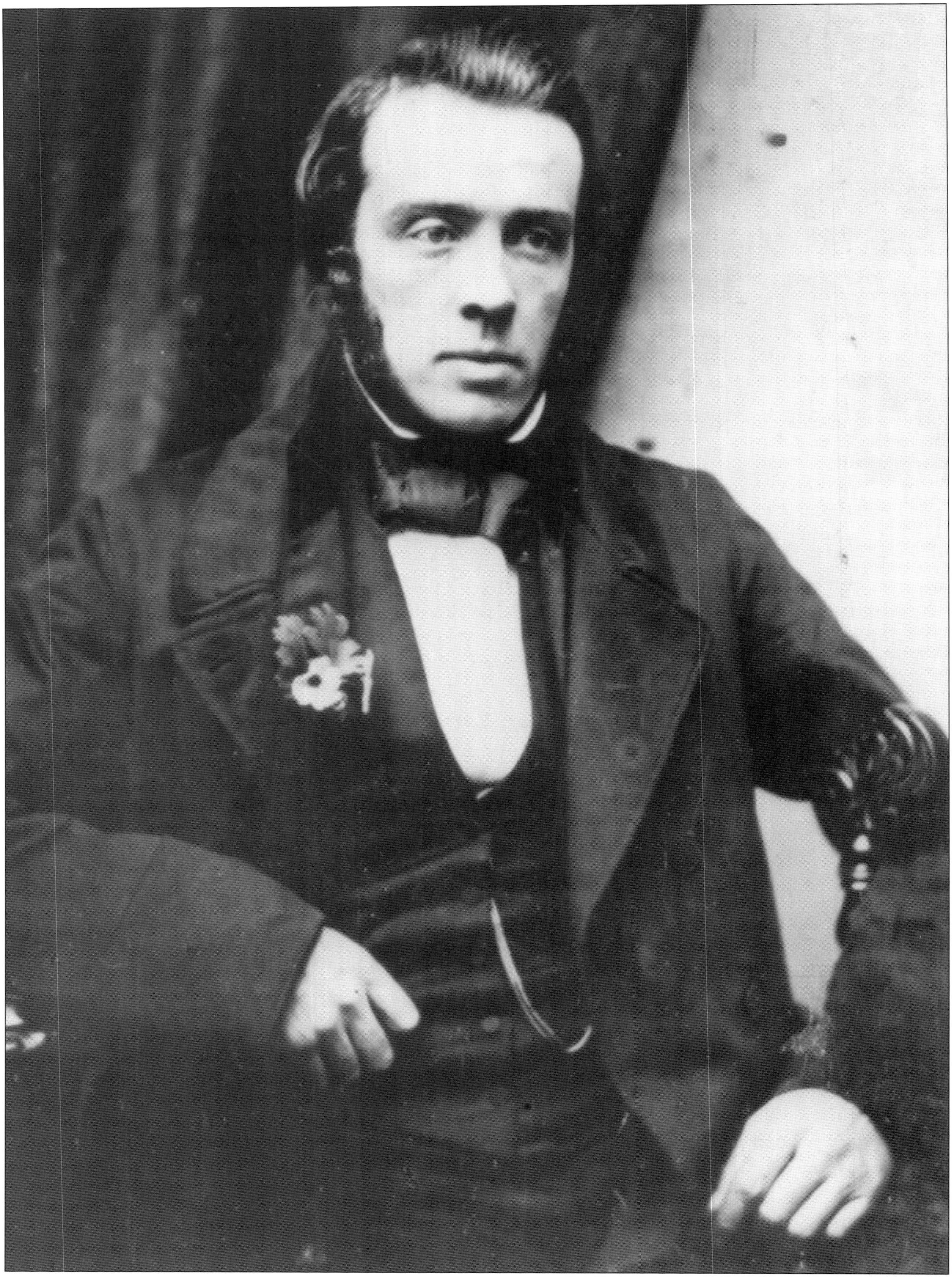

Francis Frith 1822-1898

Introduction

Francis Frith: A Victorian Pioneer

Francis Frith, the founder of the world famous photographic archive was a complex and multitudinous man. A devout Quaker and a highly successful and respected Victorian businessman he was also a flamboyant character.

By 1855 Frith had already established a wholesale grocery business in Liverpool and sold it for the astonishing sum of £200,000, equivalent of over £15,000,000 today. Now a multi-millionaire he was able to indulge in his irresistible desire to travel. As a child he had pored over books penned by early explorers, and his imagination had been stirred by family holidays to the sublime mountain regions of Wales and Scotland. "What a land of spirit-stirring and enriching scenes and places!" he had written. He was to return to these scenes of grandeur in later years to "recapture the thousands of vivid and tender memories", but with a very different purpose. Now in his thirties, and captivated by the new science of photography, Frith set out on a series of pioneering journeys to the Middle East, that occupied him from 1856 until 1860.

He took with him a specially-designed wicker carriage which acted as camera, dark-room and sleeping chamber. These far-flung journeys were full of intrigue and adventure. In his life story, written when he was sixty-three, Frith tells of being held captive by bandits, and fighting "an awful midnight battle to the very point of exhaustion and surrender with a deadly pack of hungry, wild dogs". He bargained for several weeks with a "mysterious priest" over a beautiful seven-volume illuminated Koran, which is now in the British Museum. Wearing full arab costume, Frith arrived at Akaba by camel seventy years before Lawrence of Arabia, where he encountered "desert princes and rival sheikhs, blazing with jewel-hilted swords".

During these extraordinary adventures he was assiduously exploring the desert regions of the Nile and recording the antiquities and people with his camera, Frith was the first photographer ever to travel beyond the sixth cataract. Africa, we must remember, was still the "Dark Continent", and Stanley and Livingstone's famous meeting was a decade into the future. The conditions for picture taking confound belief. He laboured for hours on end in his dark-room in the sweltering heat, while the volatile collodion chemicals fizzed dangerously in their trays. Often he was forced to work in tombs and caves where conditions were cooler.

Back in London he exhibited his photographs and was "rapturously cheered" by the Royal Society. His reputation as a photographer was made overnight. His photographs were issued in albums by James S Virtue and William MacKenzie, and published simultaneously in London and New York. An eminent historian has likened their impact on the population of the time to that on our own generation of the first photographs taken on the surface of the moon.

Characteristically, Frith spotted the potential to create a new business as a specialist publisher of photographs. In 1860 he married Mary Ann Rosling and set out to photograph every city, town and village in Britain. For the next thirty years Frith travelled the country by train and by pony and trap, producing photographs that were keenly bought by the millions of Victorians who, because of the burgeoning rail network, were beginning to enjoy holidays and day trips to Britain's seaside resorts and beauty spots.

To meet the demand he gathered together a team of up to twelve photographers, and also published the work of independent artist-photographers of the reputation of Roger Fenton and Francis Bedford. Together with clerks and photographic printers he employed a substantial staff at his Reigate studios. To gain an understanding of the scale of Frith's business one only has to look at the catalogue issued by Frith & Co. in 1886. It runs to some 670 pages listing not only many thousands of views of the British Isles but also photographs of most major European countries, and China, Japan, the USA and Canada. By 1890 Frith had created the greatest specialist photographic publishing company in the world.

He died in 1898 at his villa in Cannes, his great project still growing. His sons, Eustace and Cyril, took over the task, and Frith & Co. continued in business for another seventy years, until by 1970 the archive contained over a third of a million pictures of 7,000 cities, towns and villages.

The photographic record he has left to us stands as a living monument to a remarkable and very special man.

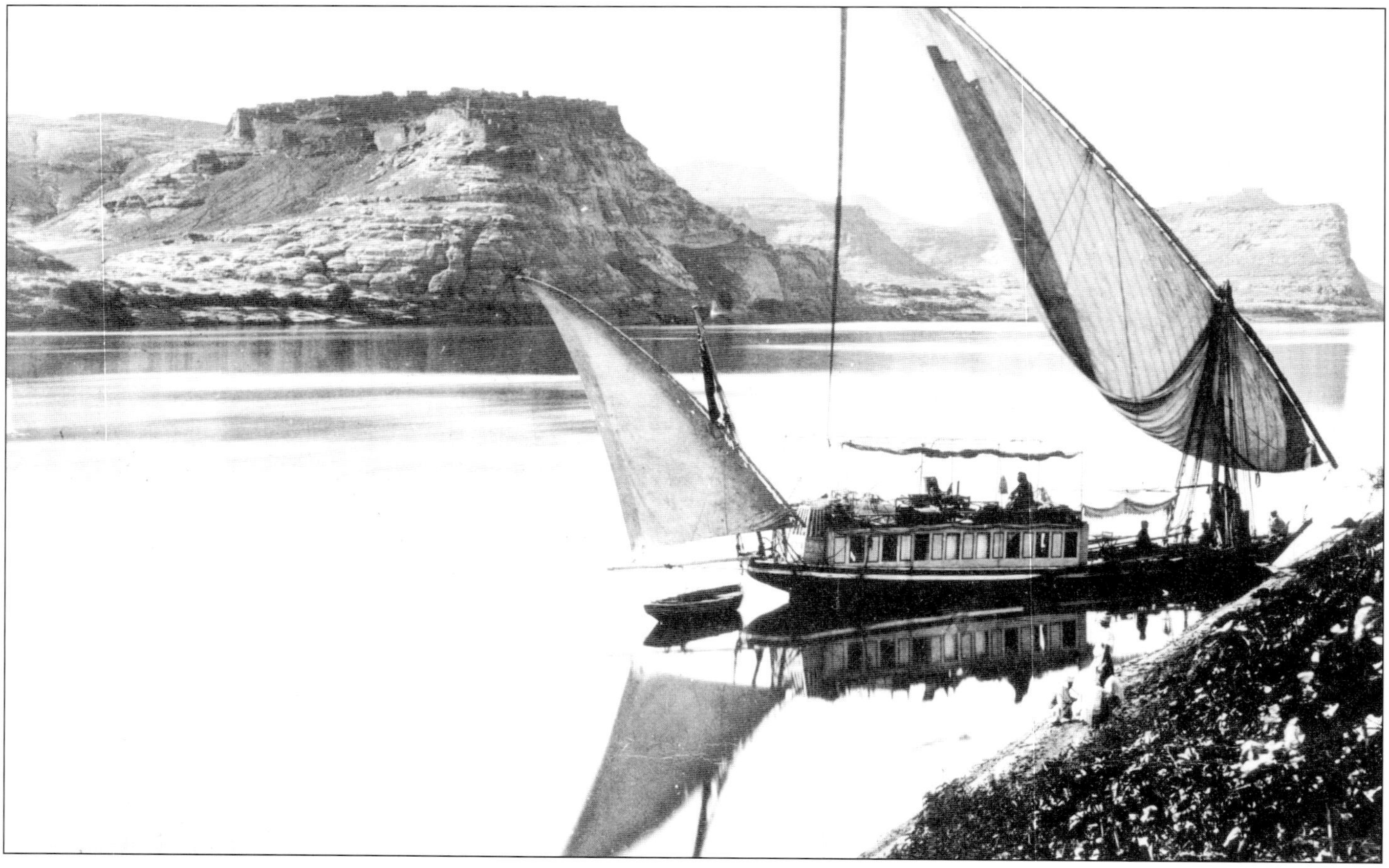

Frith's dhow in Egypt *c.*1857

INTRODUCTION TO WARWICKSHIRE

In 1974 local government reorganisation led to the creation of a number of large metropolitan boroughs, such as Merseyside and Greater Manchester. The West Midlands was created by taking territory off Warwickshire and Staffordshire. Warwickshire lost its two great cathedral cities of Birmingham and Coventry, and with them the county's manufacturing and industrial heartland. With the decline of the Warwickshire coalfield, the county was left with little in the way of industry, save for Nuneaton and Rugby. Agriculture was and still is important, and many towns owed their early wealth to sheep and wool.

The north of the county was once covered with woods but most were cut down during the early years of the industrial revolution. The Forest of Arden, on the other hand, covers over 220 square miles, but it is not a forest in the modern sense. The word forest used to mean any stretch of wild country, the woods and copses broken up by farms, villages, heaths and common land.

In the north of the county is Atherstone, where Henry of Lancaster stayed on the eve of the Battle of Bosworth. Atherstone is also where Shrovetide football is still played through the streets of the town. The only other town to carry on the tradition is Ashbourne, Derbyshire, though it survived in Derby itself until finally banned in 1846. Hence the expression a 'Derby game', when two local teams play one another.

A few miles to the south-east is Nuneaton, the name of which is derived from a priory founded in 1150. The construction of the Coventry Canal in the late-eighteenth century and the fact that Nuneaton was later a busy railway junction, made the town an attractive proposition for manufacturers. There were coal mines, brick and tile works, iron works, worsted factories, ribbon makers and cotton and silk goods manufacturers.

Modern Warwickshire's only other manufacturing centre of any consequence is Rugby. Originally a parish of Clifton-on-Dunsmore, Rugby had gained its own identity by the time the Domesday Book was being compiled. It was the founding of Rugby School in 1567 that led to the town's growth, and industrialisation came with the Oxford Canal and the railways.

To the south of the great bulge of the West Midlands lies the heart of present-day Warwickshire, centred on Warwick itself together with Kenilworth, Leamington Spa and Stratford-upon-Avon all close-by.

In Kenilworth and Warwick are two of England's most famous castles: Kenilworth, a majestic ruin, and Warwick, a stately home second only to Windsor. Around the year 1122 Henry I gave Kenilworth to his chamberlain and treasurer Geoffrey de Clinton. Over the next few years, de Clinton is thought to have built a motte and bailey; but it was his son who set about the task of transforming Kenilworth by building its stone keep and defensive wall.

During the reign of Henry II, the de Clintons leased Kenilworth to the Crown, who eventually obtained ownership outright. Under the Plantagenets massive sums were spent to turn Kenilworth into one of the greatest fortresses in the Midlands. The Inchford and Finham brooks were dammed to create water defences on three sides, which covered a total of 111 acres.

In 1248 Henry III gave Kenilworth to his sister Eleanor and her husband Simon de Montfort. By the 1260s de Montfort was leading the barons against the King; it could only end on the field of battle. At Evesham on 4 August 1265, the last battle of the Barons' War was fought, ending in defeat and death for de Montfort. The remnants of the rebel army retreated to Kenilworth where they withstood a six-month siege, surrendering only when supplies had been exhausted and disease had broken out. The castle was once again in royal hands and was given to Henry III's younger son Edmund, founder of the House of Lancaster. In 1399 the castle became state property once more with the accession of the Lancastrian Henry IV.

Over the next 200 years or so Kenilworth was slowly transformed from a fortress to a palace. John of Gaunt spent large sums building a banqueting hall, residential apartments and a chapel. Henry VIII ordered structures on the south side of the inner ward demolished and had them replaced with a building known as King Henry's Lodgings.

The last building phase came after 1563 when Elizabeth I presented Kenilworth to her favourite, Robert Dudley. He was responsible for building Leicester's Gate and some buildings at the south-east corner of the inner ward. Kenilworth returned to the Crown during the reign of James I when it was bought back for £14,000. However it was hardly ever used and in 1626 it was leased to the Earl of Monmouth. The castle may well have already been in a serious state of disrepair when it was ordered to be slighted by Parliament in 1648. The north side of the keep was blown up and breaches blasted in the outer walls. At the end of the Civil War, Kenilworth was given to a group of officers in lieu of pay. They divided the land between themselves, a certain Colonel Hawkesworth draining the lake for pasture. After the Restoration the castle was returned to the Crown, though Charles II presented it to the family of the Earl of Clarendon. They could do little with it and nature was allowed to take its course.

The history of Warwick Castle is somewhat different. It was Henry de Newburgh, one of Henry I's councillors, who was responsible for building a large motte and bailey on the site of the present castle. Before his death in 1123, de Newburgh may well have replaced his wooden keep with a stone-built shell keep, and either he or his son replaced the palisading with a stone wall.

Eventually the male line of the de Newburghs became extinct and by 1263 the castle was in the hands of William Maudit, the son of the last earl's aunt Alicia. Drawn into the Royalist cause during the Barons' War, Earl William was attacked by de Montfort's troops from Kenilworth. Warwick was sacked, the de Newburgh fortifications being completely destroyed.

Maudit died in 1268, the earldom passing to the son of his sister who had married William Beauchamp. The Beauchamps set about the complete rebuilding of Warwick, though much of what remains today dates from the second half of the fourteenth century and the rebuilding undertaken by Sir Fulke Greville in the seventeenth century. Sir Fulke rebuilt the residential block, which overlooks the river on the south side of the castle. Warwick was spared from being slighted after the Civil War, as the second Lord Brooke had fought for Parliament and had been killed at Lichfield.

Another link with Warwickshire's warlike past is a round tower built in 1750 at Edge Hill as a memorial to the Civil War battle fought there on 23 October 1642. Charles I was marching toward London, leaving Parliament little choice but to attempt to intercept him. Parliament charged the Earl of Essex with the task. Both sides had only the vaguest of ideas where the other was. Just how close they were to one another was discovered at the village of Wormleighton, when quartermasters from both armies met in the street.

Essex had 14,800 troops, while the king's forces numbered 14,300. The Parliamentarians had two things in their favour. Firstly, they were better equipped and armed due to Parliament having secured the weapons held in the magazines at the Tower of London and at Hull. Secondly, they had the support of the locals who, where possible, gave the troops food, drink and shelter. The Royalists were left to fend for themselves.

The battle itself was a shambles, though it did involve some bloody hand-to-hand fighting during which the Knight Marshal, Sir Edmund Varney was killed and the Banner Royal captured. Neither side could claim a victory, though Essex had failed to stop the King's march on London.

As early as January 1643 a pamphlet entitled *Apparitions and Prodigious Noyses of War and Battels seen on Edge Hill near Keinton in Warwickshire* was published. This was the first account of the ghostly re-enactments of the battle which have been reported over the past 350 years. King Charles sent a party under Colonel Kirke to Edge Hill to investigate. When Kirke returned he reported that they had witnessed the battle being refought and had been able to identify some of the people taking part, including Sir Edmund Varney.

But for most people today Warwickshire is about Stratford-upon-Avon and William Shakespeare. Stratford, which originally built its wealth on sheep, is now the most visited literary shrine in the world. The first Shakespeare festival was organised by the actor David Garrick in 1769, but it was not until 1824 that the Shakespeare Club was founded. In 1827 the town's first Shakespeare Theatre was opened in Chapel Lane but proved to be a financial disaster, and it was 37 years before another festival was held. The Shakespeare Memorial Association was founded in 1874 and the annual Shakespeare festival began with the opening of a new theatre in 1879.

William Shakespeare was born in a house in Henley Street, Stratford-upon-Avon, on 23 April 1564. In his day the building was really two houses: one where the family lived, the other where John Shakespeare worked as a glover and wool merchant. Over the years there were many changes. The family home finished up as a butcher's shop and John Shakespeare's wool shop became an inn. Even so it is thought that the timber framework, floors and the internal walls remained unaltered from William's day.

In 1848 the buildings were purchased for restoration into a style representative of the period when the Bard was alive. One of the things missing from the restored building is the muck-heap outside the front door. Apparently John Shakespeare was fined on a number of occasions for not having the evil-smelling mound cleared away.

There was once another house in the town where Shakespeare lived. In 1597 he purchased a large house in Church Street known as New Place. He retired here in 1609 at the age of 45. This house was said to have been built around the year 1490 by Sir Hugh Clopton but it was demolished between 1755-59 by the Reverend Francis Gastrell. Gastrell was so full of his own importance that he even cut down the poet's mulberry tree in 1756 to avoid 'the importunities of visitors.'

CHAPTER 1

NUNEATON

Once famous for the manufacture of ribbons, Nuneaton's industrial base diversified to include ironworks, worsted factories, cotton and silk goods. There were also coal mines, brickworks and tile making. The town's name derives from a priory founded in 1150.

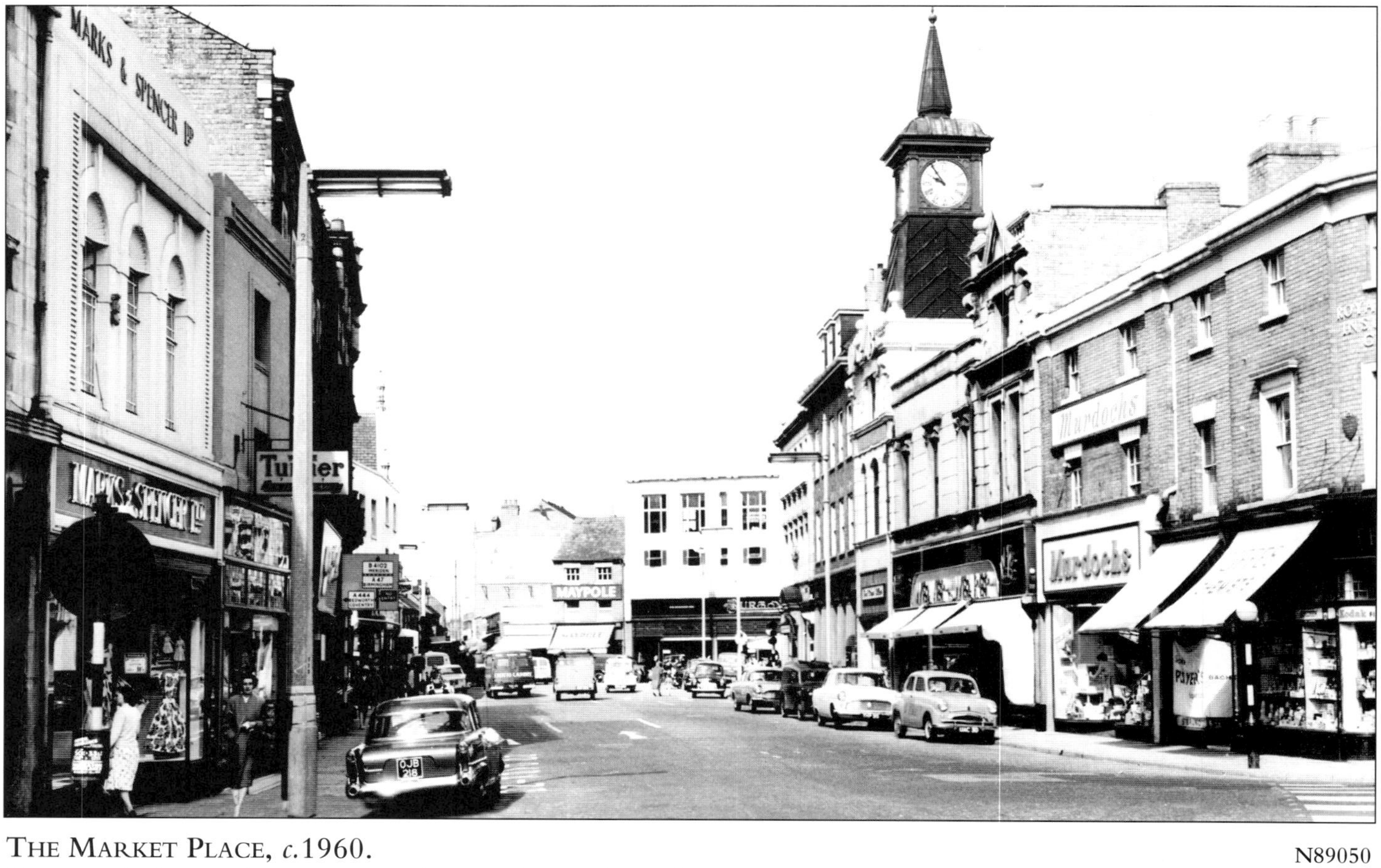

THE MARKET PLACE, *c*.1960. N89050

Nuneaton's first market was granted to the local prioress by Henry III. Among the market traders who used to draw the crowds were Mrs Gee, who literally sold crockery at knock-down prices by shouting out the price and banging on an old tea chest. There was also a man who sold foot oils. He demonstrated the effectiveness of his products by jumping barefoot on a wooden block studded with nails.

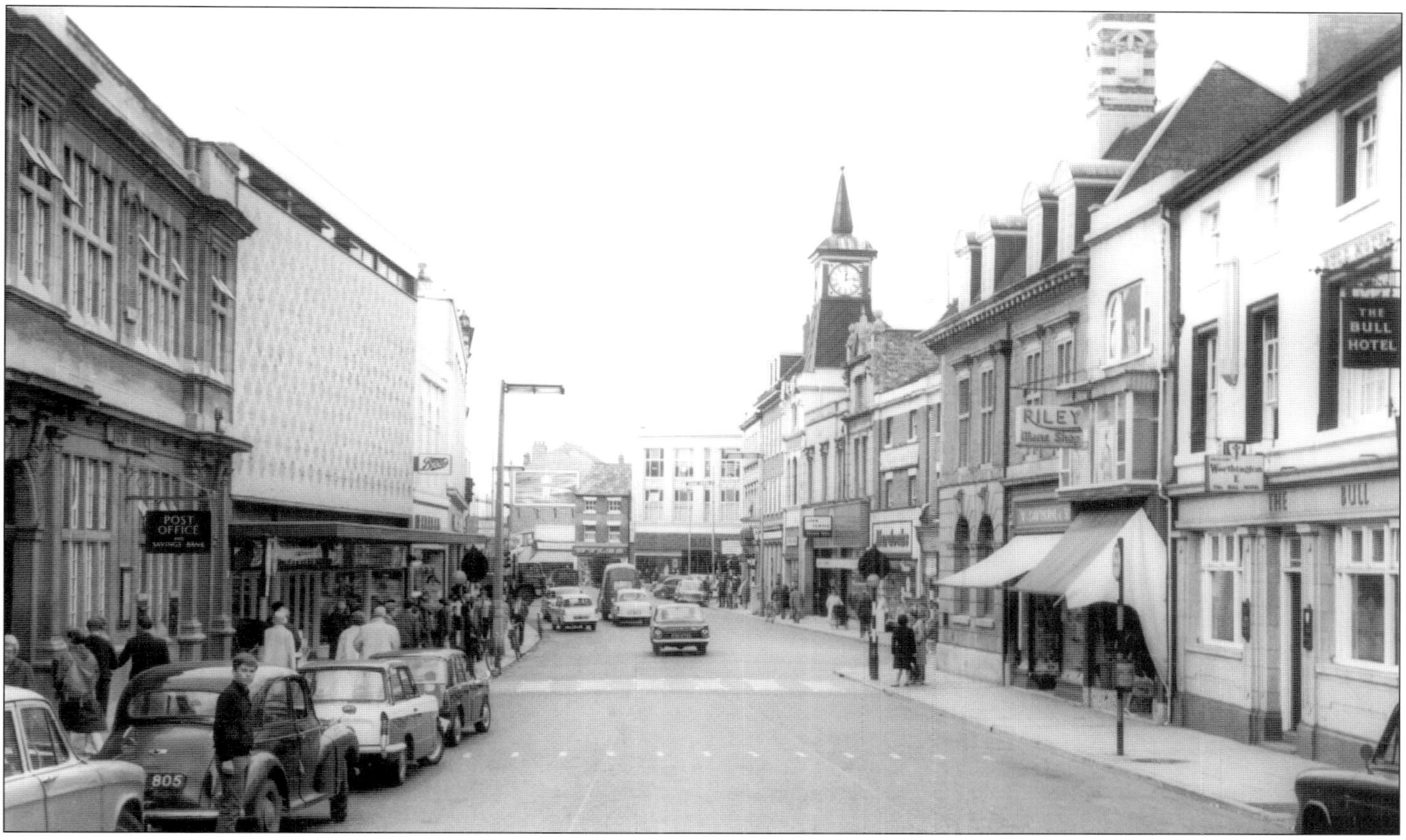

THE MARKET PLACE, *c.*1965 N89084

In this view, Market Place shows signs of a limited amount of redevelopment. A new retail block has been built between the post office and Marks & Spencer, replacing Lesters and the White Swan. Boots has moved from its previous location next to Woolworths.

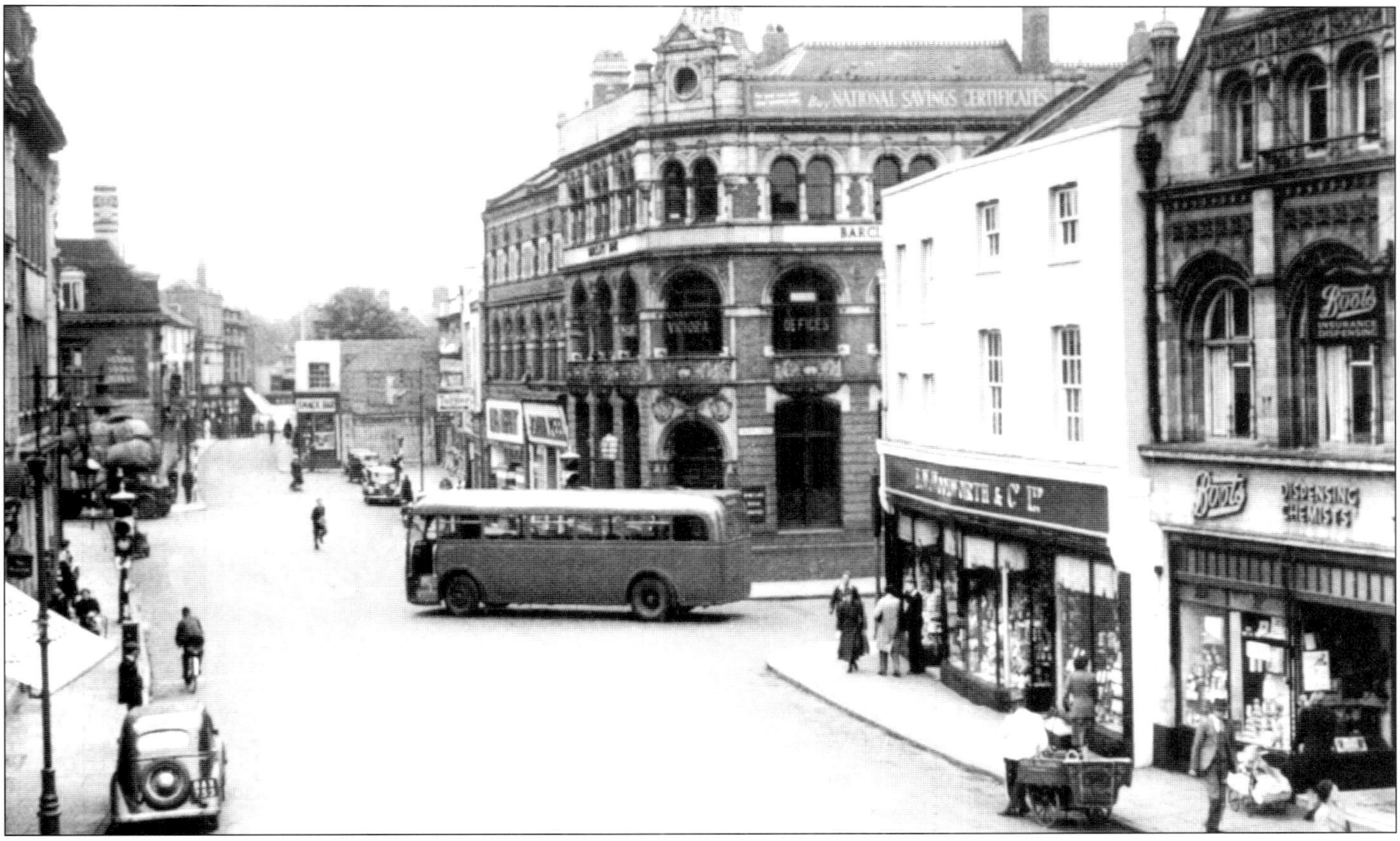

TOWN CENTRE, *c.*1960. N89401

A Midland Red bus makes its way through the town. The bus station was built on the site where the amusement fairs used to set up when they came to town. If the fairs were particularly big, rides and stalls would spill over and occupy land next to the cattle market.

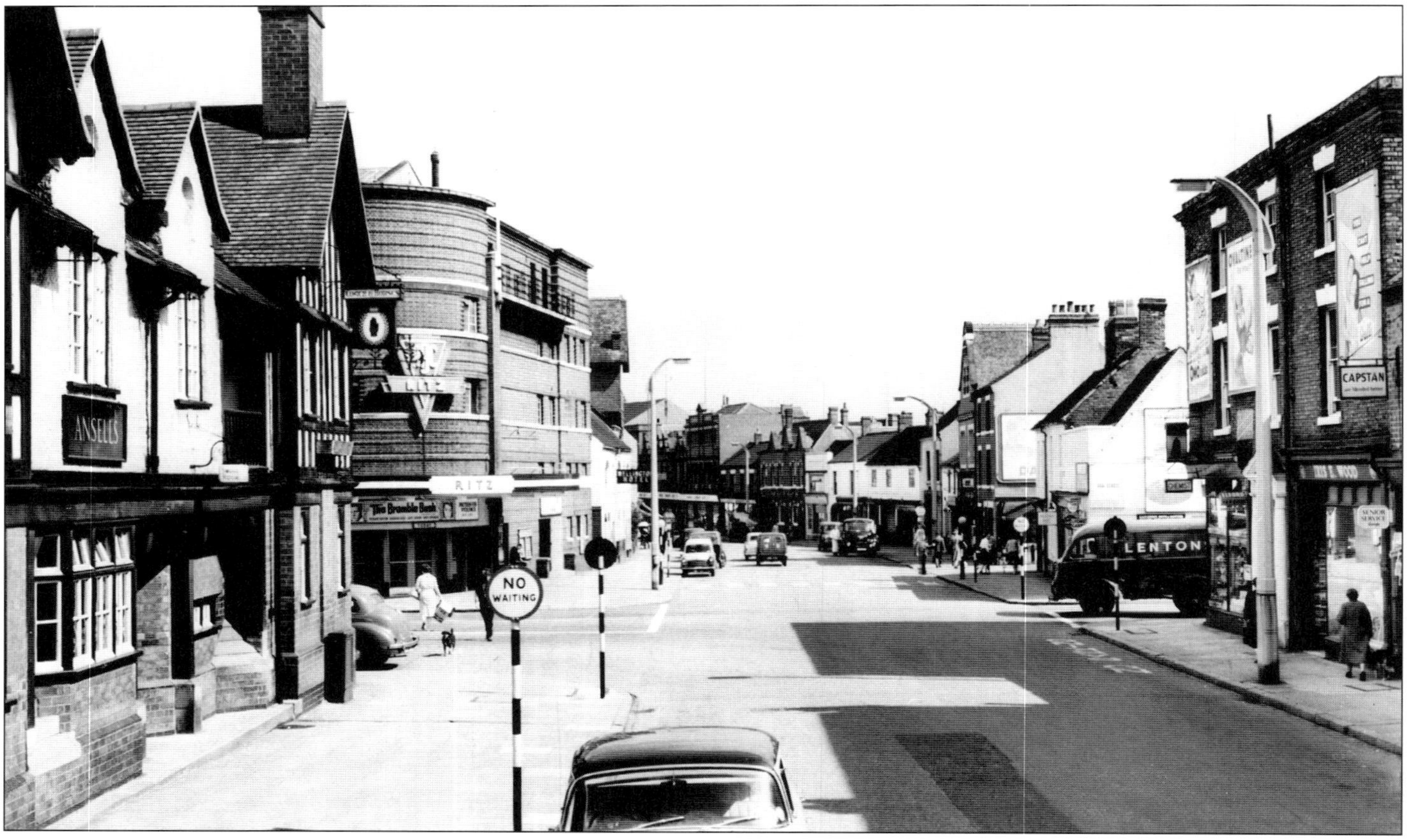

ABBEY STREET, *c.*1960. N89038

It was in Abbey Street during the Great War that Palladinos had their ice-cream business. Michael Palladino used to go round the town with his ice-cream barrow and charged a penny for a wafer and just a halfpenny for a cup.

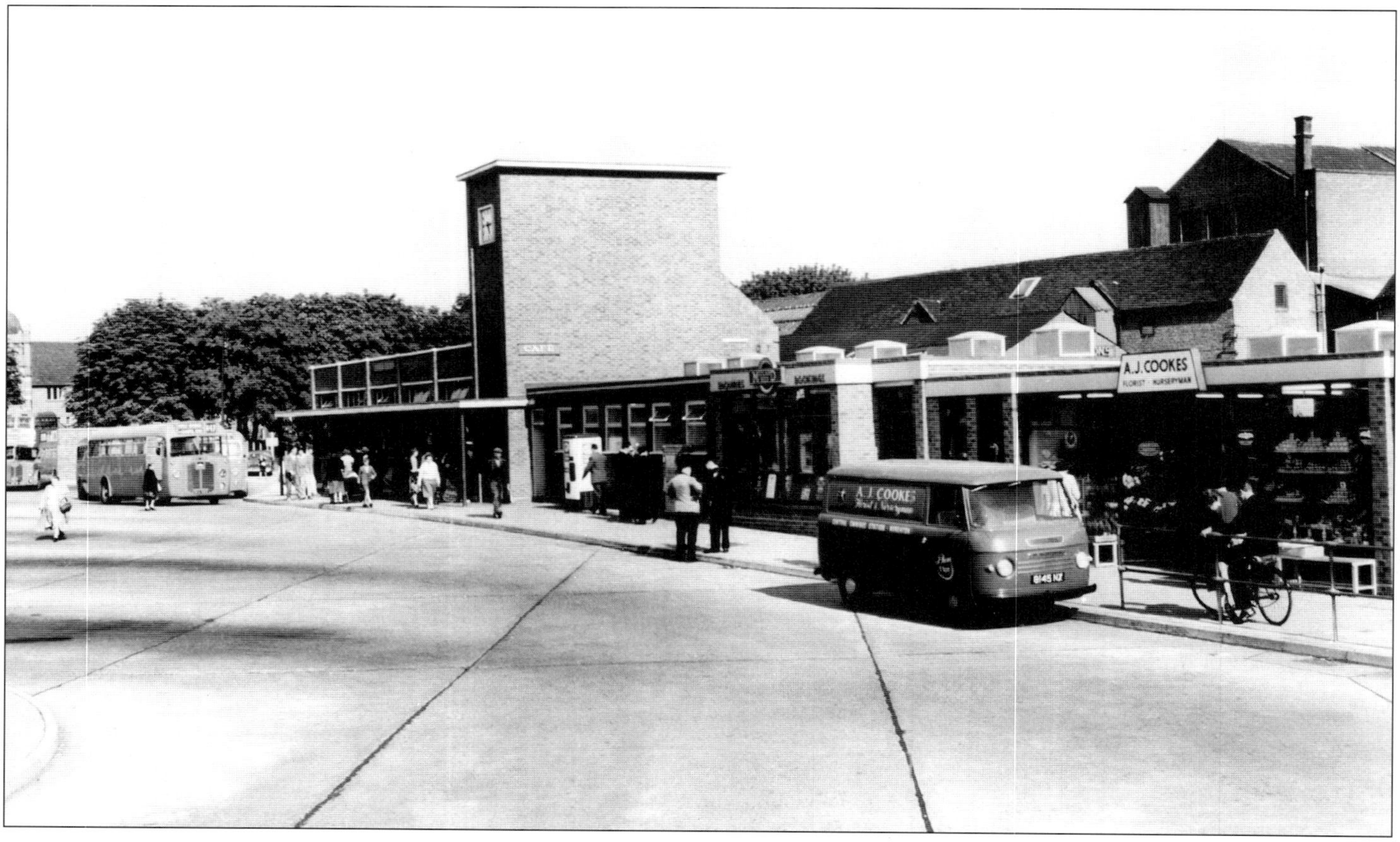

NUNEATON BUS STATION, *c.*1960. N89044

Until the late-1920s there was only a handful of regular bus services around Nuneaton. When Midland Red started operating in the area it bought out the local firms with the exception of Monty Moreton, who continued to run his services to Hinckley.

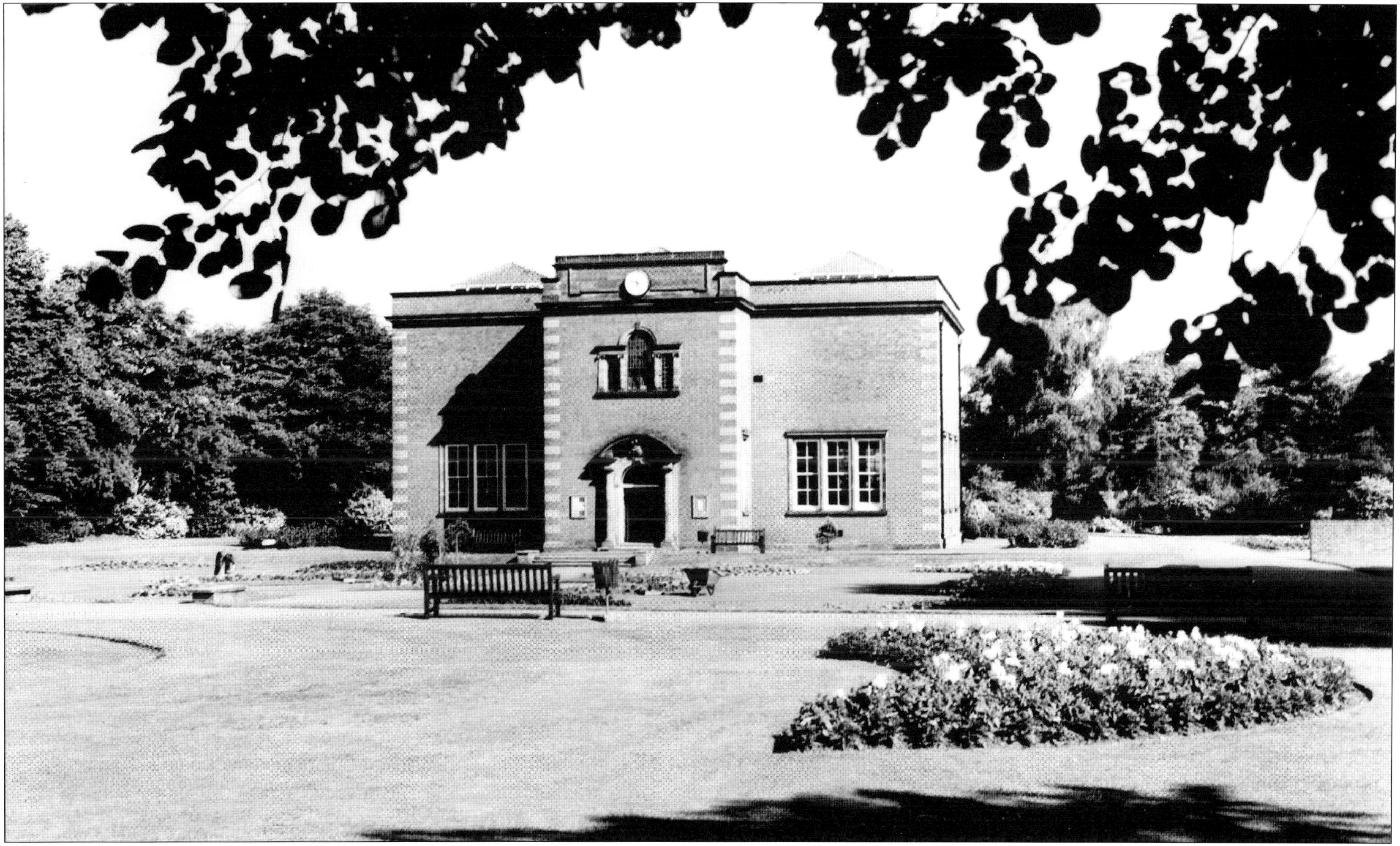

THE ART GALLERY AND MUSEUM, RIVERSLEY PARK, *c.*1960. N89046

The archaeological exhibits range from prehistoric to medieval times and were all discovered locally. There is also a collection dedicated to the novelist George Eliot.

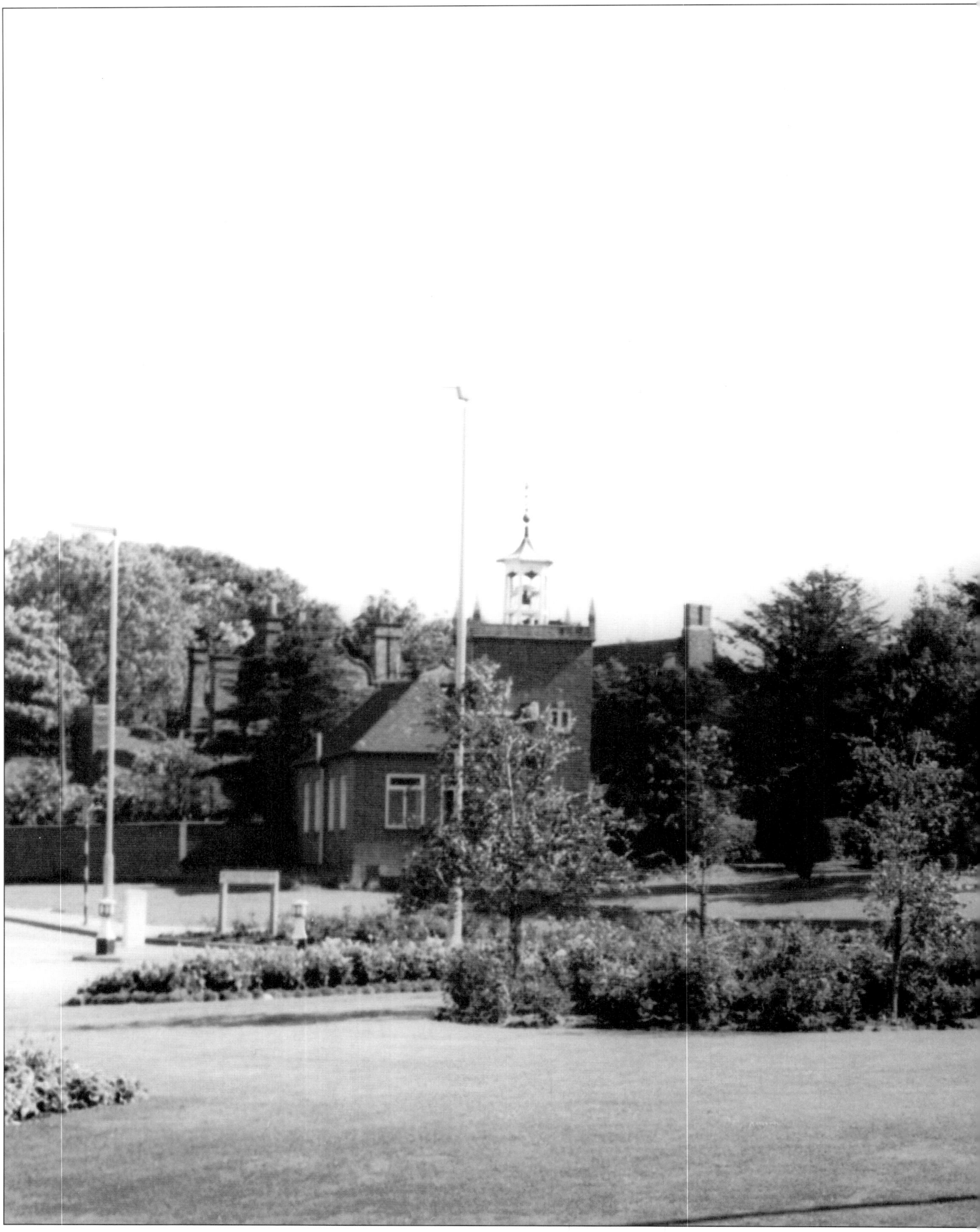

THE CHURCH OF ST NICHOLAS, *c.*1960.
The church consisted of a nave, chancel and aisles, with a square embattled tower having pinnacles at the angles.

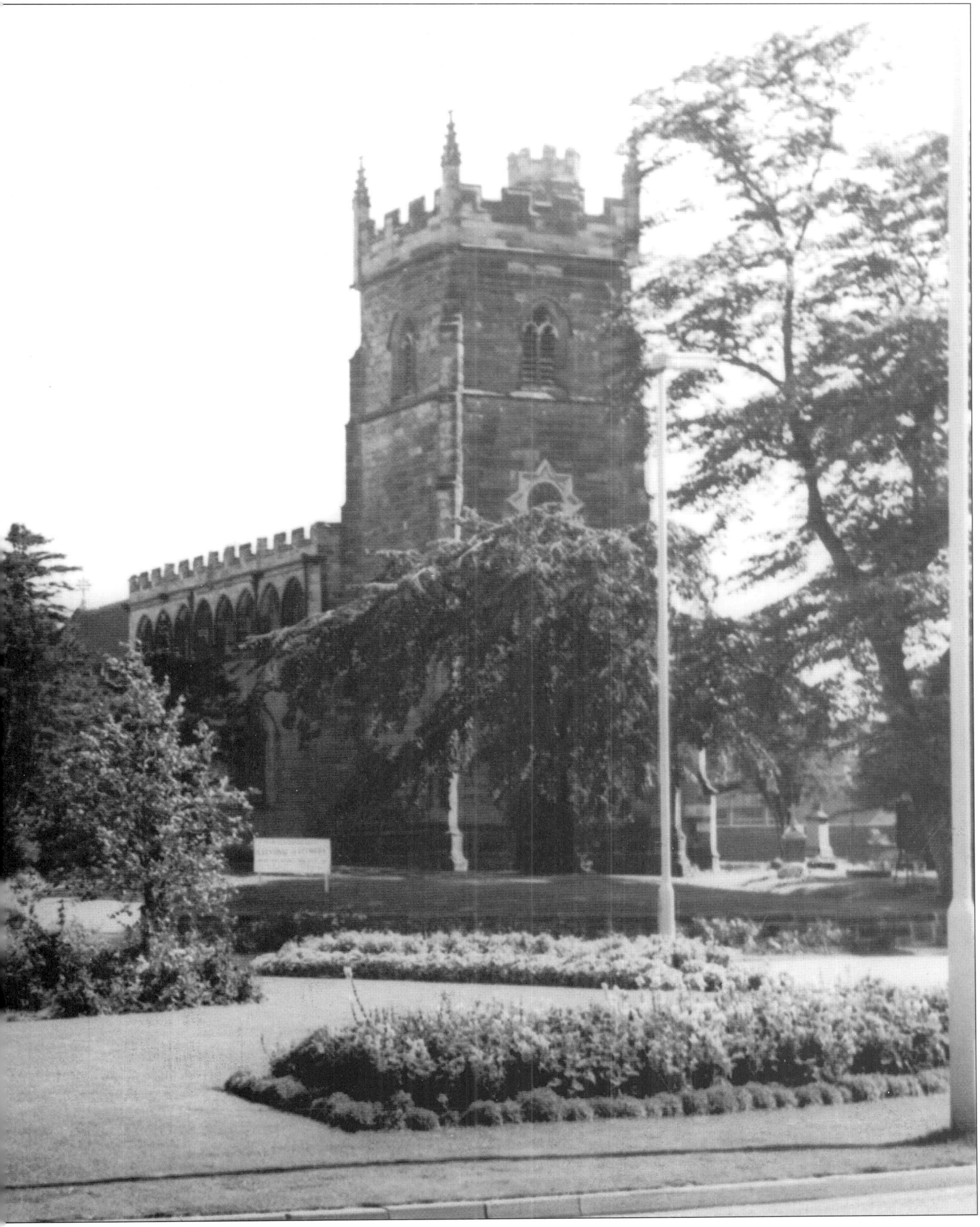

N89082

Chapter 2

RUGBY

It was the founding of Rugby School in 1567 that led to the town's growth. The endowment was bequeathed in the will of Laurence Sheriff and comprised his manor house in Rugby, one-third of his lands in Middlesex and the parsonage of Brownsover. The school had moved to its present site to the south of the town by 1750 and rebuilding began in 1809. Under the guidance of Dr Thomas Arnold, headmaster from 1828-1842, Rugby grew to become one of the country's leading public schools. Arnold became famous thanks to two books which proved influencial in educational circles. They were Arthur Stanley's *Life and Correspondence of Dr Thomas Arnold* and Thomas Hughes's *Tom Brown's Schooldays.*

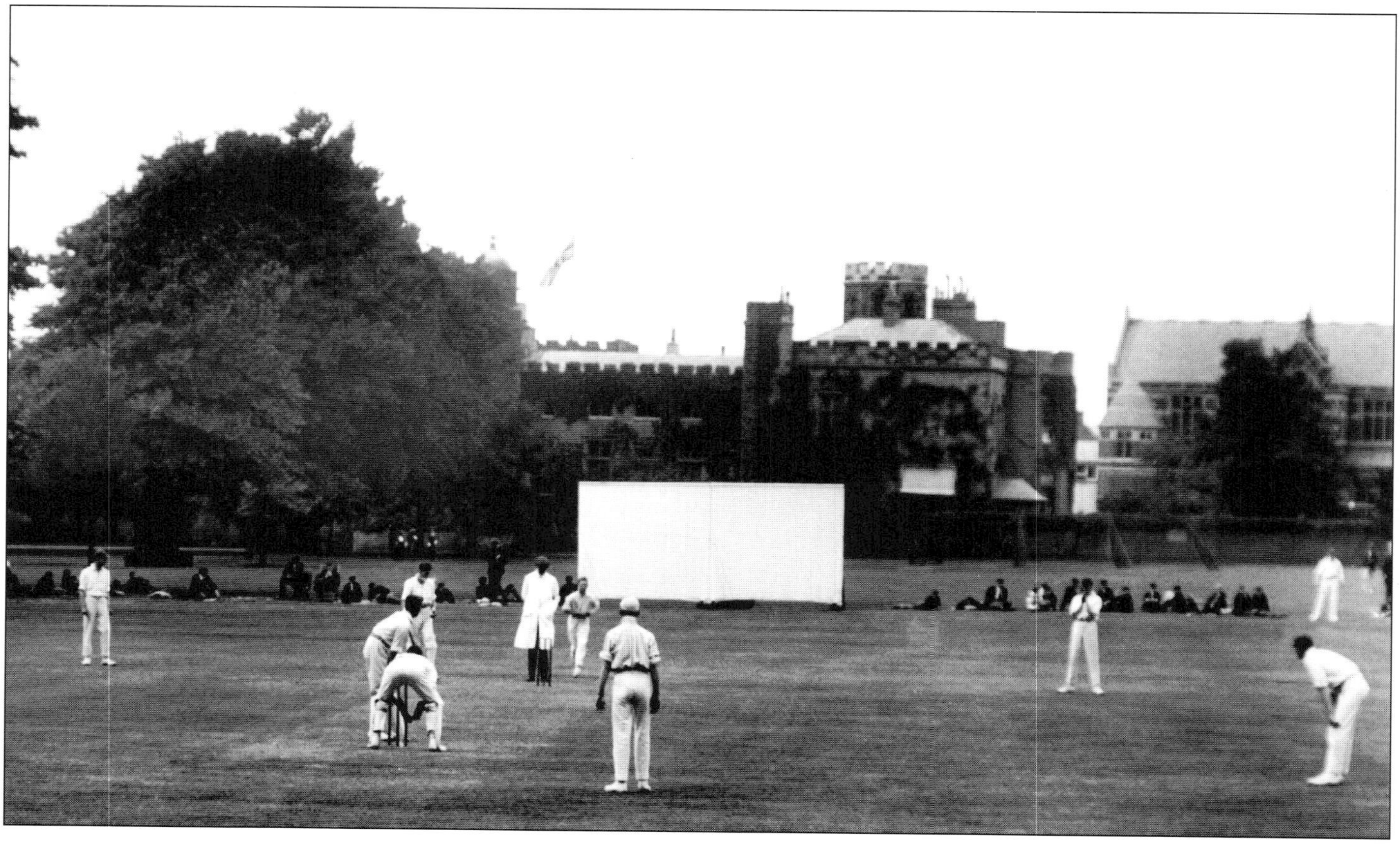

Rugby School, 1922. 72142A
It was during the headmastership of Dr William Temple from 1857-1869 that many of the school's buildings were constructed.

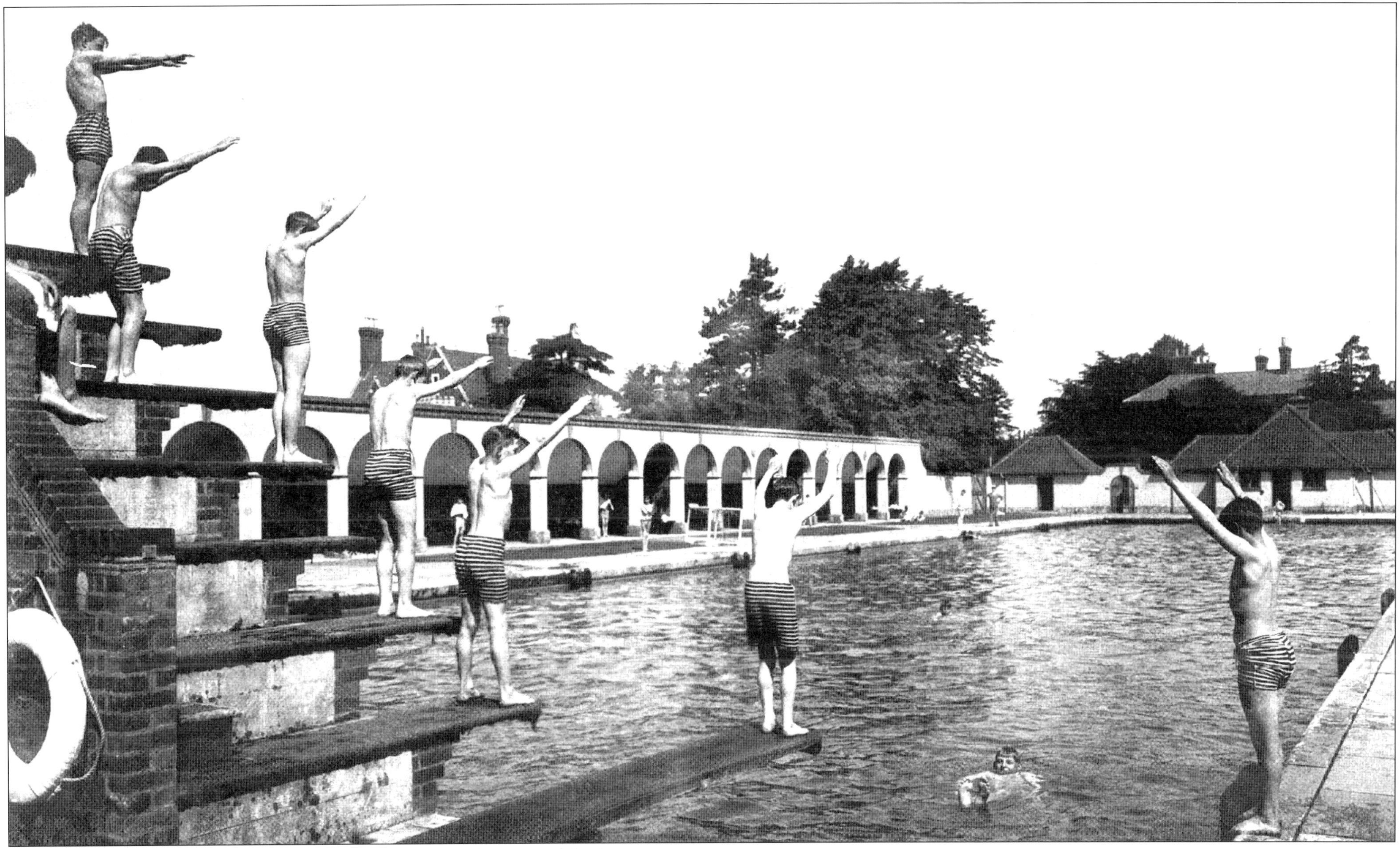

RUGBY SCHOOL SWIMMING BATHS, 1932. 85188

It was under Dr Thomas Arnold, appointed headmaster in 1828 that the face of the English public school was to change. It was his influence that led to public schools becoming places that trained character.

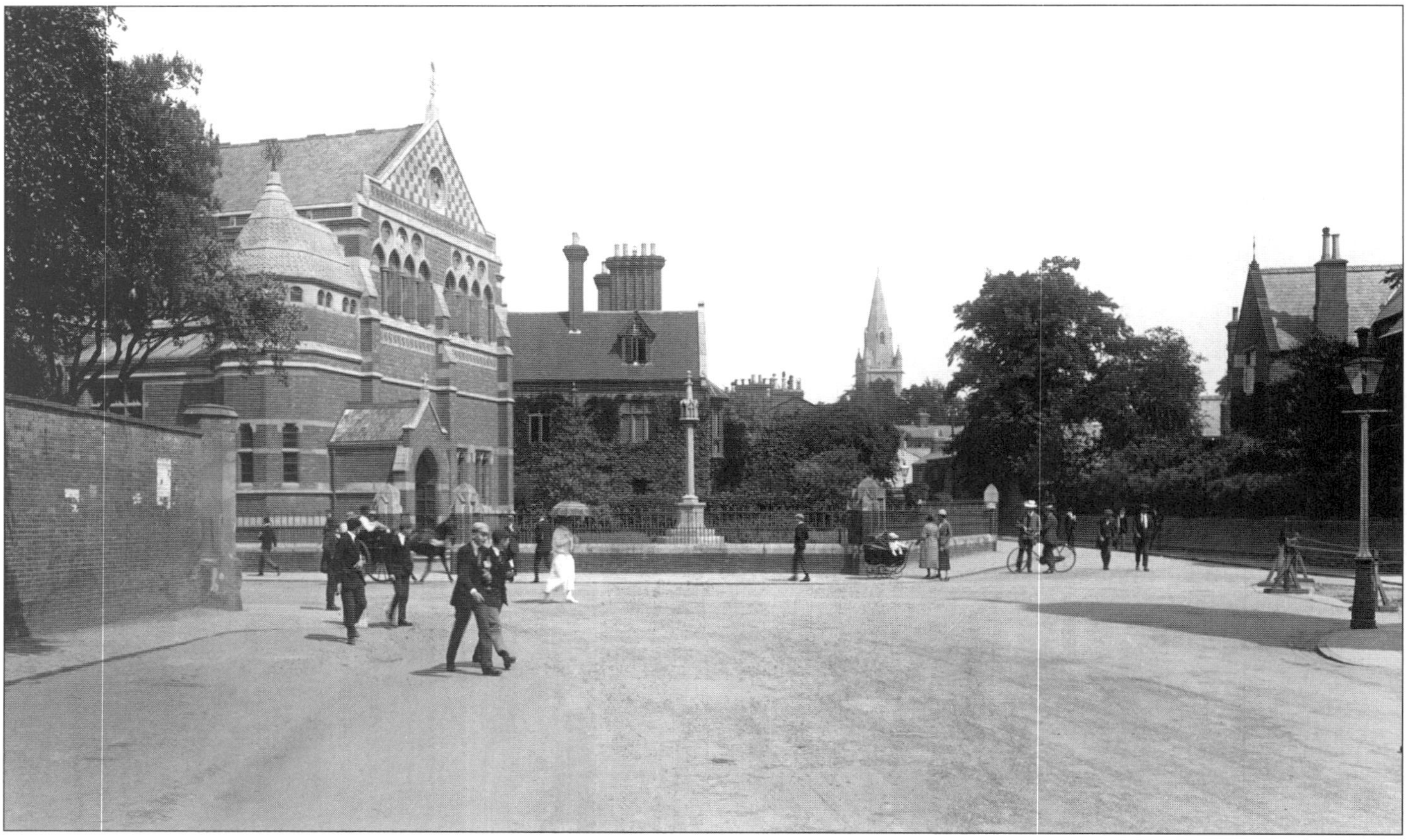

RUGBY SCHOOL, 1922. 72123

The school was originally located in premises opposite the parish church but moved to its present site during the mid-eighteenth century.

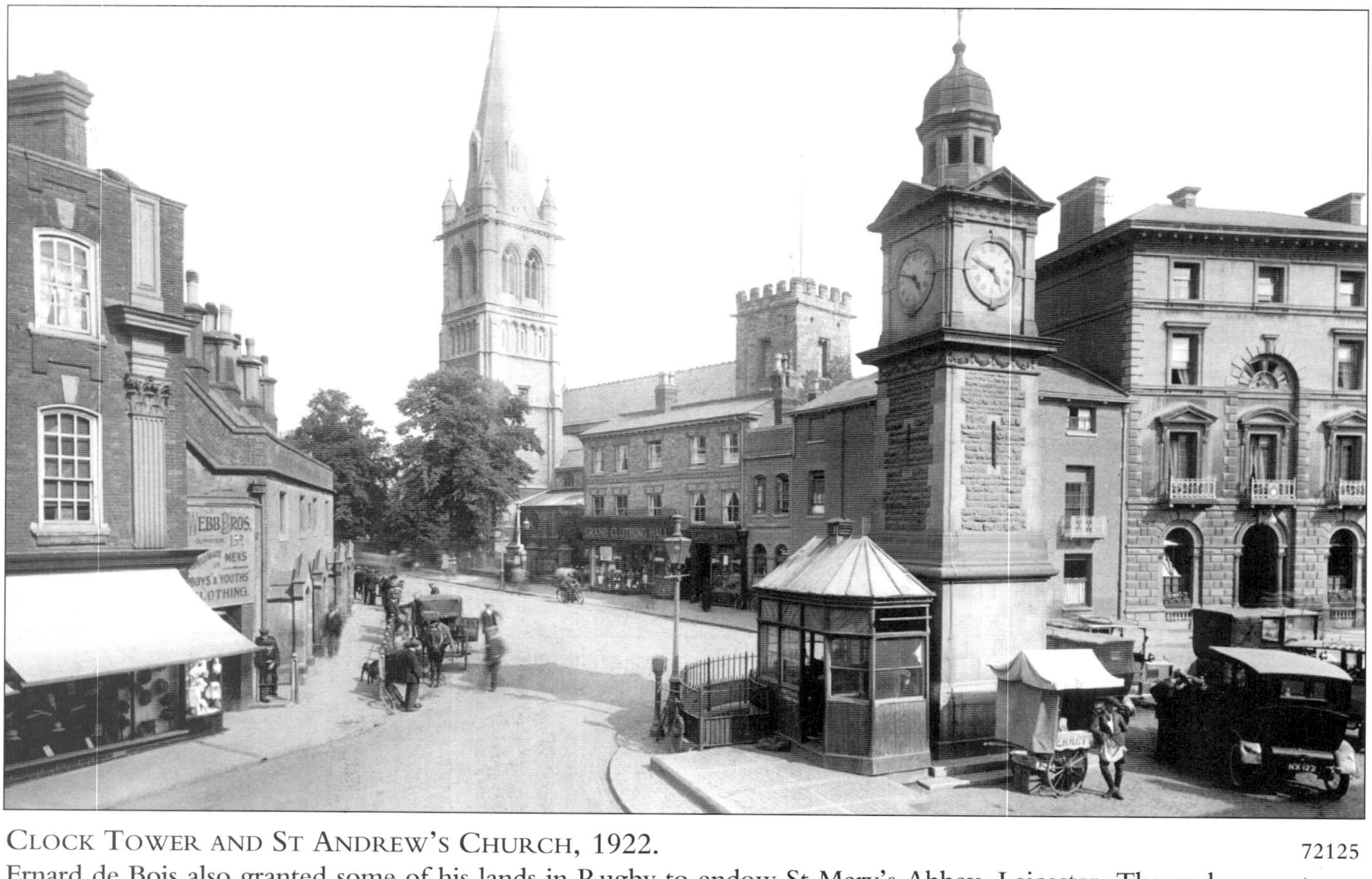

CLOCK TOWER AND ST ANDREW'S CHURCH, 1922. 72125

Ernard de Bois also granted some of his lands in Rugby to endow St Mary's Abbey, Leicester. The endowment was eventually confirmed by a royal charter of Henry II.

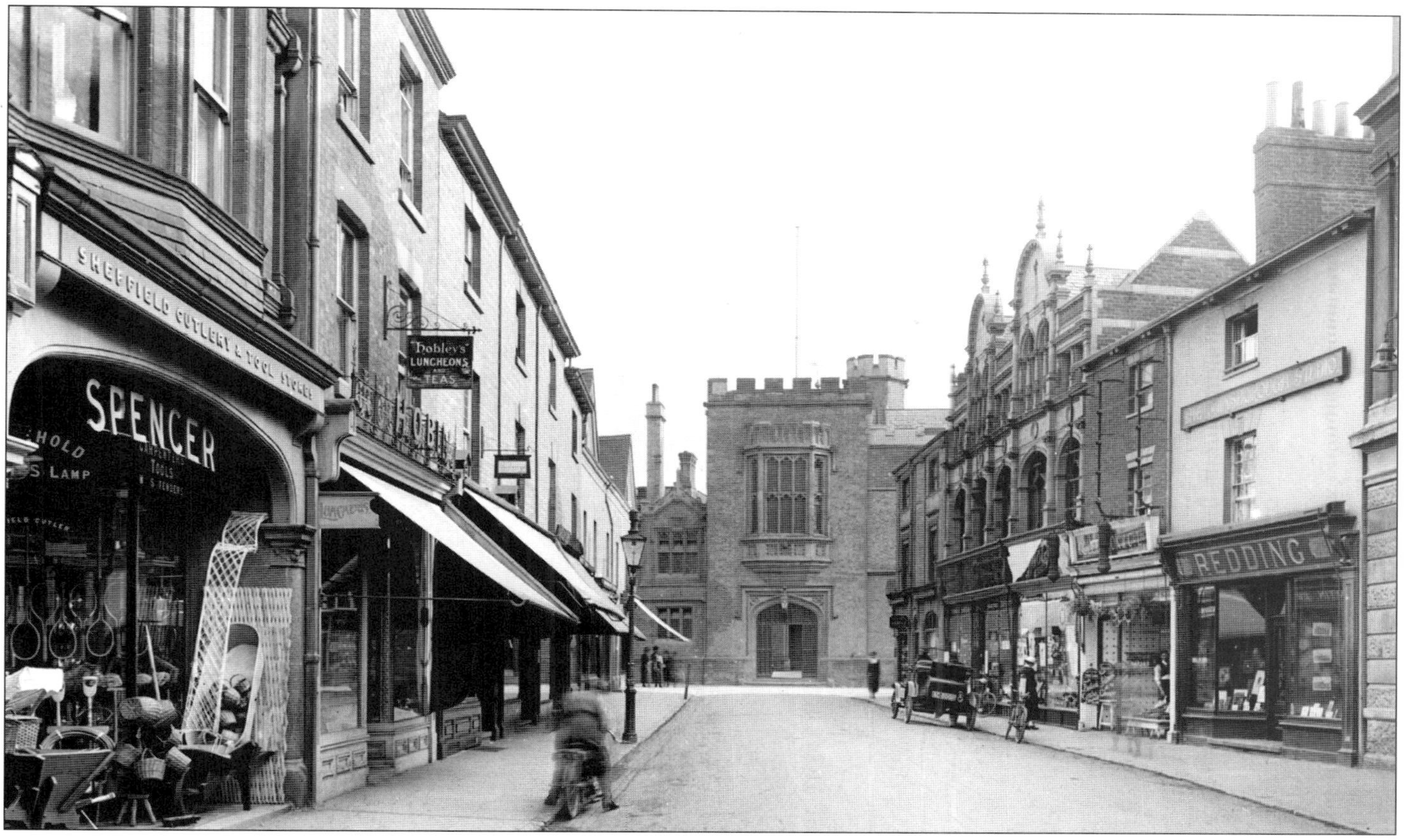

HIGH STREET, 1922. 72124

At this date the town had just one hotel recommended by the *Dunlop Motorists Guide*. This was the 25-bedroom Royal George.

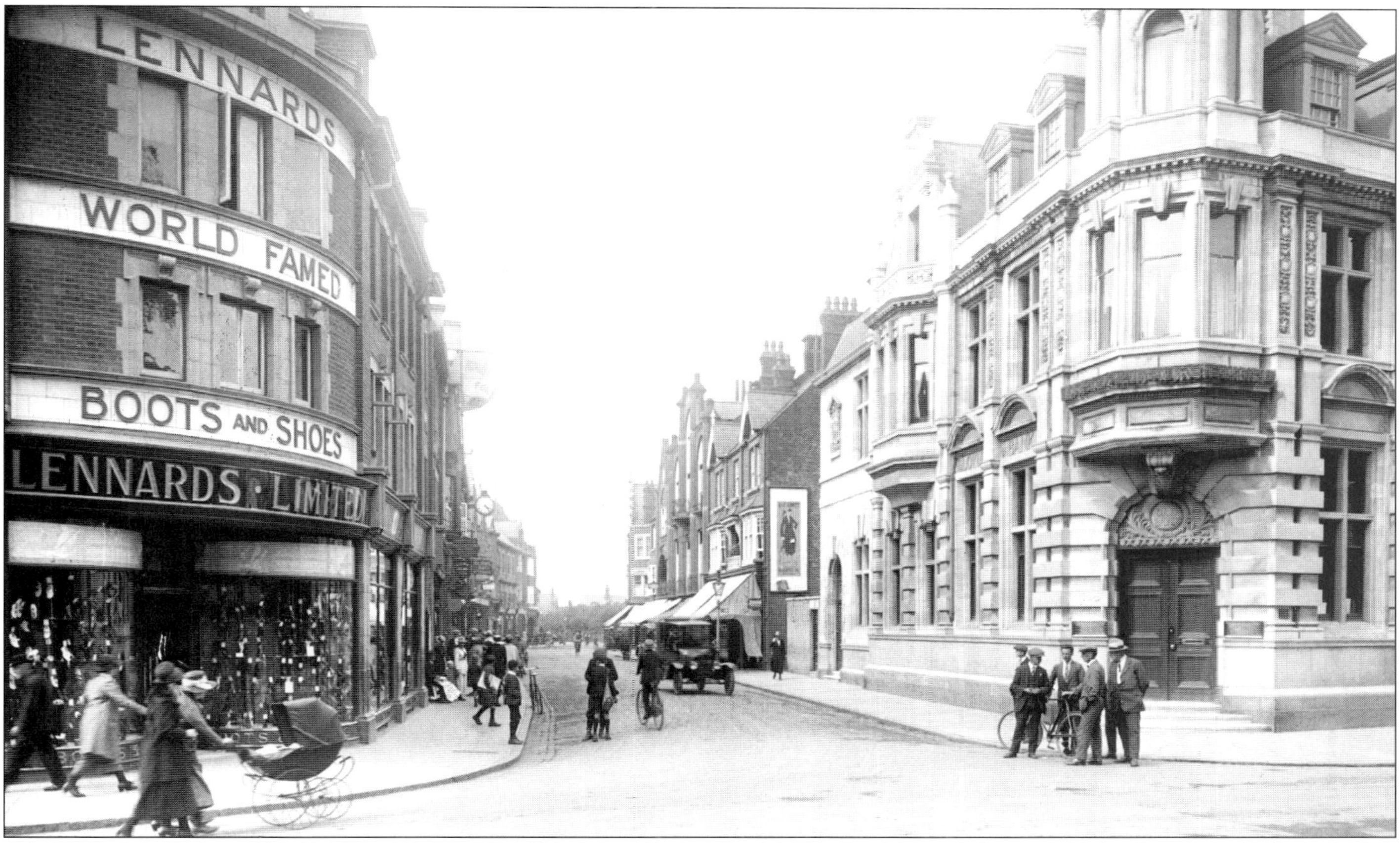

REGENT STREET, 1922. 72128

Rugby had become an important railway junction with routes radiating out to Birmingham, Nuneaton, Leicester, Sheffield, Northampton, Warwick and Marylebone.

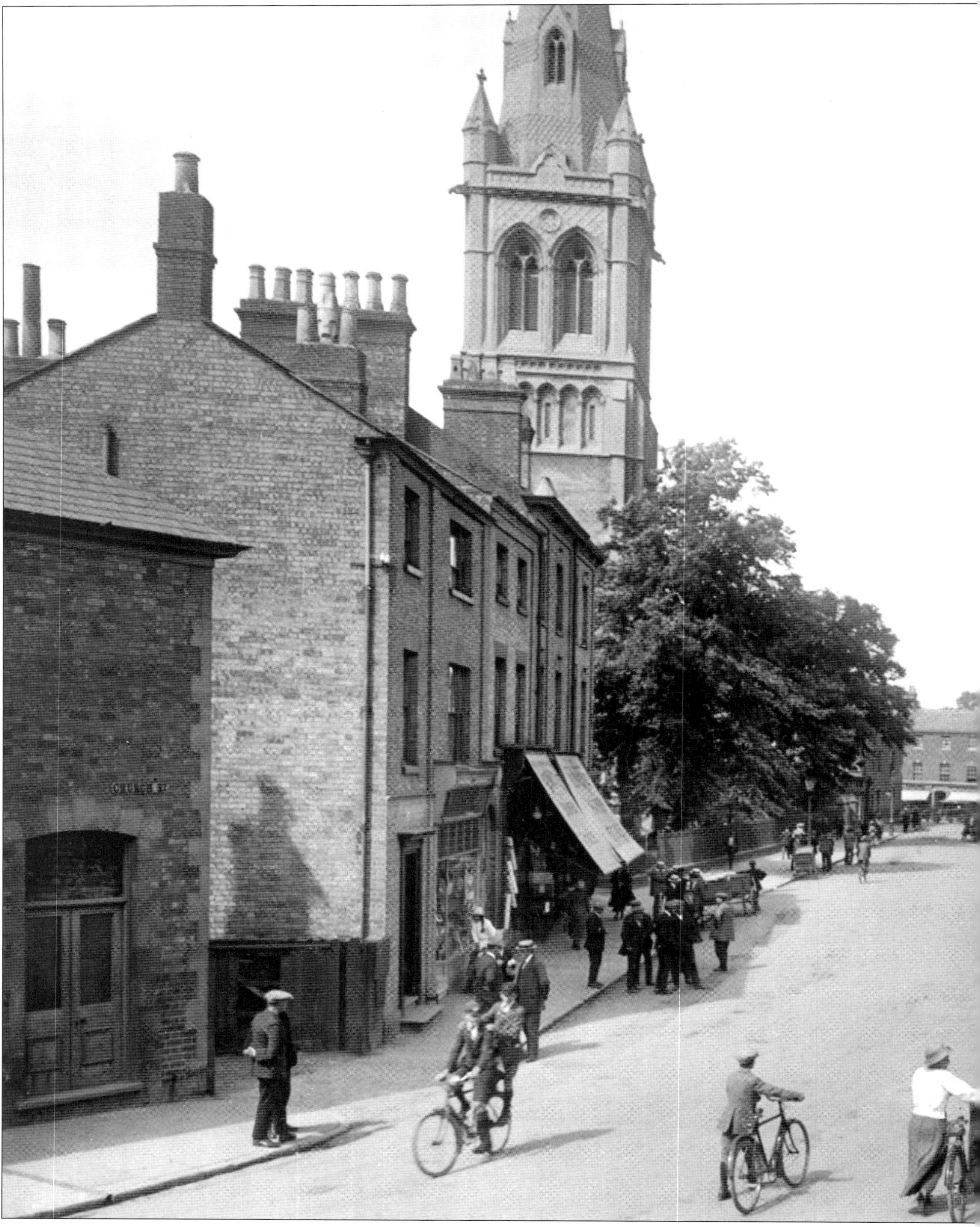

CHURCH STREET, 1922.
Ernard de Bois, lord of the manor of Clifton-on-Dunsmore, built the first chapel in Rugby around the year 1140.

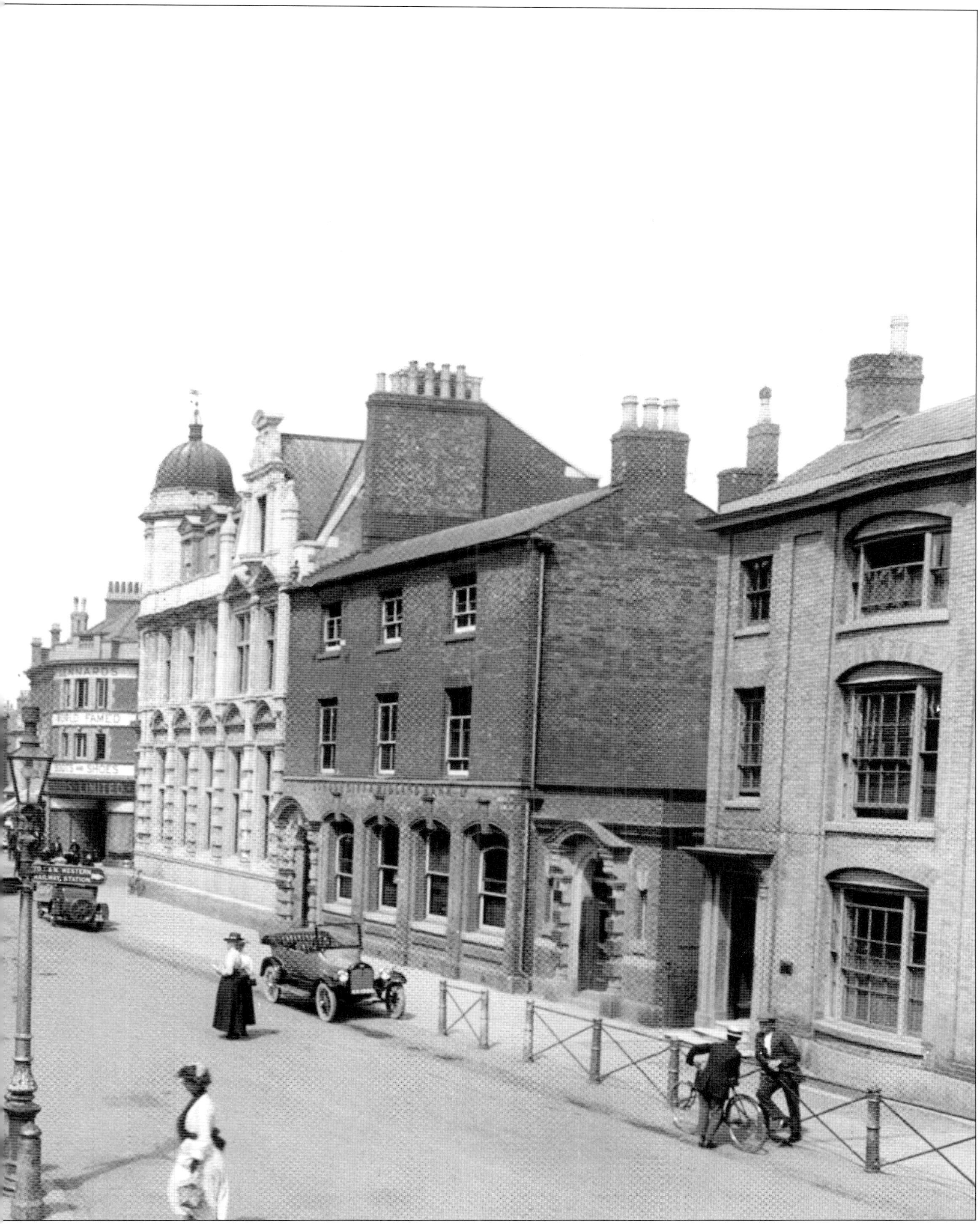

72117

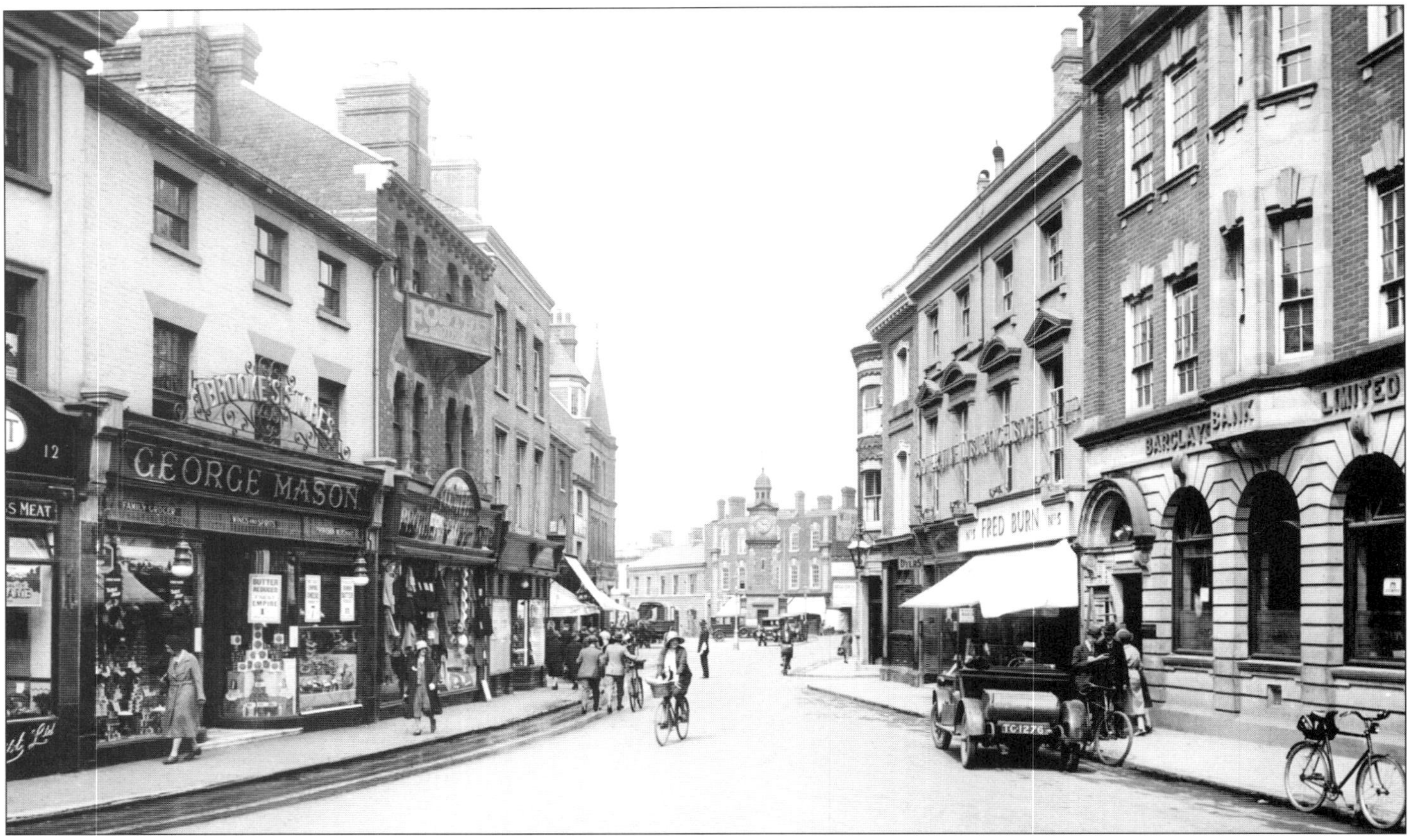

THE MARKET PLACE, 1932. 85177

The population by this date was in excess of 22,000. Market day was held on Saturdays, half-day closing was on Wednesdays.

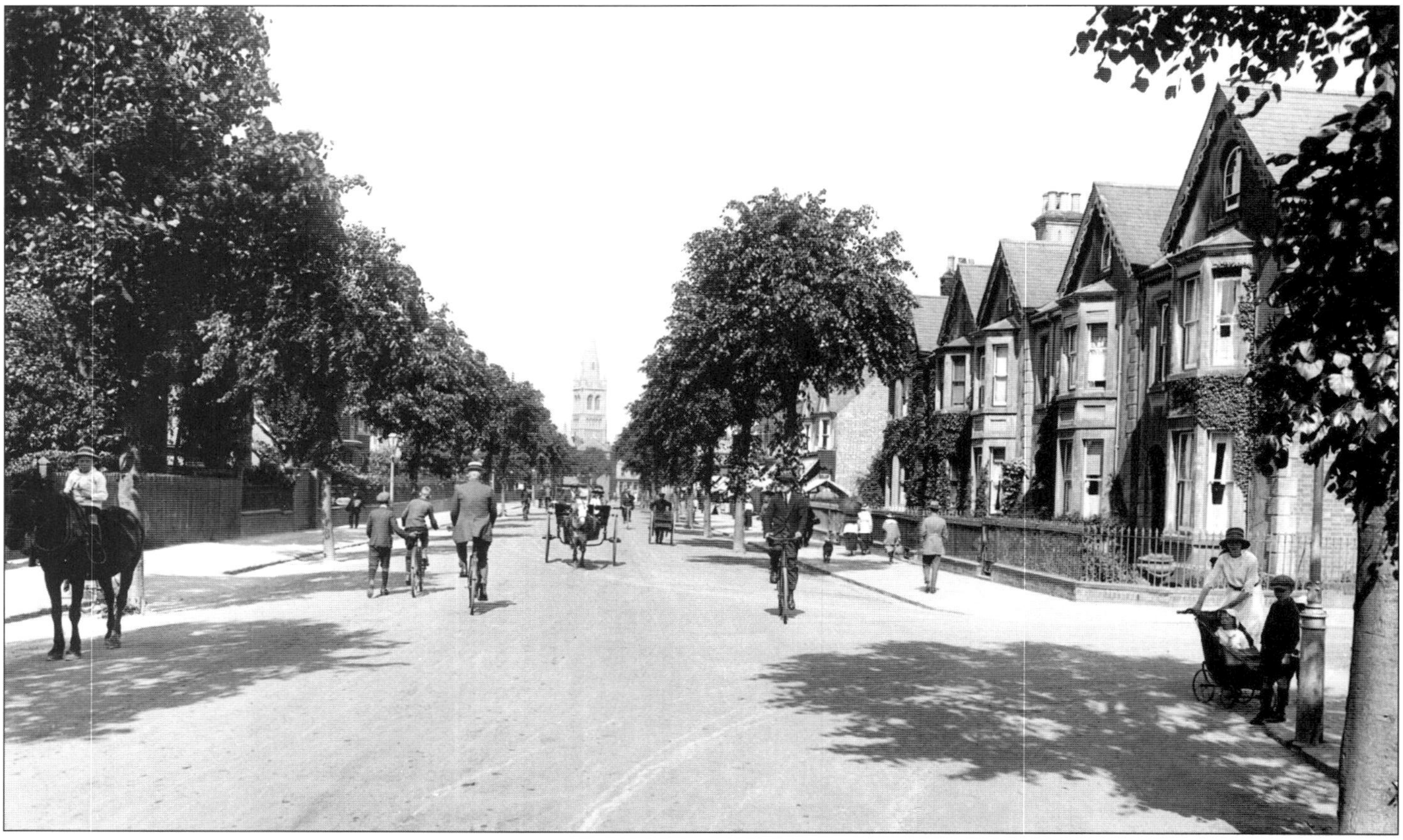

CLIFTON ROAD, 1922. 72121

Rugby was originally a hamlet within the parish of Clifton-on-Dunsmore; but by the time the Domesday Book was compiled it was treated separately.

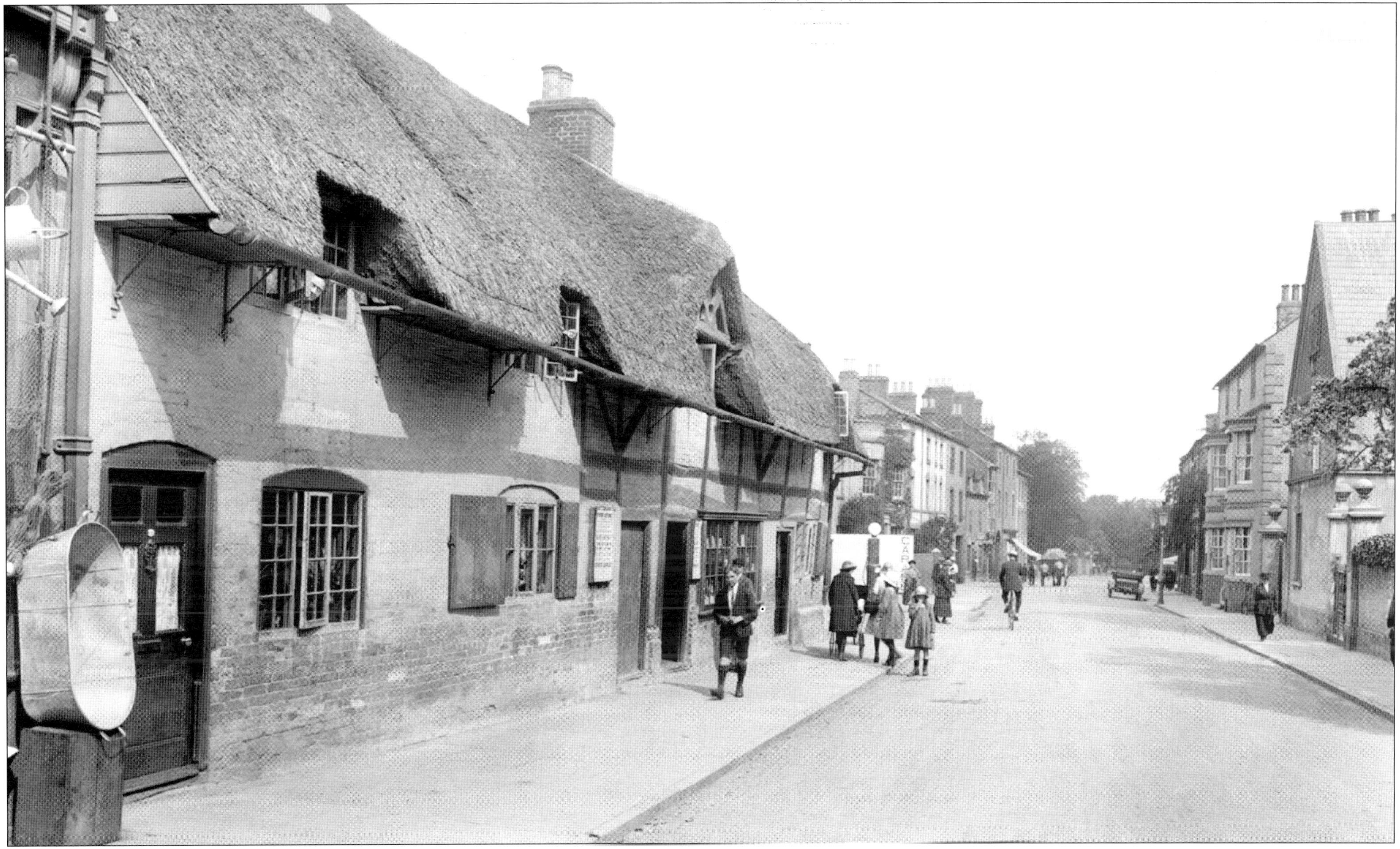

OLD HOUSES IN NORTH STREET, 1922. 72120

Built-in bathrooms for most people were still something of a novelty. For the majority bathnight was held in a zinc tub in front of the kitchen fire and two or three people might share the same water – though not at the same time. Emptying the things could be fun, the knack was to avoid creating a mini tidal wave when trying to move a bath full of water.

Chapter 3

ROYAL LEAMINGTON SPA

The natural springs at Leamington were known about in the seventeenth century and were mentioned by a number of writers. In 1656 Dugdale wrote of 'a spring of salt water (not above a stone's throw from the Leam) whereof the inhabitants make much use for seasoning their meats'. However, Leamington's development as a spa did not begin until 1789 when William Abbotts discovered a mineral spring on his land in what is now Bath Street. Following a favourable report on the medicinal properties of the waters, a baths and hotel were built and Leamington was on the spa trail. By the end of the Napoleonic Wars a number of other springs had been discovered and developed.

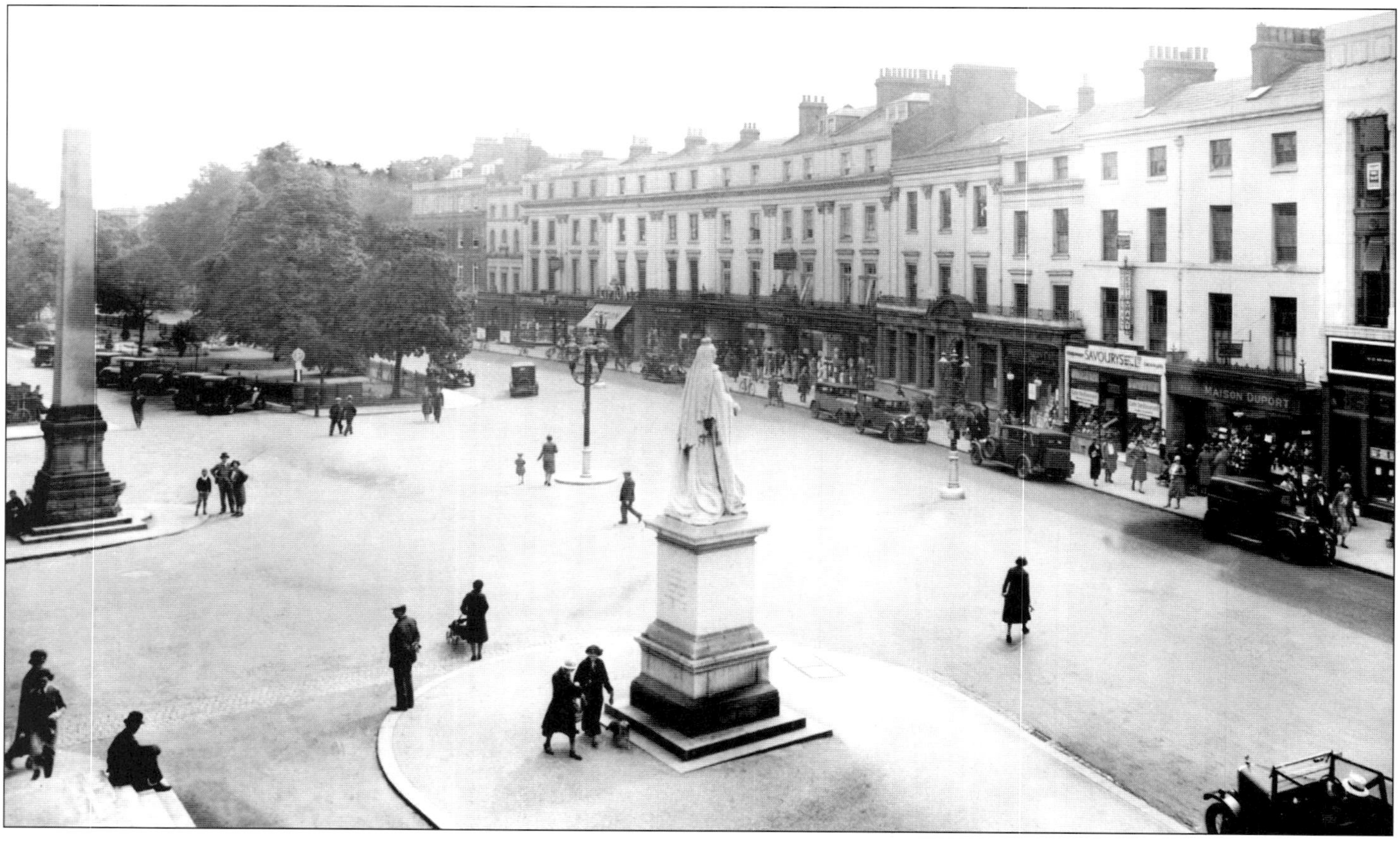

Leamington Spa, 1932. 85204

In 1838 Queen Victoria came to drink the waters. She was received by Dr Henry Jephson, an outstanding surgeon in his day and also the man responsible for planning much of the town. It was Victoria who allowed the town to assume the name of Royal Leamington Spa.

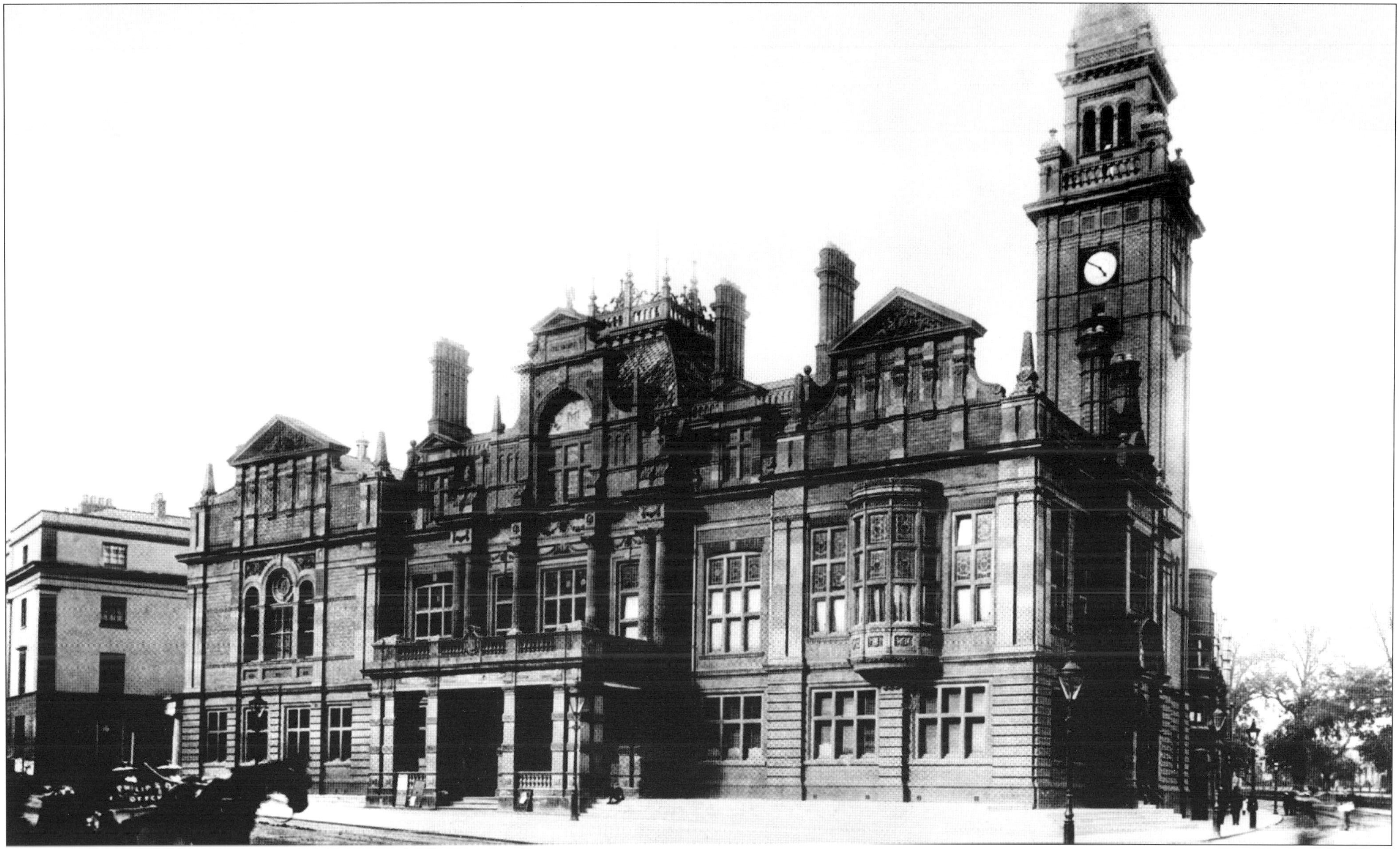

Renaissance-style Town Hall with Campanile, 1892. 30953

In 1801 the population was just 315; during the 1820s it rose to around 6,000 and by 1840 it was nearly 12,000.

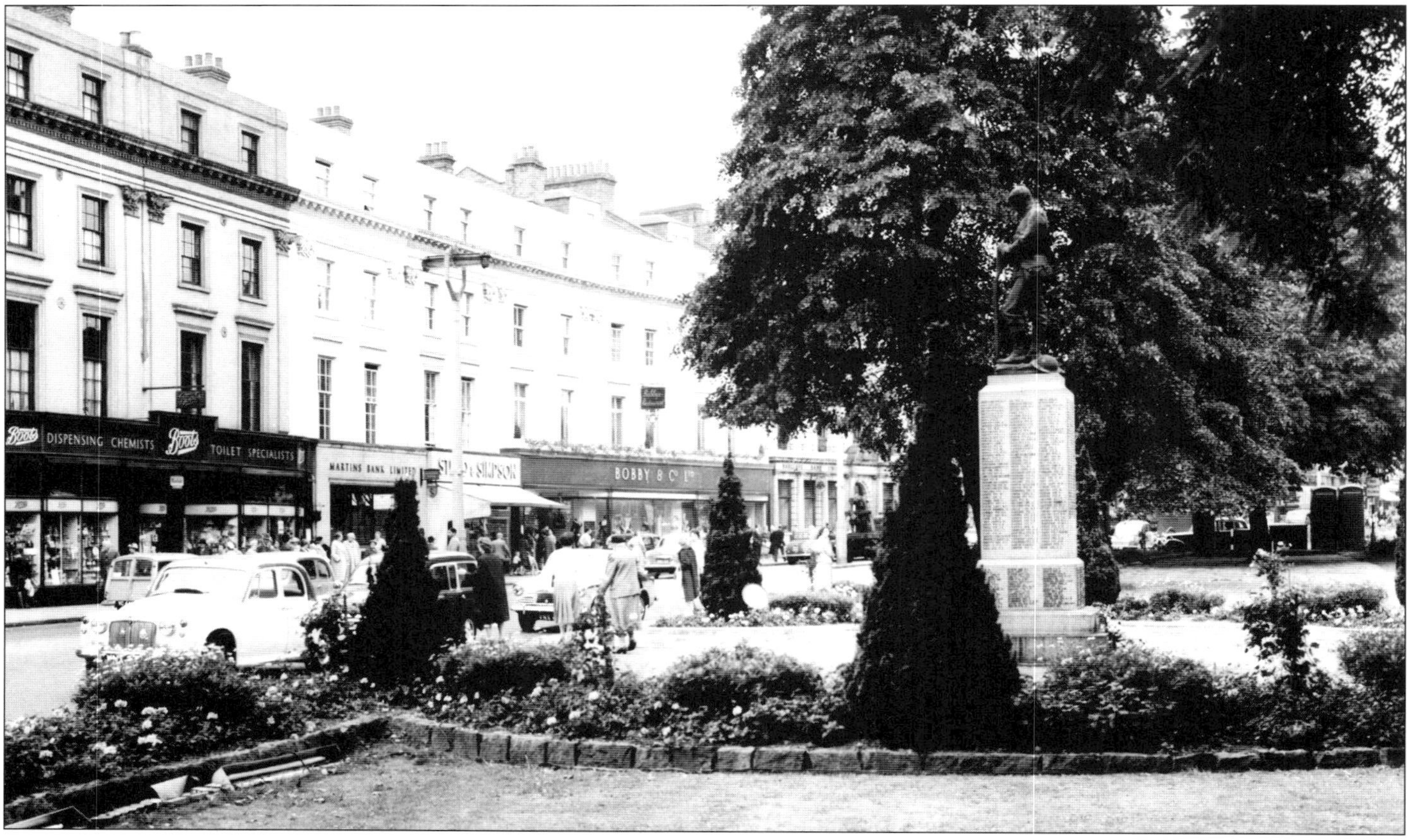

THE PARADE AND WAR MEMORIAL, *c.*1960. L25070

Among Leamington's famous residents was Napoleon III of France, who came to the town for a short period following France's defeat at the hands of Prussia in 1871. The American author Nathaniel Hawthorne spent some time at 10 Lansdowne Crescent.

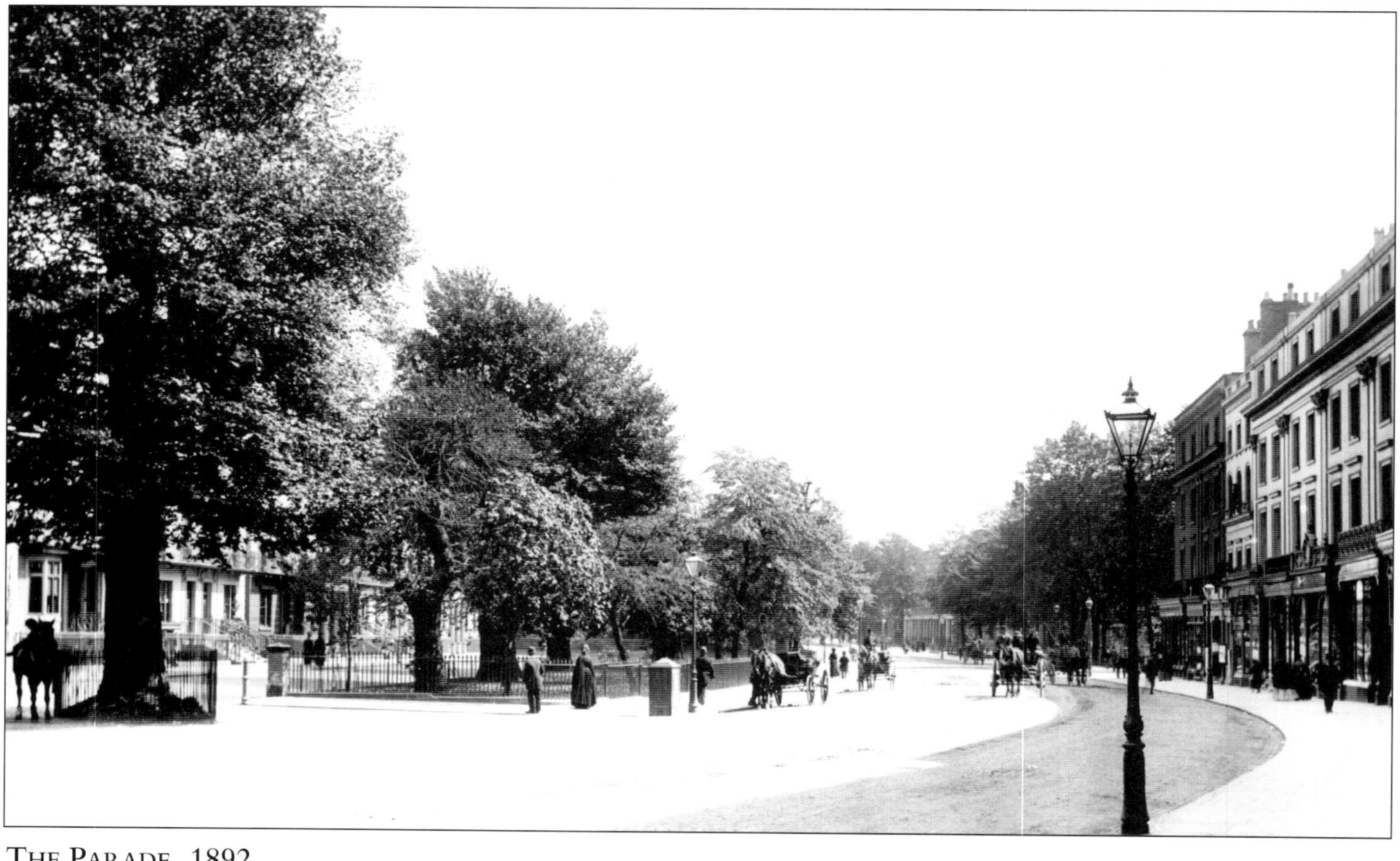

THE PARADE, 1892. 30956

Horse-drawn cabs were fairly expensive. The fare per mile for 1-2 persons was 1*s,* for 3-4 persons, 1*s* 6*d,* and each additional half-mile was 6*d.* Cabs could be hired by the hour for 2*s* 6*d,* each additional half-hour was 1*s.* Each article of luggage carried on the outside cost 2*d.*

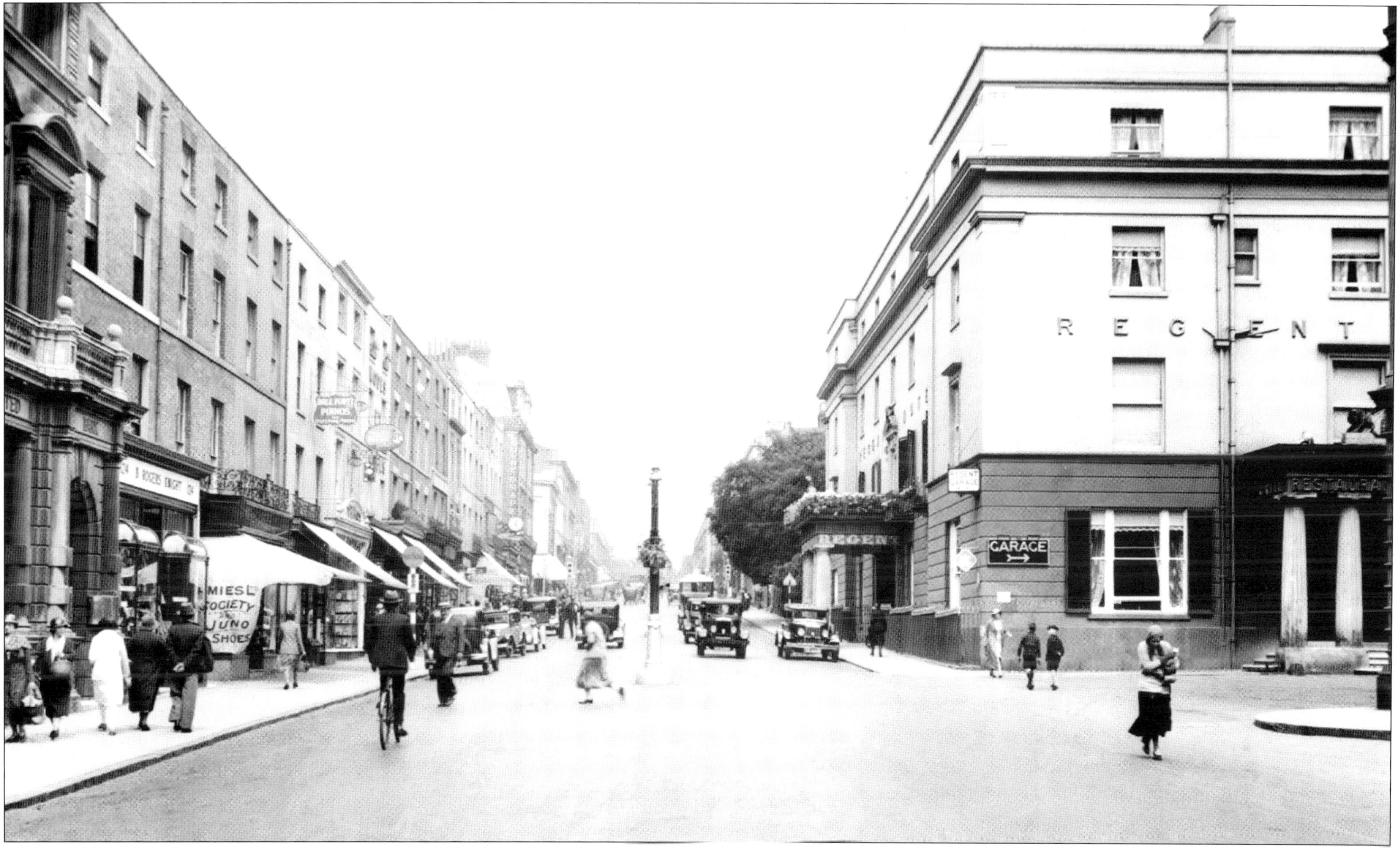

THE REGENT HOTEL, 1922. 85200

On 10 September 1819, the Prince Regent came to stay at the recently opened William's Royal Hotel. As a result the hotel was renamed The Regent.

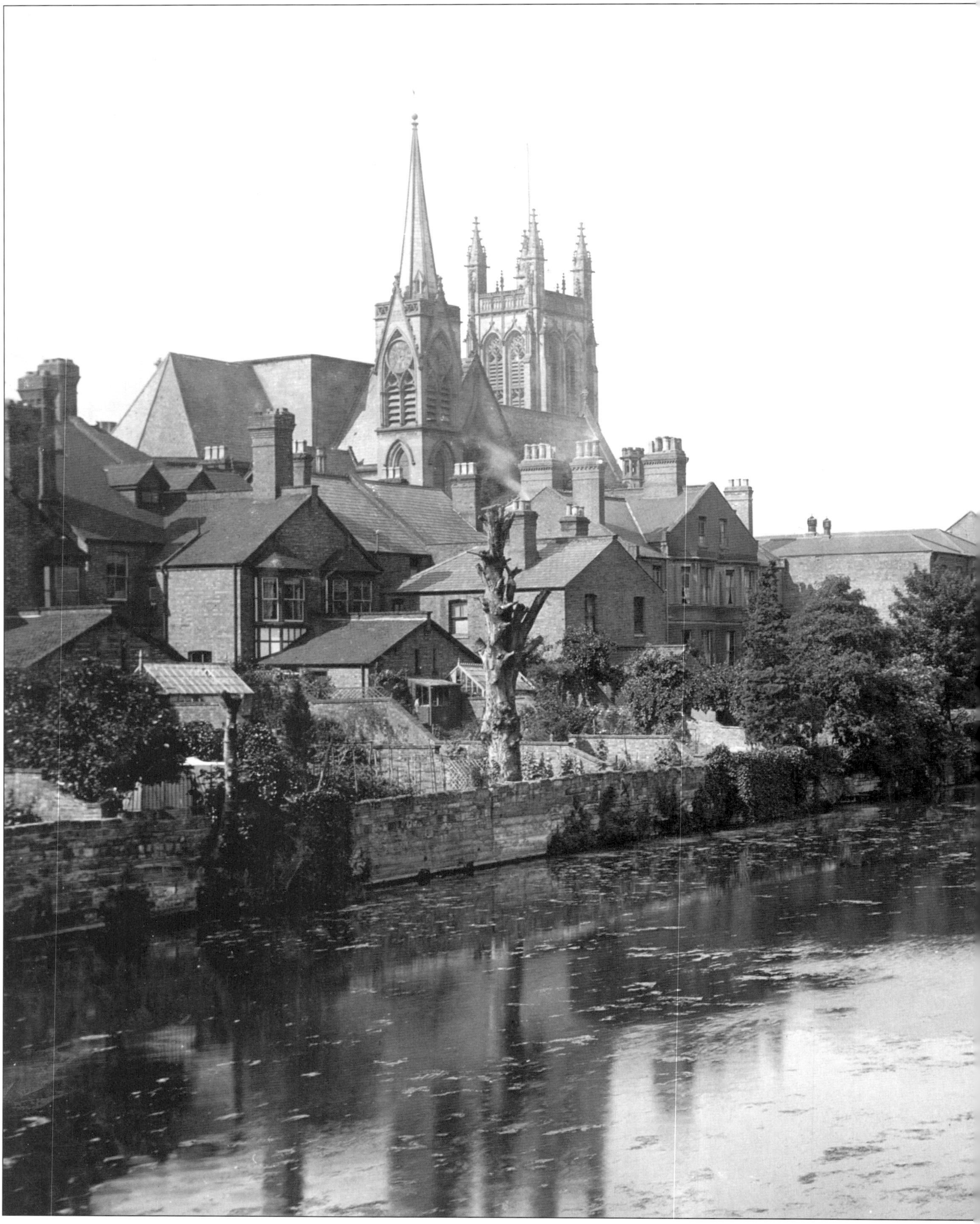

LEAMINGTON SPA, 1922.
In the 1780s Leamington was little more than a village with a population of around 300 people. The village was confined to the south bank of the river; the development of the north bank did not take place until the building of the Victoria Bridge.

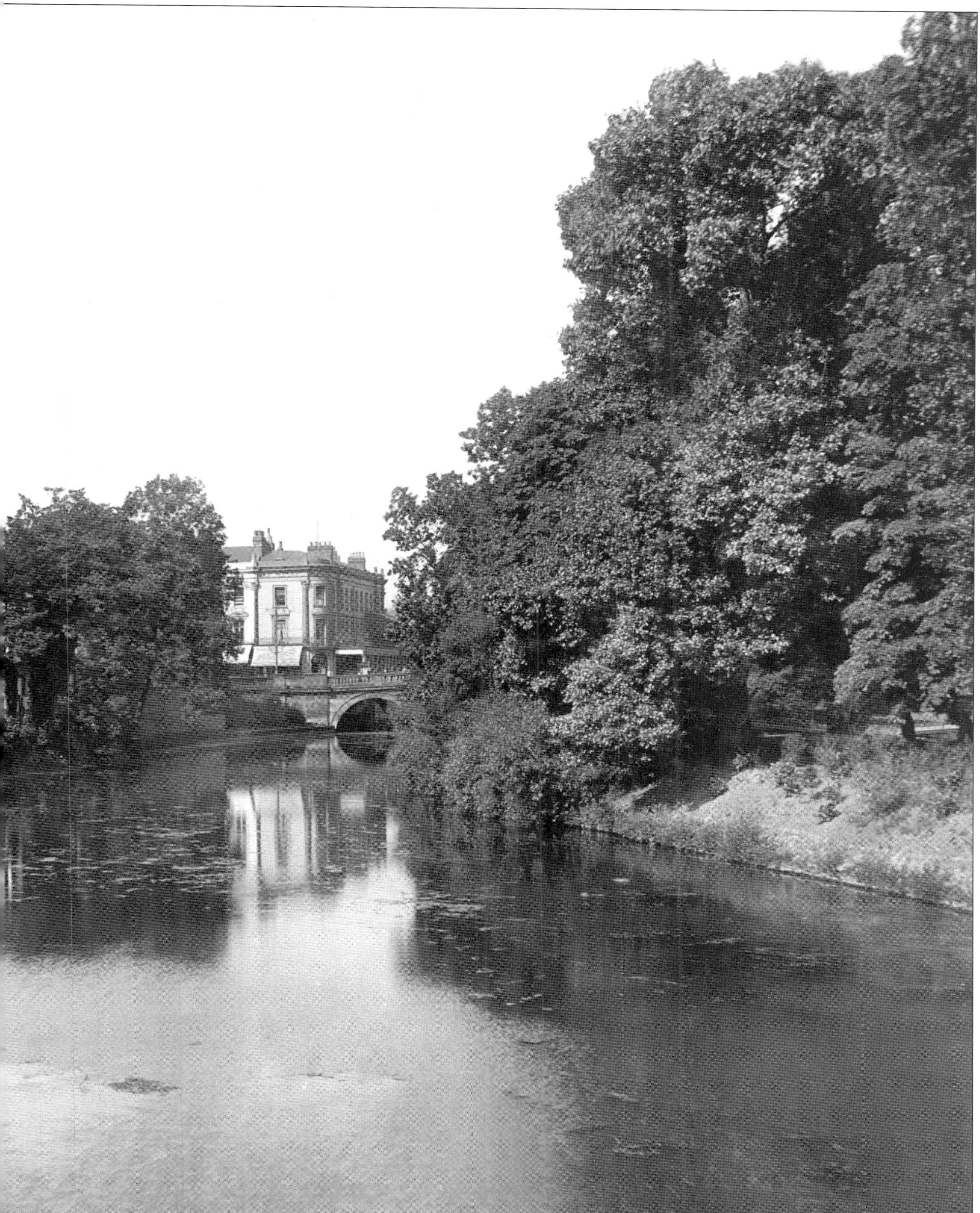

72436

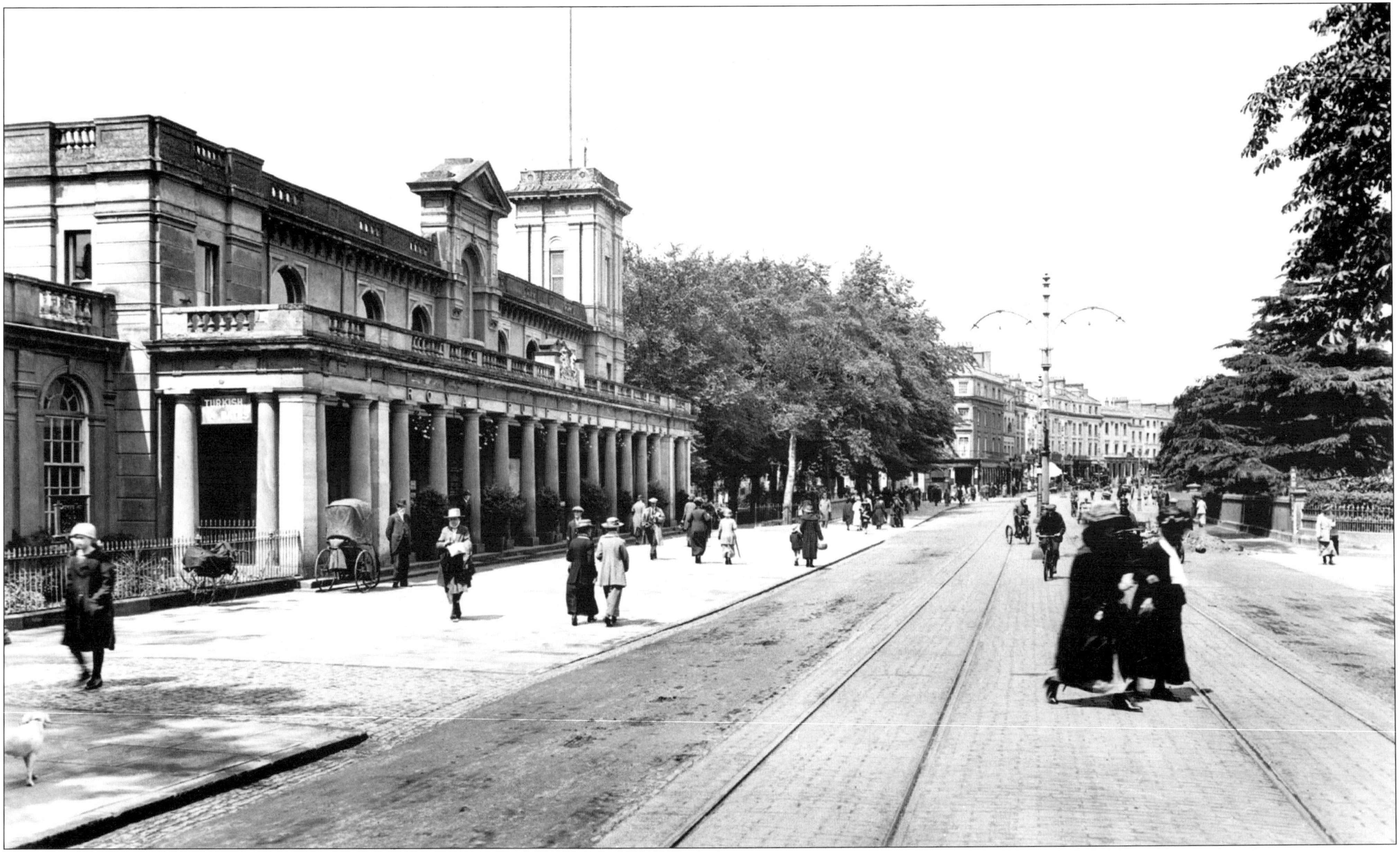

LEAMINGTON SPA, 1922. 72443

In 1905 the horse-drawn tramway linking Leamington and Warwick was converted to electric traction. The gauge between the rails was 3ft 6ins, the same as the tramways of Birmingham, Coventry, Walsall and Wolverhampton.

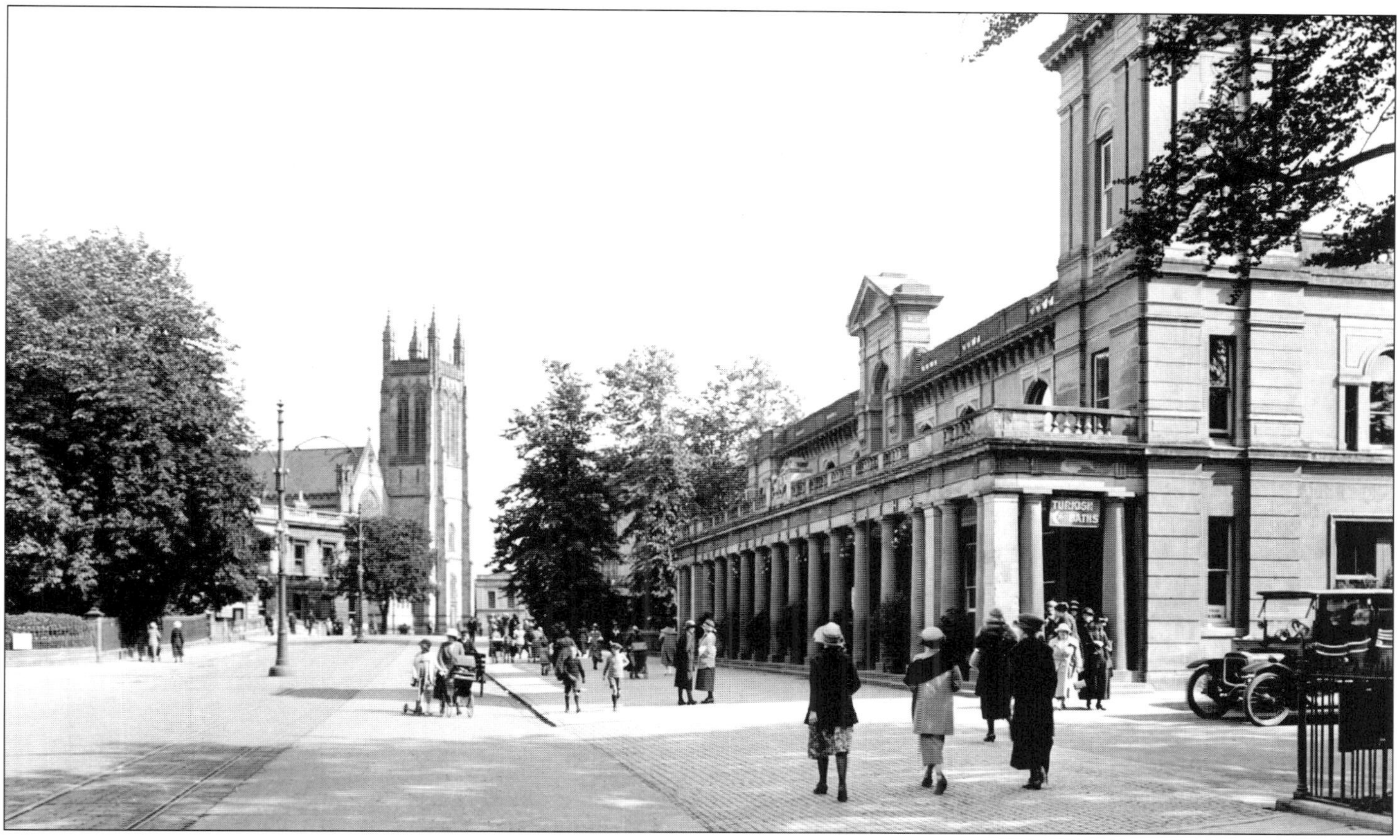

BATH AND PUMP ROOMS, 1922. 72442

On the right is the Royal Leamington Bath & Pump Rooms, with swimming pool and Turkish baths. Other baths were Hudson's Sulphur & Saline Springs; the Old Pump Room (Earl of Aylesford's) and Oldham's Open-air Swimming Baths.

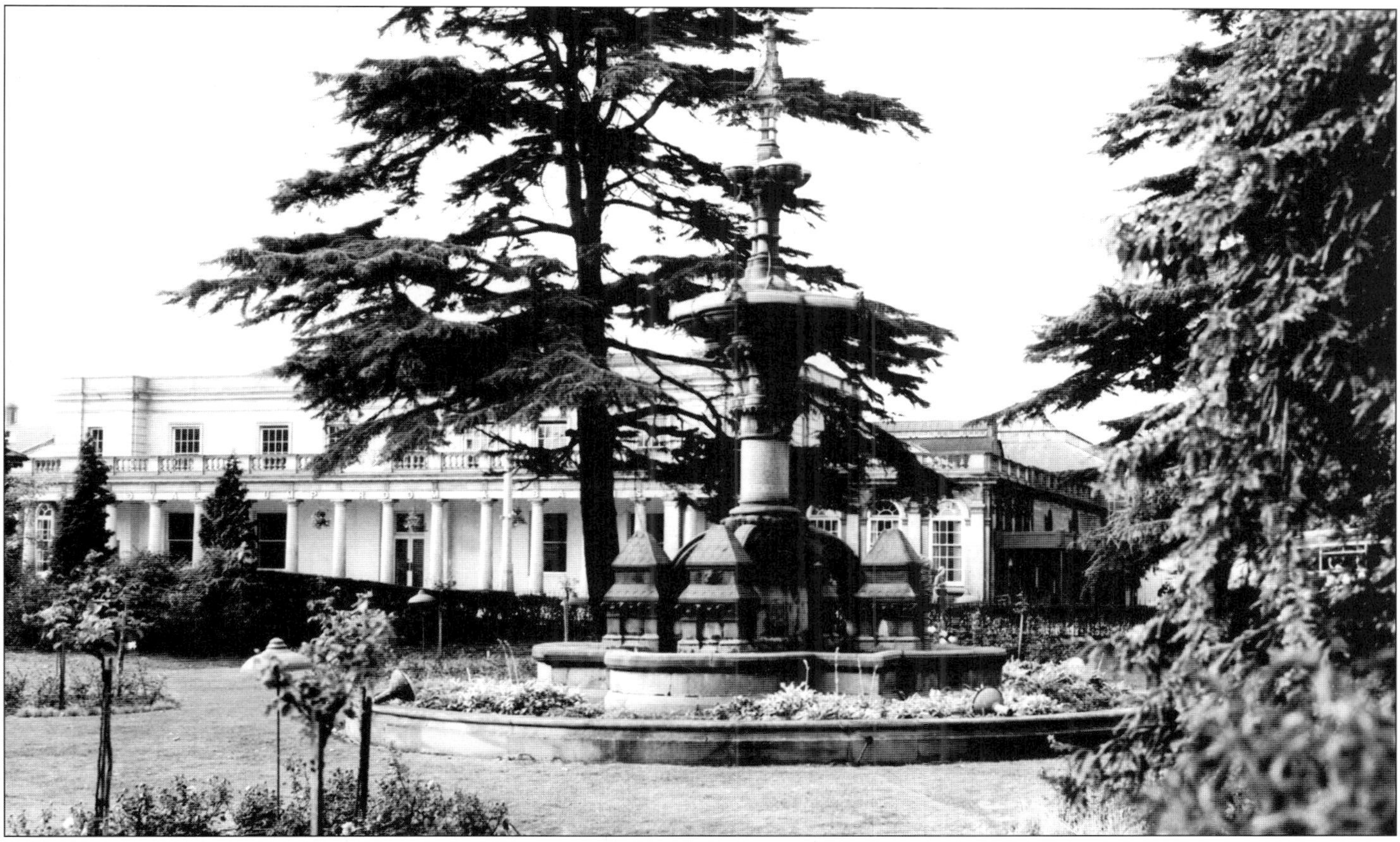

LEAMINGTON SPA, *c.*1960. L25063

For those taking the waters in Edwardian times, there were plenty of hotels. The most expensive was the Clarendon with rooms 6*s* 6*d,* breakfast 3*s,* dinner 5*s*. Those on a restricted budget could avail themselves of the York, a temperance establishment on Spencer Street where a room could be had for 1*s* 6*d*.

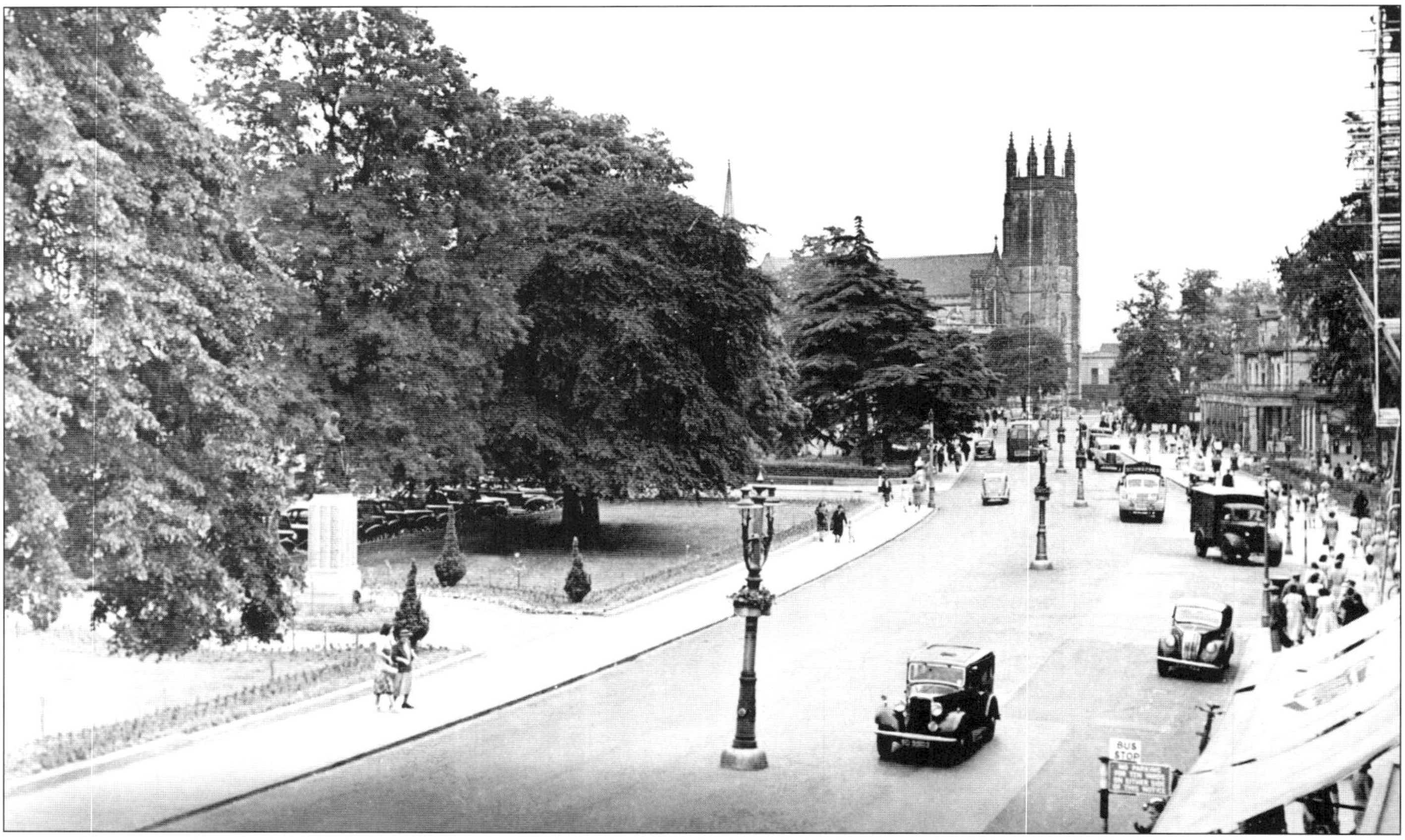

LOWER PARADE, 1960. L25029

All Saints provides the backdrop to this view of the parade.

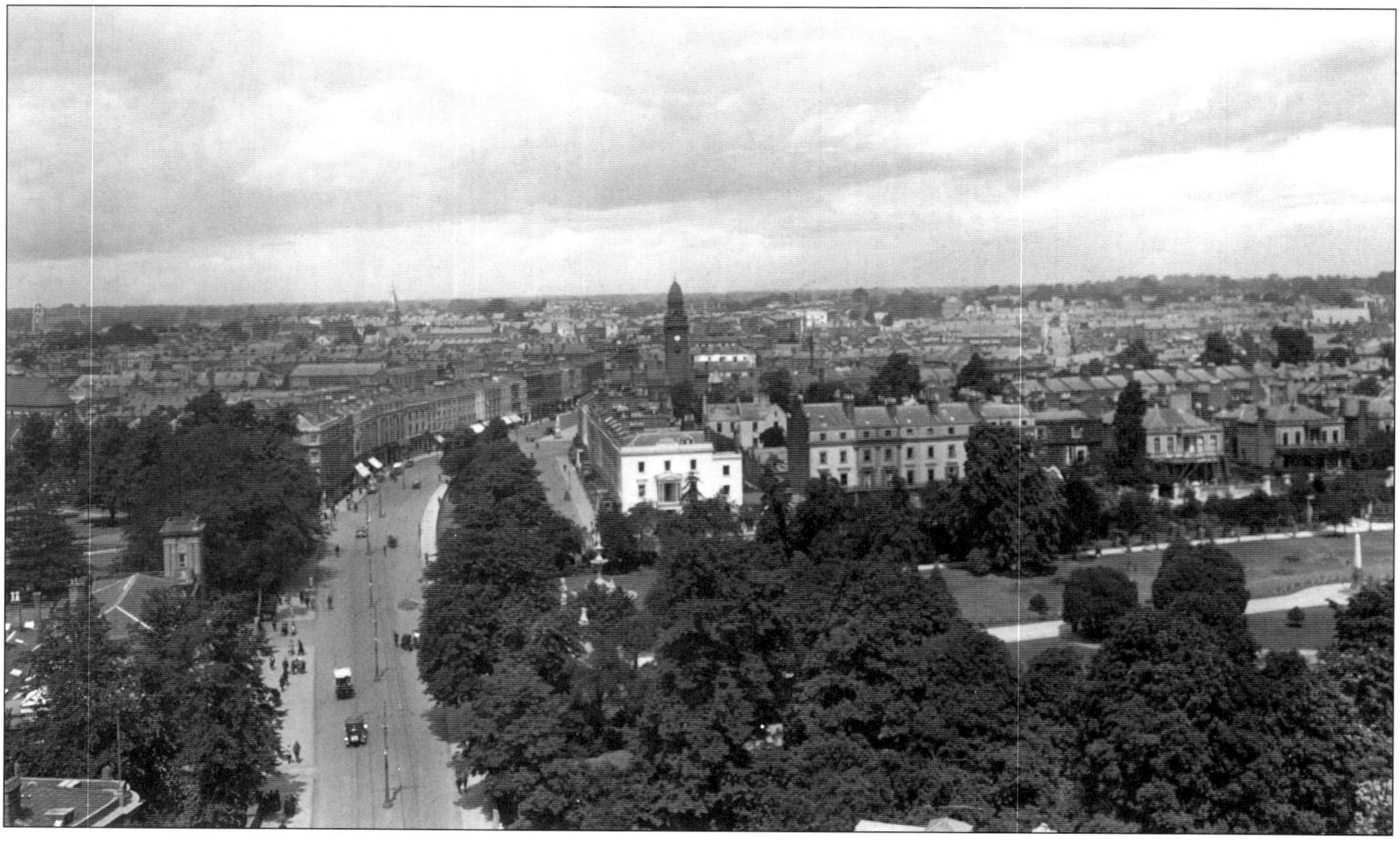

ROYAL LEAMINGTON SPA FROM THE TOWER OF ALL SAINTS, 1922. 72435

The view takes us along The Parade, with the Royal Pump Room on the left and the campanile of the town hall in the centre of the picture.

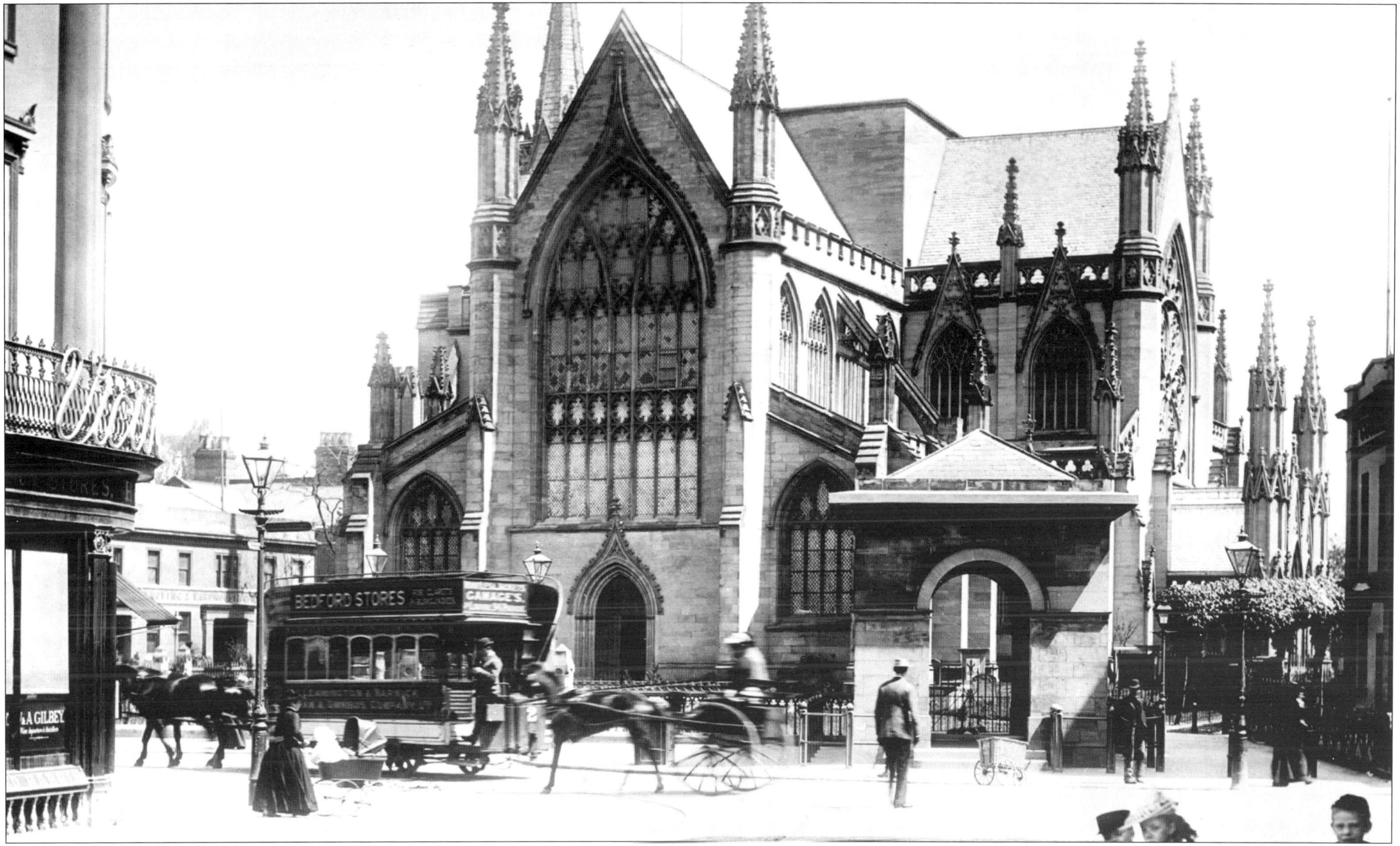

ALL SAINTS CHURCH, 1892. 30961

A horse-tram belonging to the Leamington & Warwick Tramway Co trundles by the parish church of All Saints. The church was built in the French-Gothic style between 1843-1869. The picture was taken during the period when the side chapel, vestries and organ chamber were added.

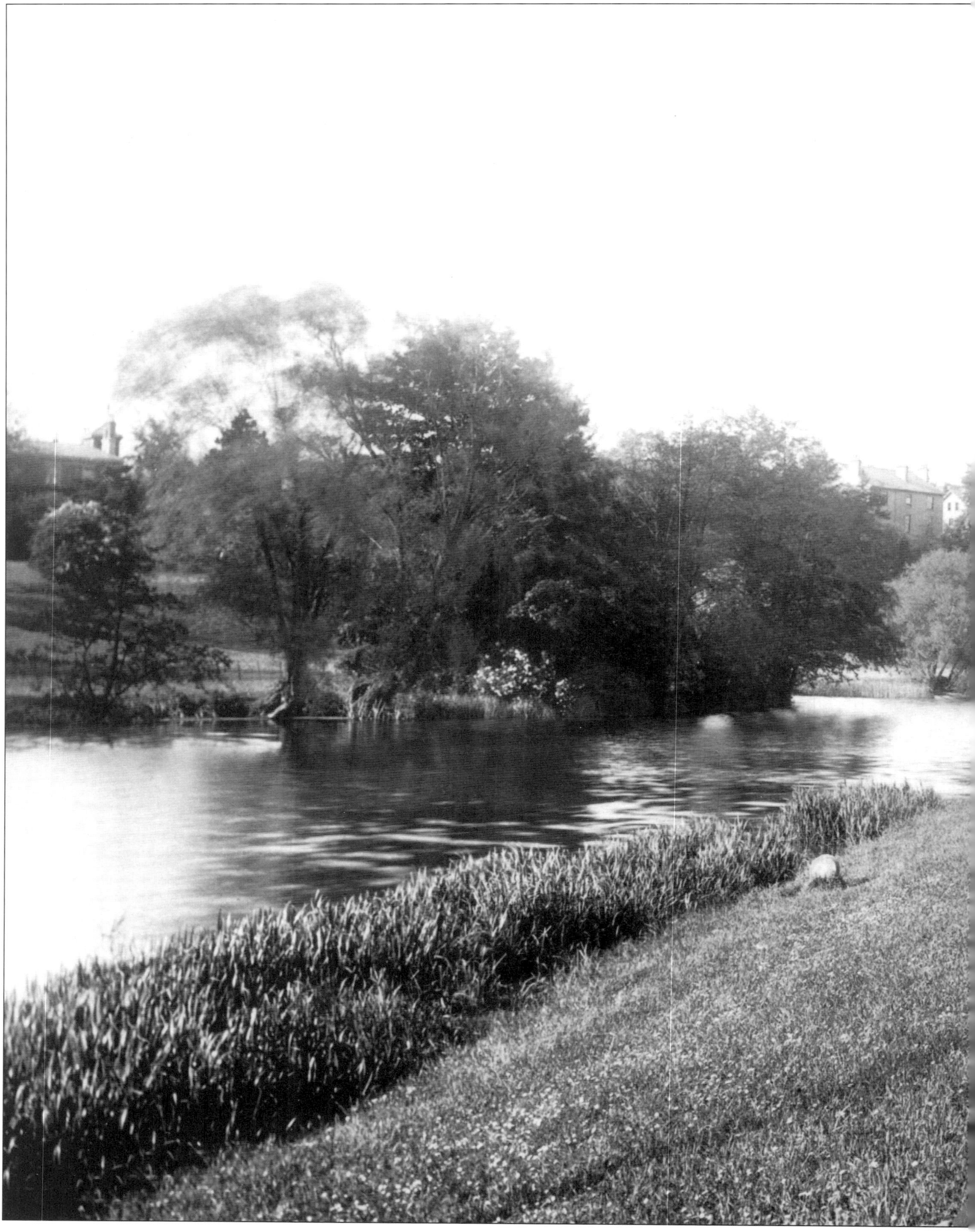

River Leam, 1892.
A quiet moment on the banks of the Leam. Jephson Gardens were laid out on land leased from Edward Willes of Newbold Comyn. Willes charged a rent of just one peppercorn on the understanding that the ground would never be built on or the trees destroyed.

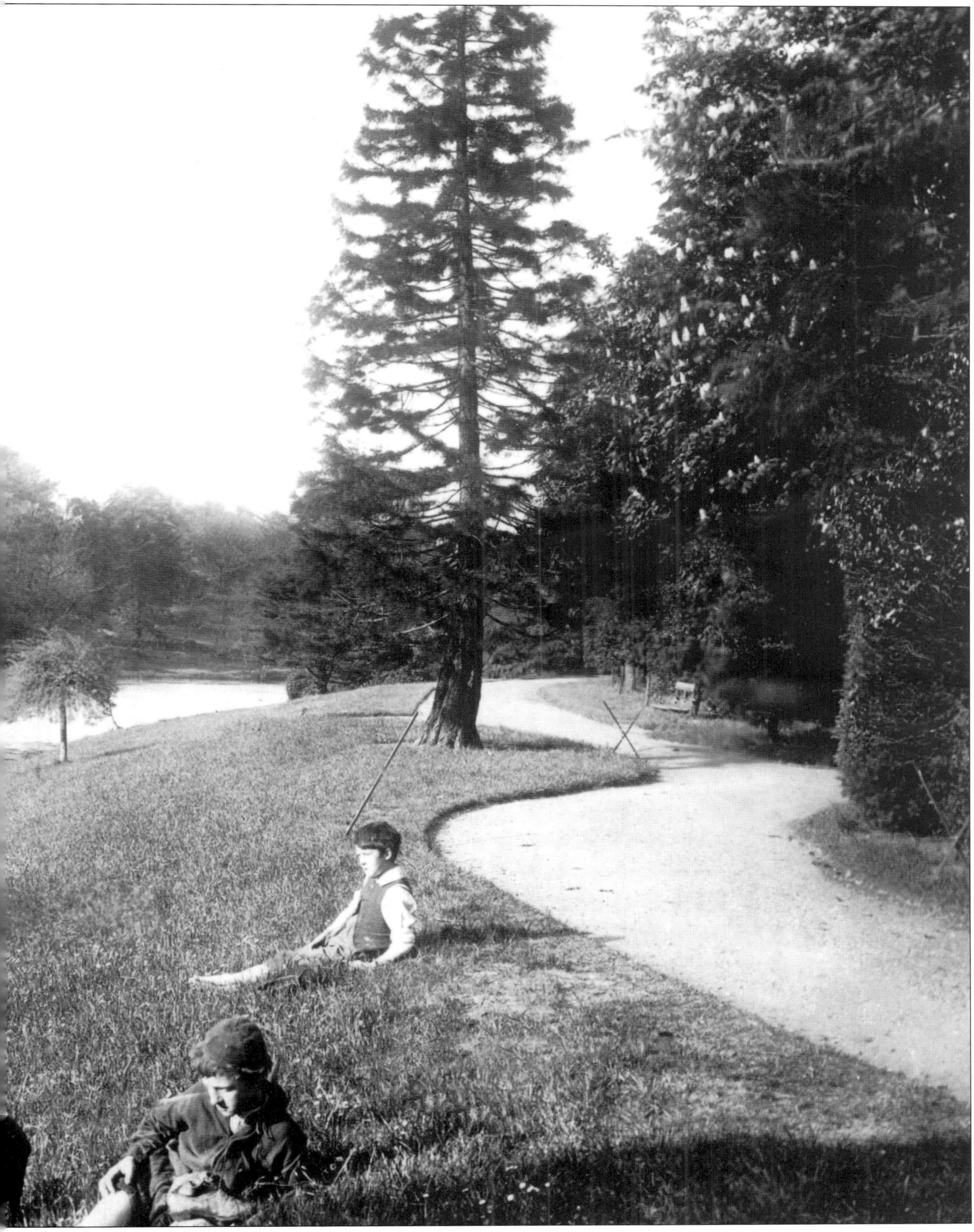

30984

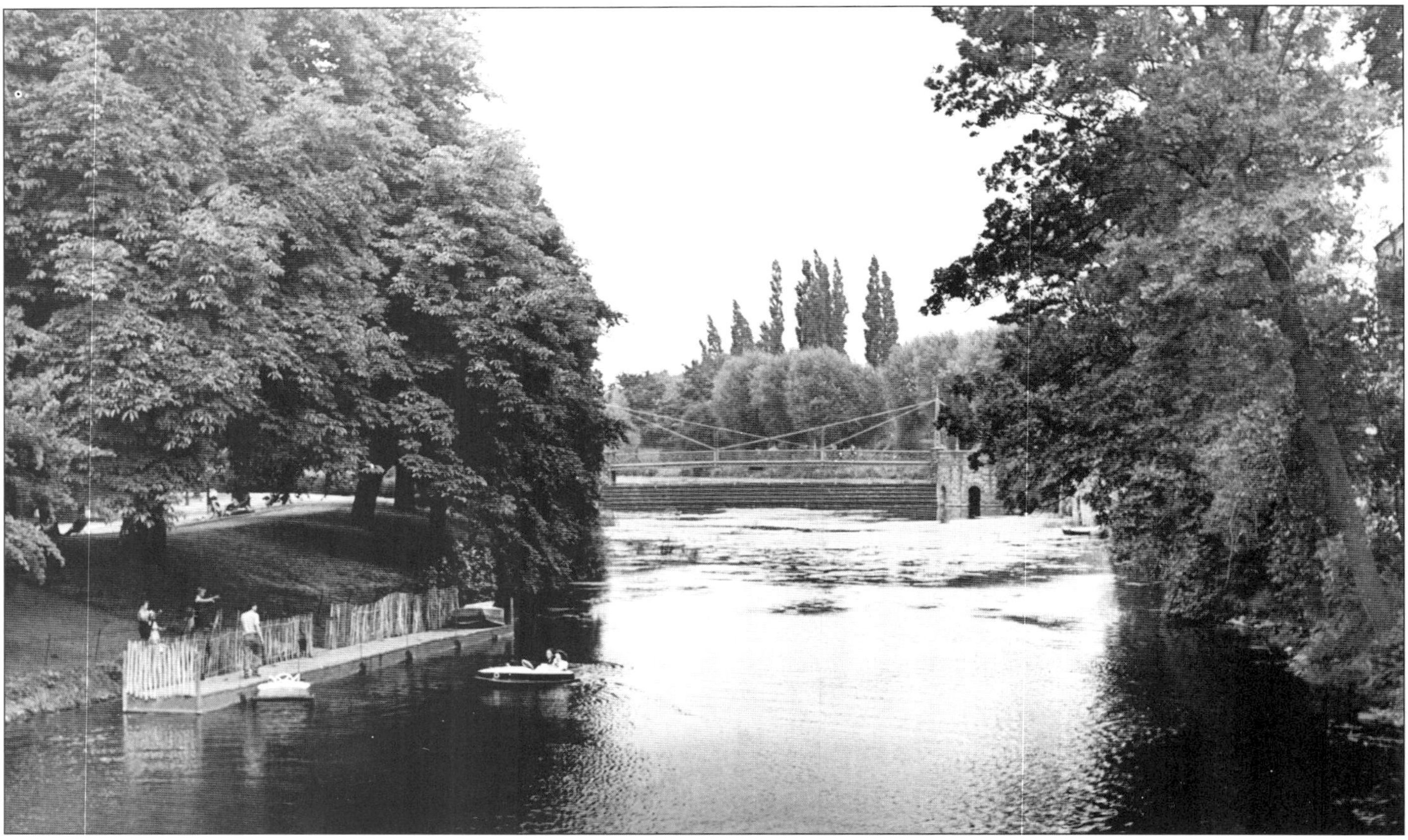

MOTORBOATS ON THE LEAM AT JEPHSON GARDENS, 1960. L25036

The gardens are now looked after by the Corporation and feature two fountains, which are replicas of those at Hampton Court, as well as superb floral displays.

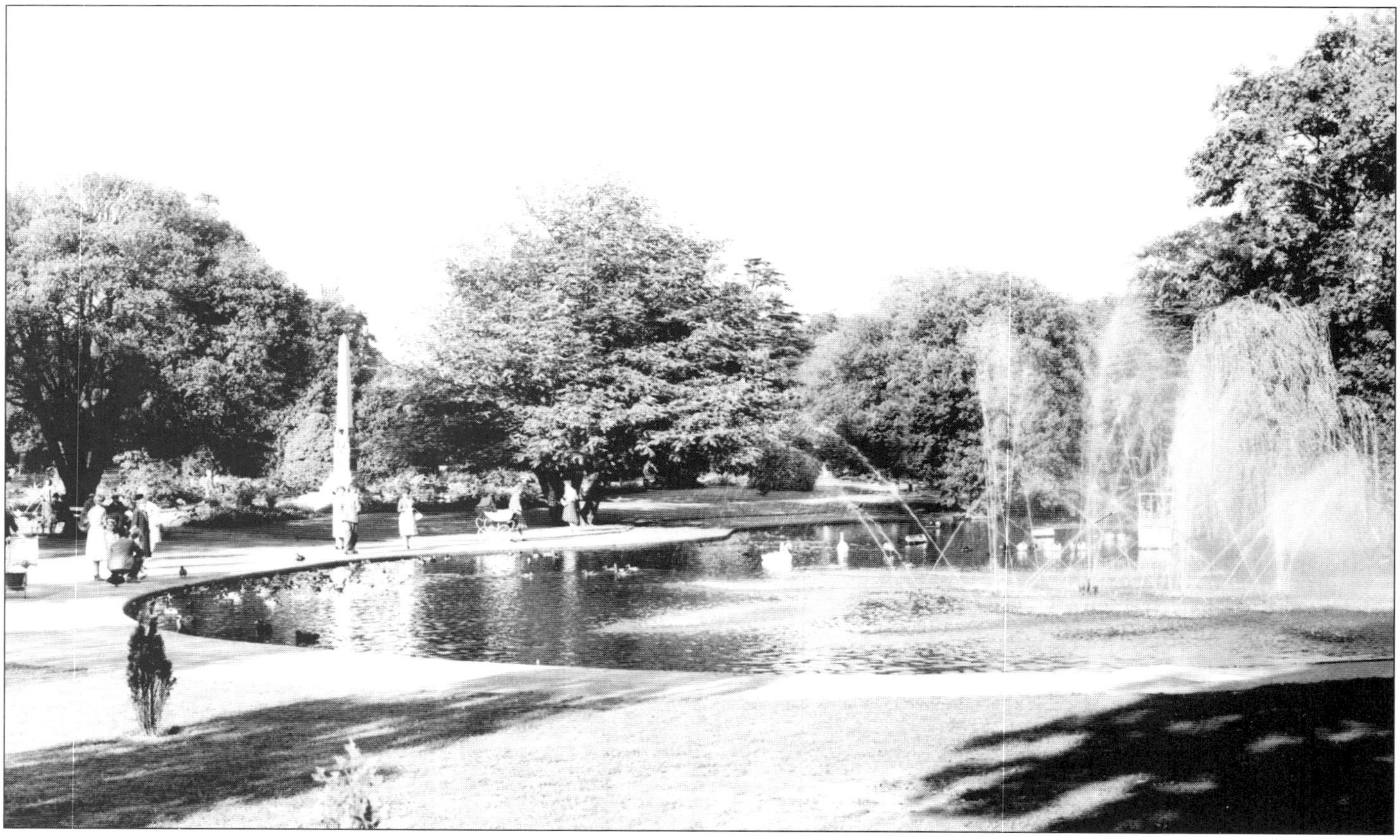

THE JEPHSON GARDENS, *c*.1960. L25076

The gardens on the banks of the Leam were laid out from the 1830s onwards. They are named after Dr Henry Jephson who was responsible for planning much of the town.

Chapter 4

KENILWORTH

Being just 19 miles from Birmingham, 6 miles from Coventry and only 5 miles from both Warwick and Lemington Spa, Kendilworth has grown into a dormitory town of over 20,000 people, it is probably most famous for its castle, it began life as a fairly basic motte and bailey castle built by Geoffrey de Clinton in the 1120s. During the reign of Henry II the castle was leased to the Crown, who eventually gained ownership outright. Under the Plantagenat Kings, vast sums were spent transforming Kenilworth into a fortress, the work included daming two brooks to create water defences on three sides covering 111 acres.

After it had seen many battles, the castle returned to the Crown and it was transformed over a two hundred year period into a palace. The last building phase came after 1563 when Elizabeth I gave it to Robert Dudley, Earl of Leicester. By the end of the Civil War, Kenilworth was in a poor state. It was given to a group of officers who divided up the land between themselves, drained the lake and dismantles several towers.

After the Restoration it became Crown property again, but was soon given to Robert Hyde. In 1937 Kenilworth was donated to the nation by Sir John Siddeley.

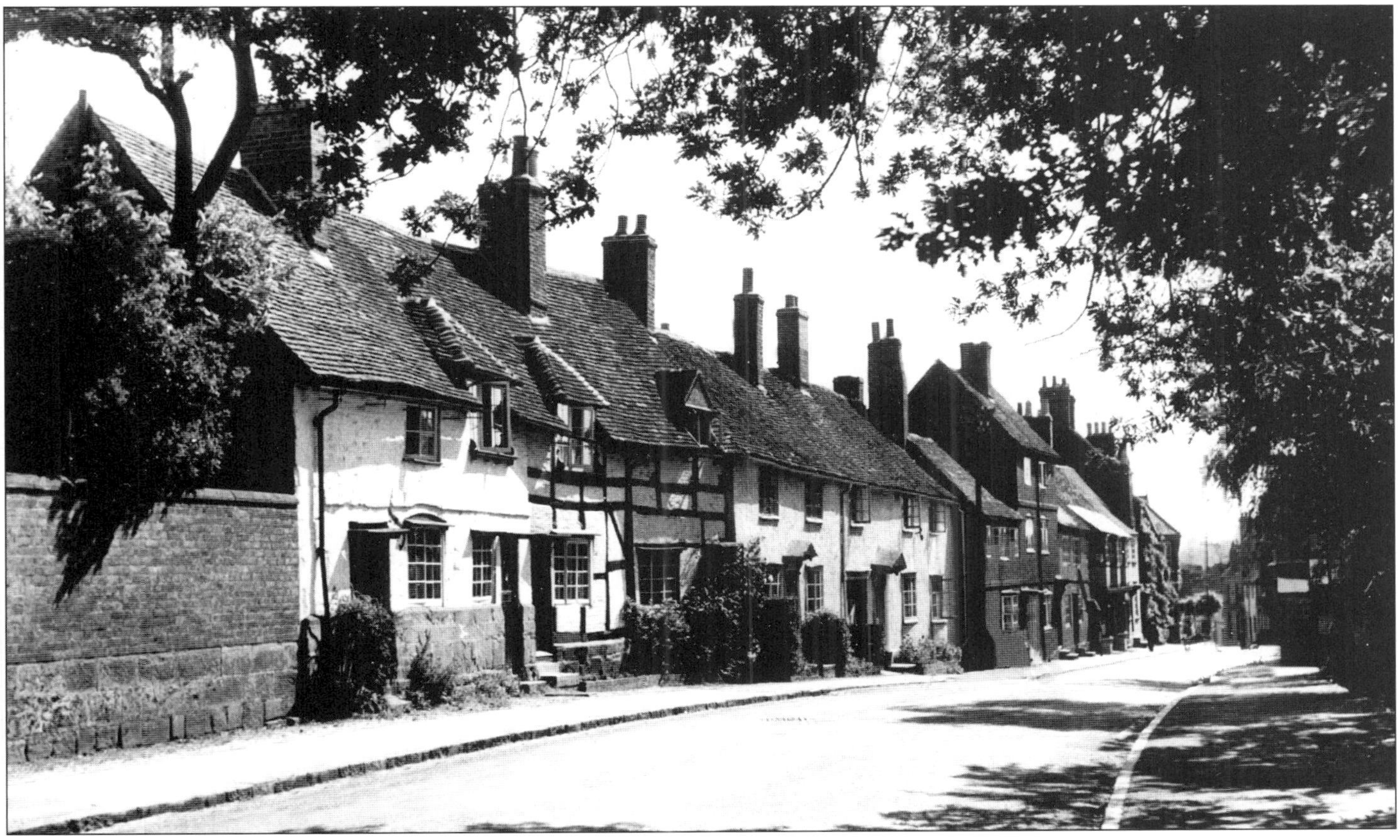

Kenilworth Town, *c.*1955. K5022

At the beginning of the twentieth century, Kenilworth was a small town with about 4,500 inhabitants. Visitors to the castle and surrounding area could avail themselves of the accommodation offered at The Abbey: rooms 4*s*, dinner 3-5*s*; or at The King's Arms Inn: rooms 3*s*, dinner 2*s* 6*d*.

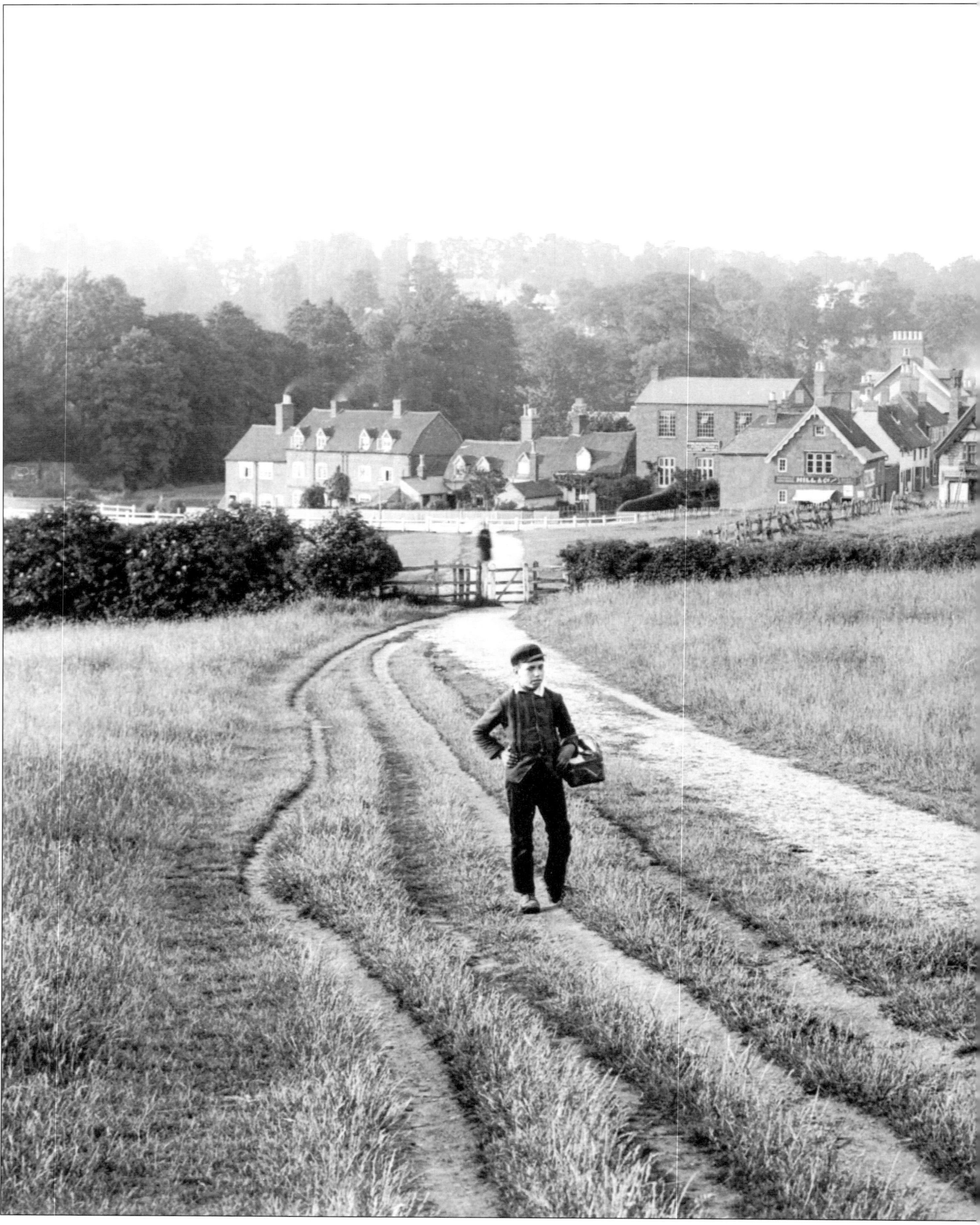

THE VILLAGE, 1892.
In 1906 it was possible to hire a horse and carriage at Warwick for a trip to Kenilworth and back for 10*s* 6*d,* though with two horses the price went up to £1, including the driver's fee. For 17*s* 6*d* a round trip via Leamington and Stoneleigh Abbey could be had.

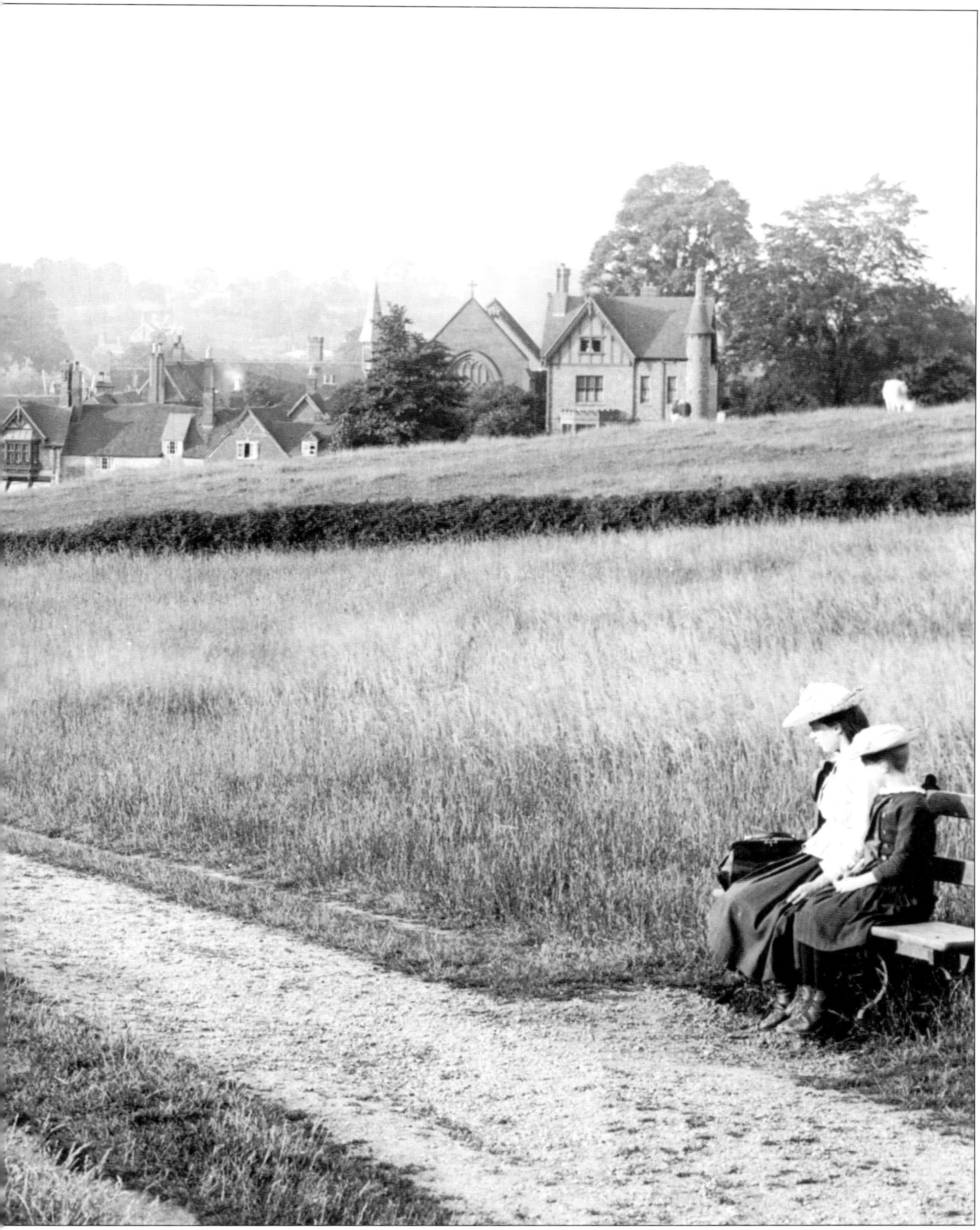

30945

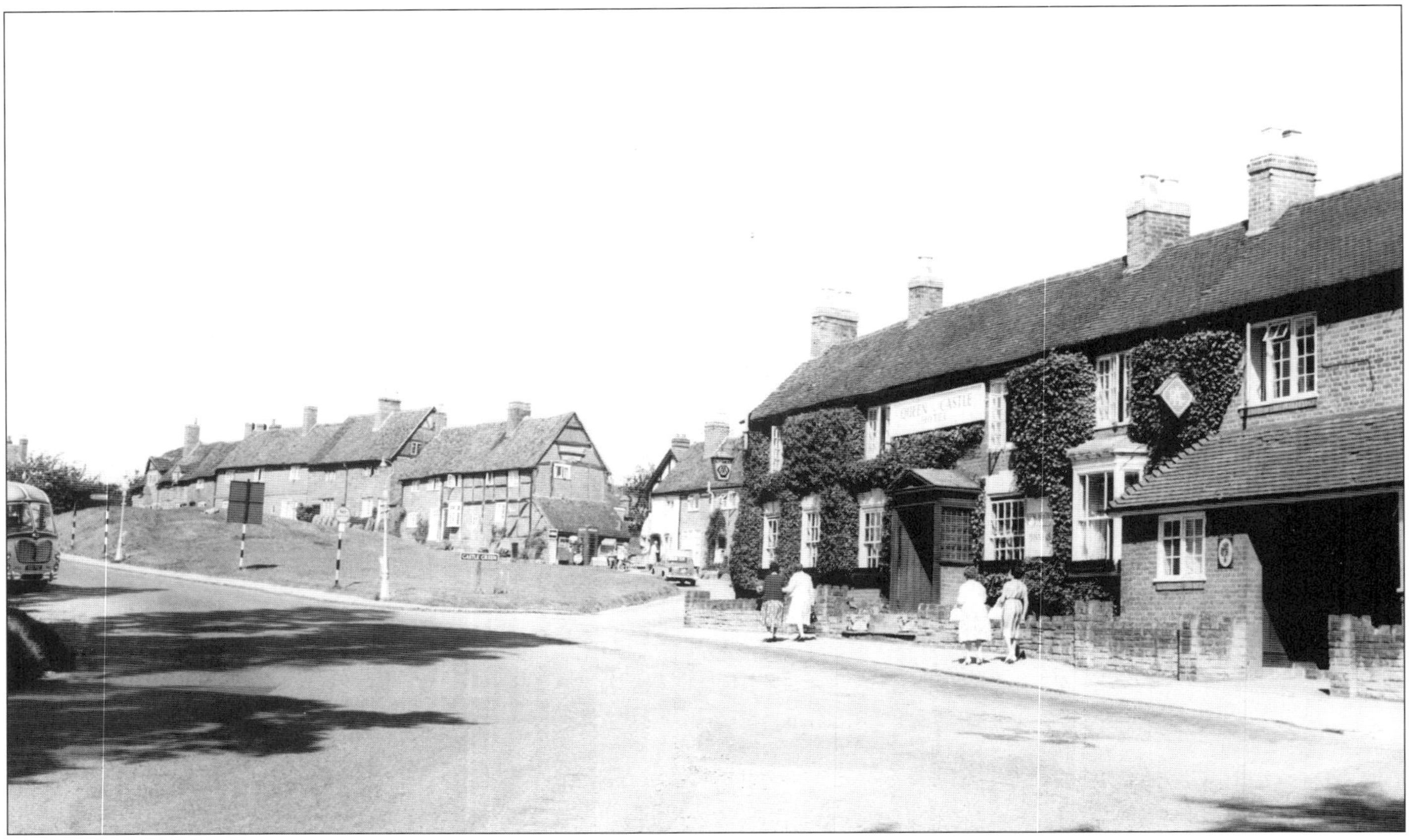

THE QUEEN & CASTLE HOTEL, *c.*1960. K5047

A quite corner of Kenilworth. It was in another of the towns inns, The King's Arms that Sir Walter Scott did the preparatory work and outline for his classic novel *Kenilworth*.

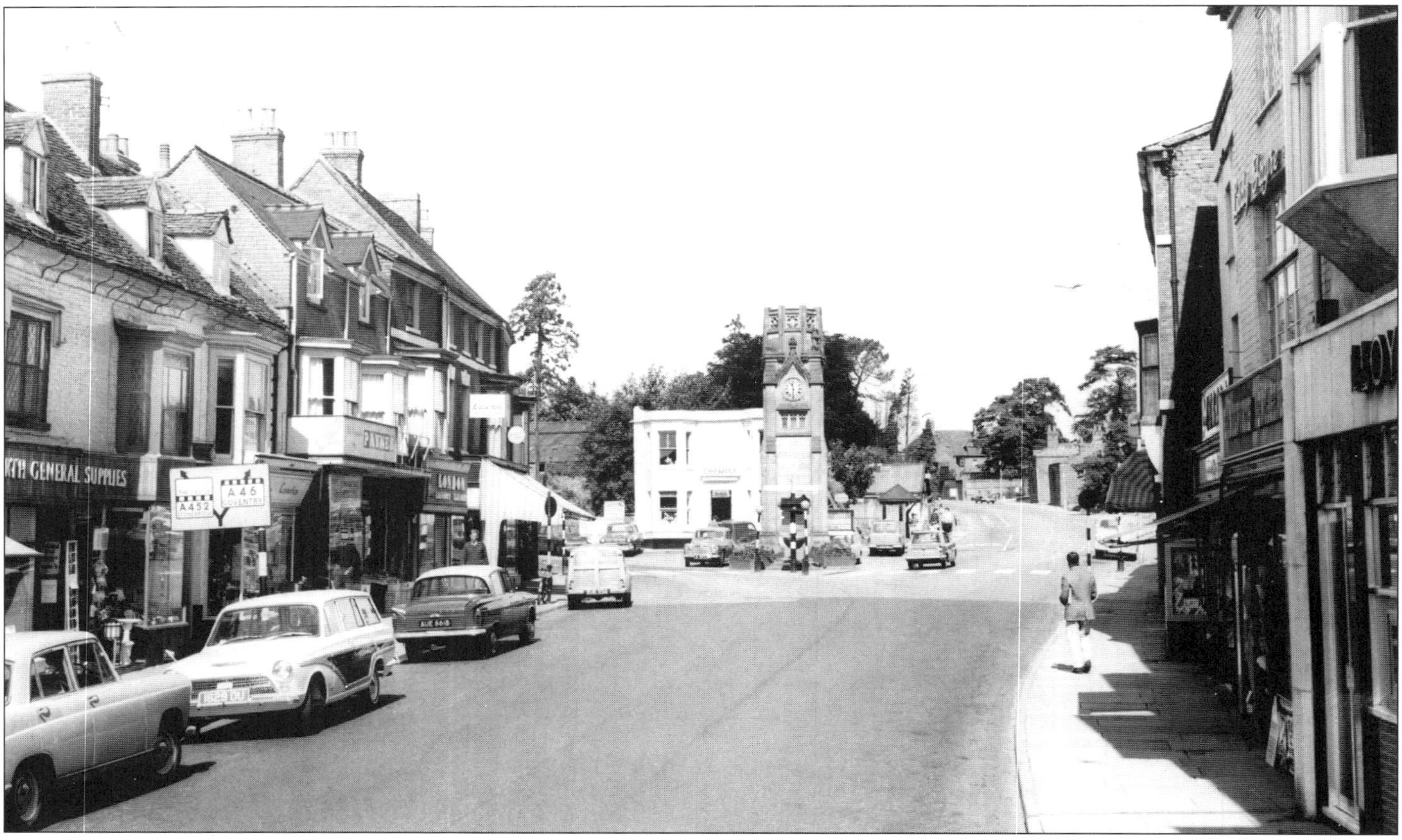

WARWICK ROAD, *c.*1960. K5049

Within a few years the road layout was changed to incorporate a traffic island. The white building in the centre background was demolished and a large block of drab-looking flats replaced the trees on the left.

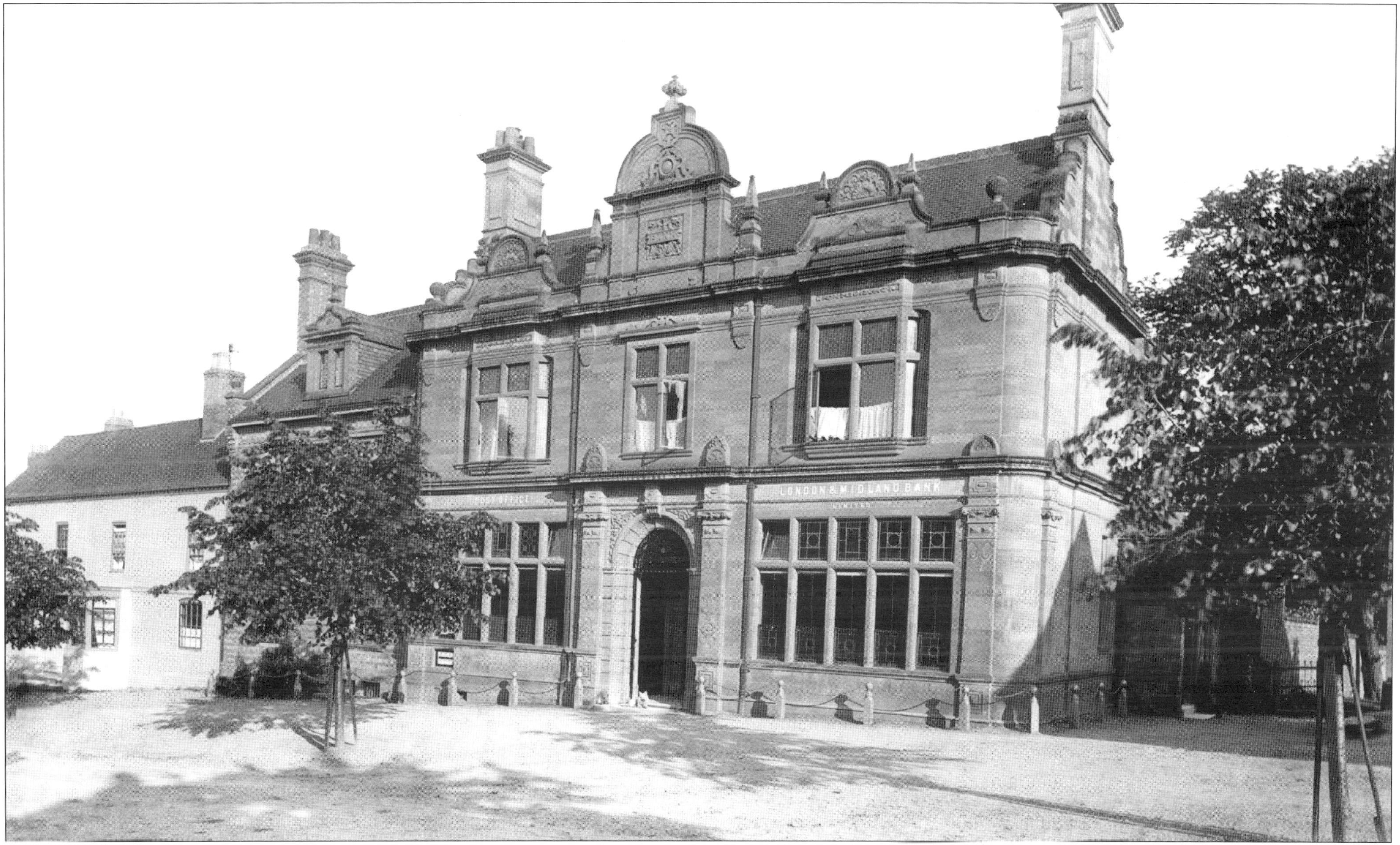

THE BANK AND POST OFFICE, 1892. 30949

In the 1880s and 90s post offices often opened longer hours than they do today, 7.00am to 9.00pm was common. On Sundays, telegraph offices opened 8.00am to 10.00am and 5.00pm to 6.00pm.

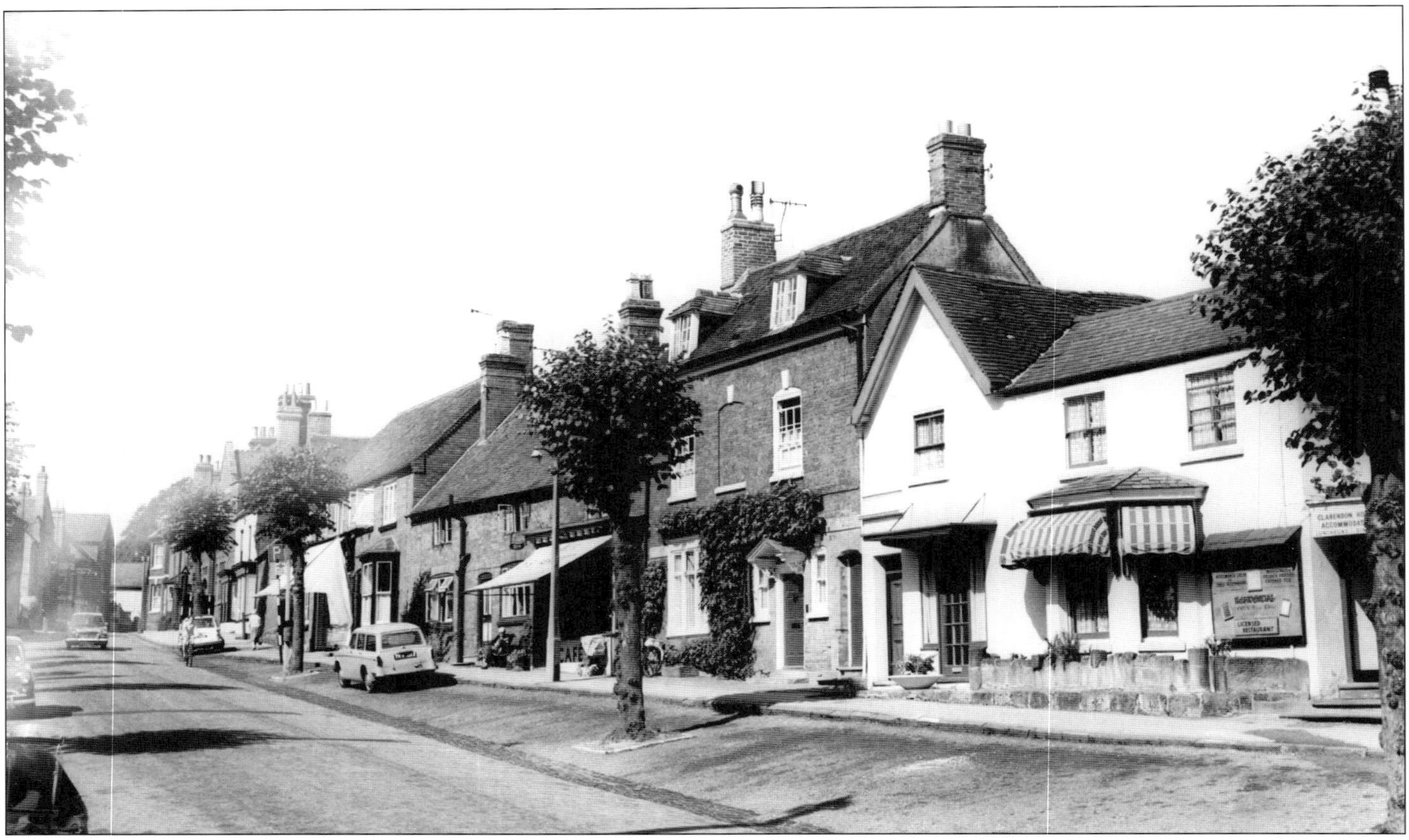

HIGH STREET, KENILWORTH, *c.*1955. K5041

When the Domesday Book was being compiled, Kenilworth came under the jurisdiction of the royal manor of Stoneleigh and was made up of two holdings – that of Alberic the Clerk and Richard the Forester. In 1122 Henry I united the holdings and gave them to Geoffrey de Clinton.

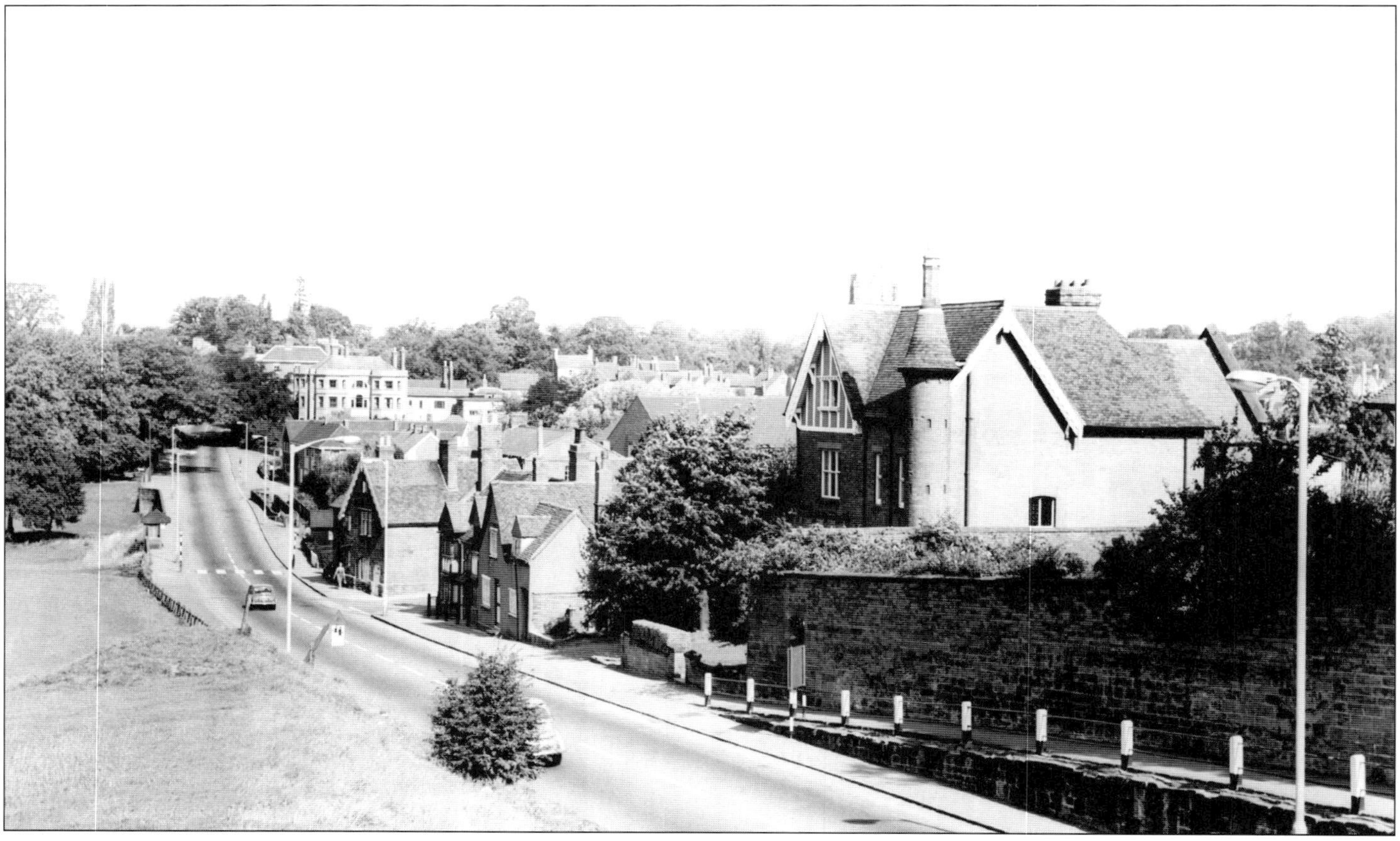

BRIDGE STREET, *c.*1960. K5040

On the left are the Abbey Fields at the end of which stands the late-thirteenth century church of St Nicholas. Nearby are the ruins of Kenilworth Abbey, founded and endowed by Geoffrey de Clinton in 1122.

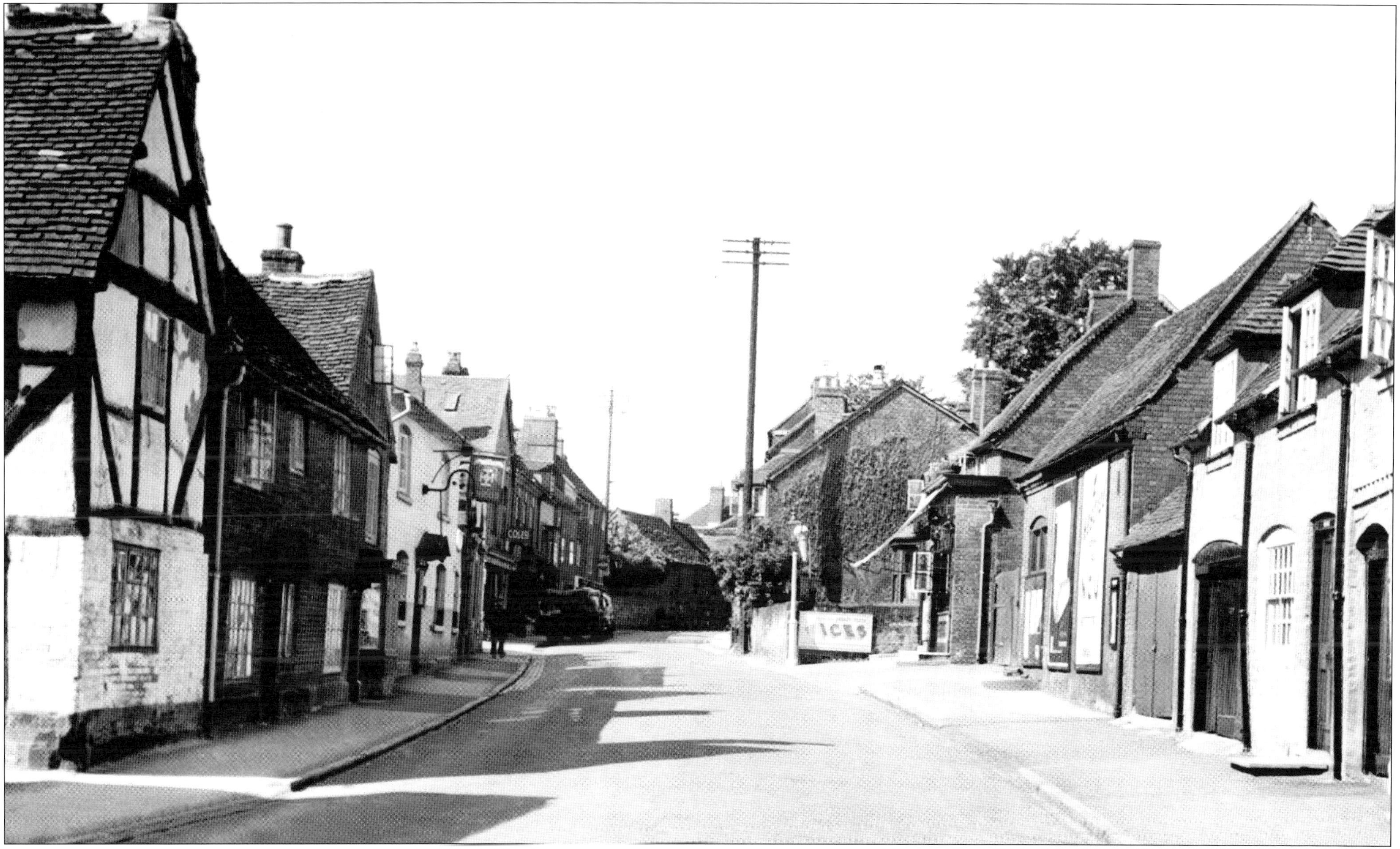

NEW STREET, KENILWORTH, *c*.1960. K5019

A mixture of building styles rangeing from the seventeenth to the nineteenth centuries. New Street is a continuation of Castle Hill and High Street and leads to Coventry Road.

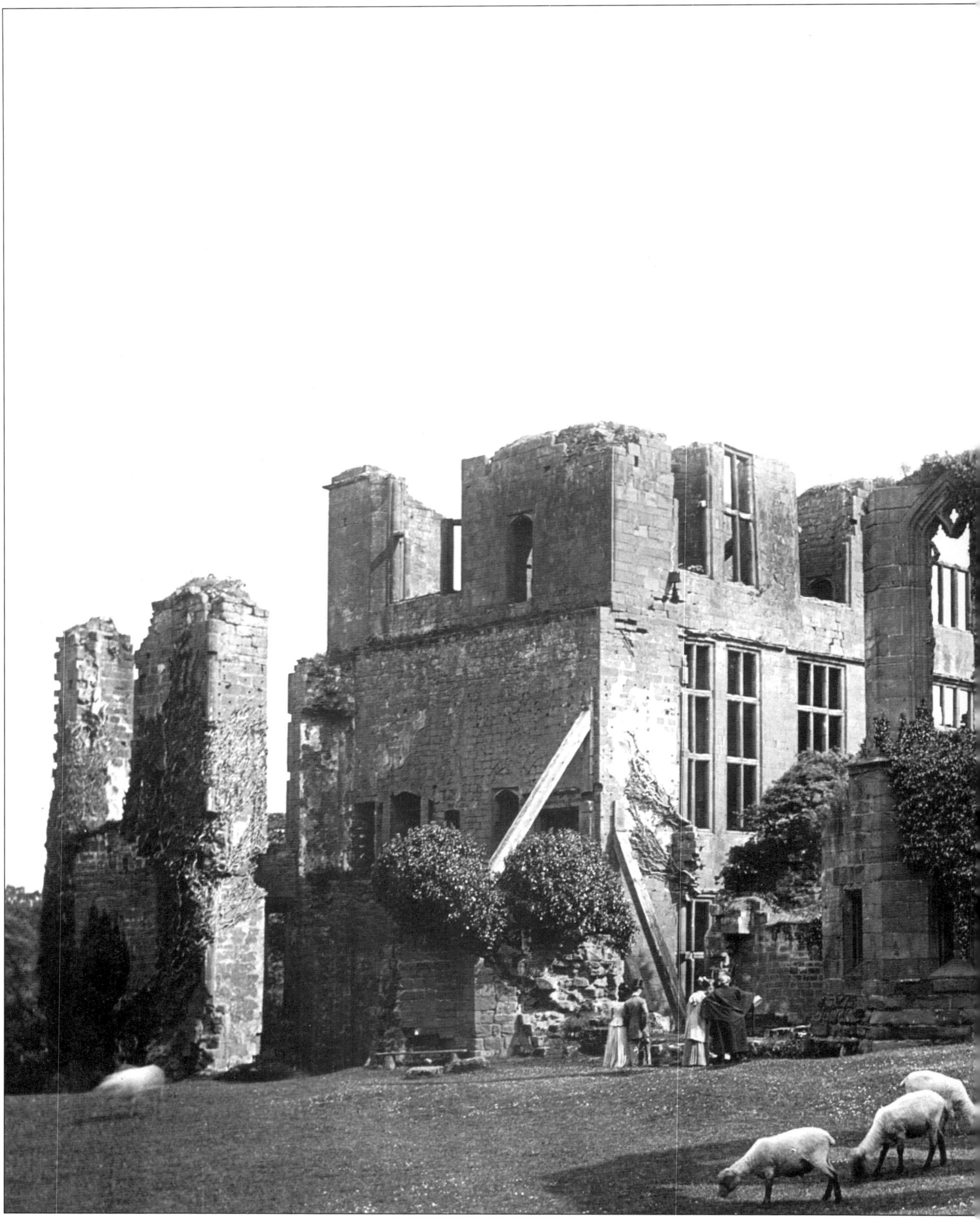

KENILWORTH CASTLE, 1892.
The first castle to be built at Kenilworth is thought to have been a motte and bailey constructed between 1122-1127 by Geoffrey de Clinton. It was de Clinton's son who built the keep. One of Kenilworth's prisoners was the deposed Edward II, who was held here prior to his transfer to Berkeley Castle, where he was murdered with a red-hot poker.

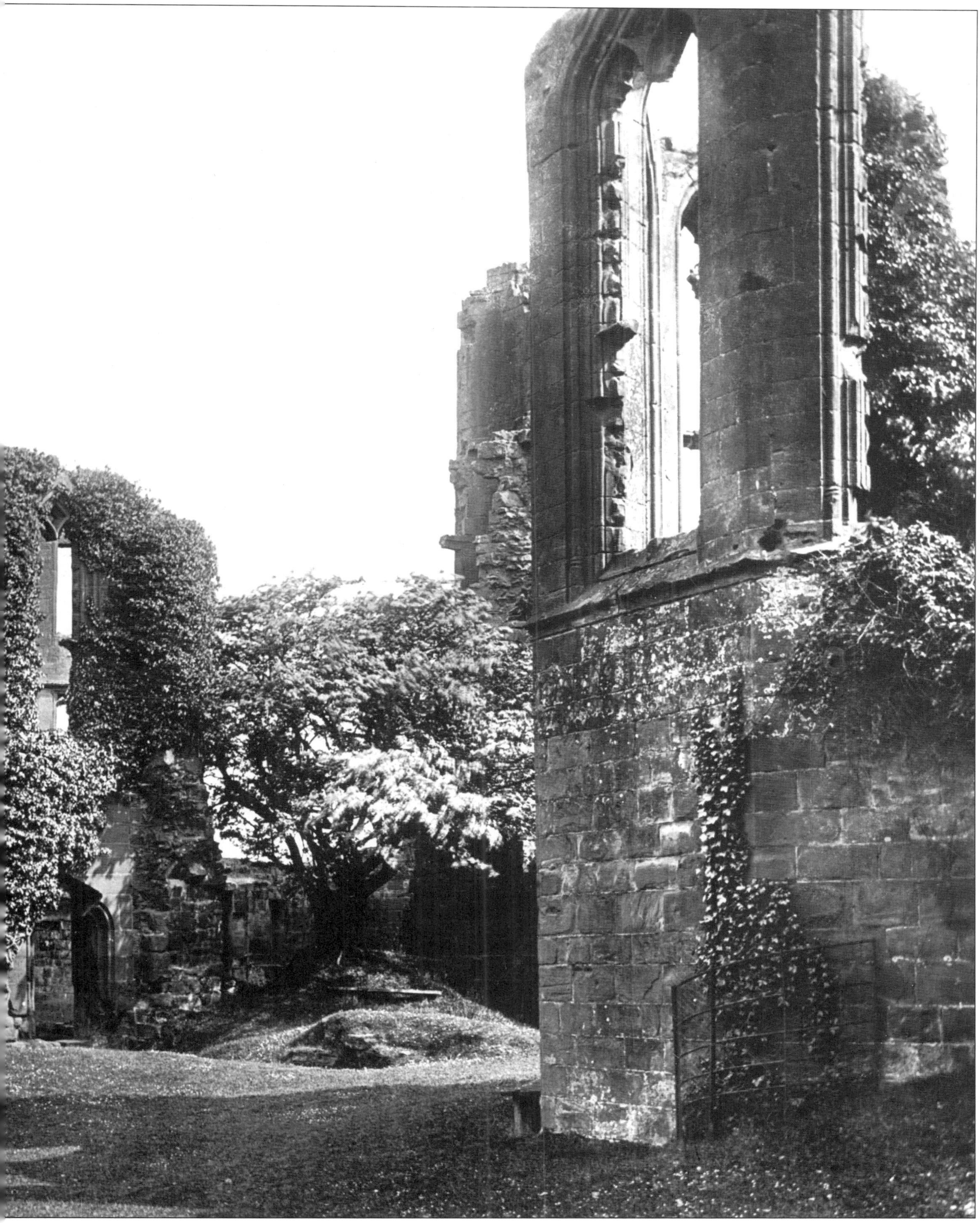

30935

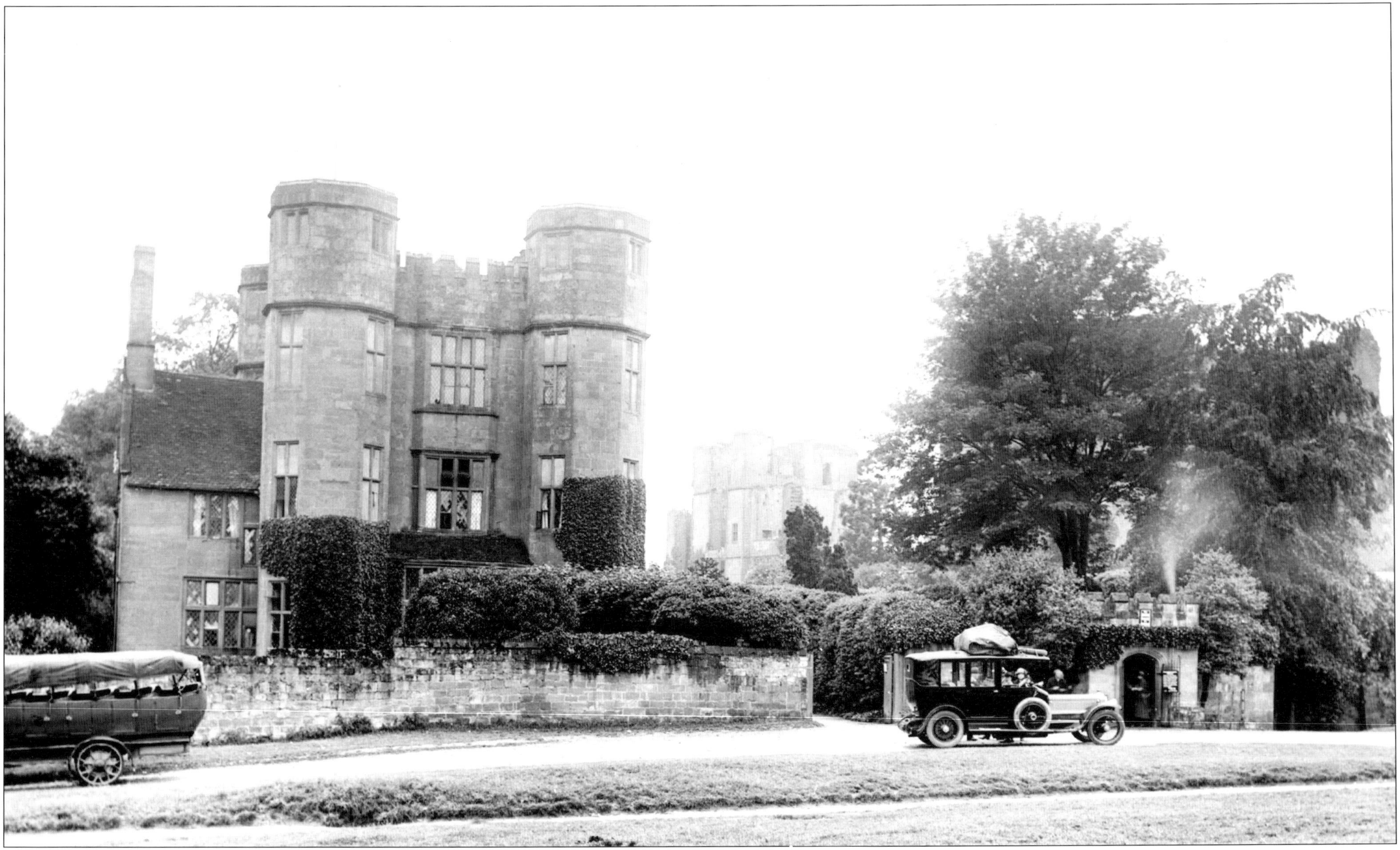

KENILWORTH CASTLE, 1922. 72405

The entrance is the small gateway just in front of the car. On the left is Leicester's gatehouse, which had been converted into a private dwelling.

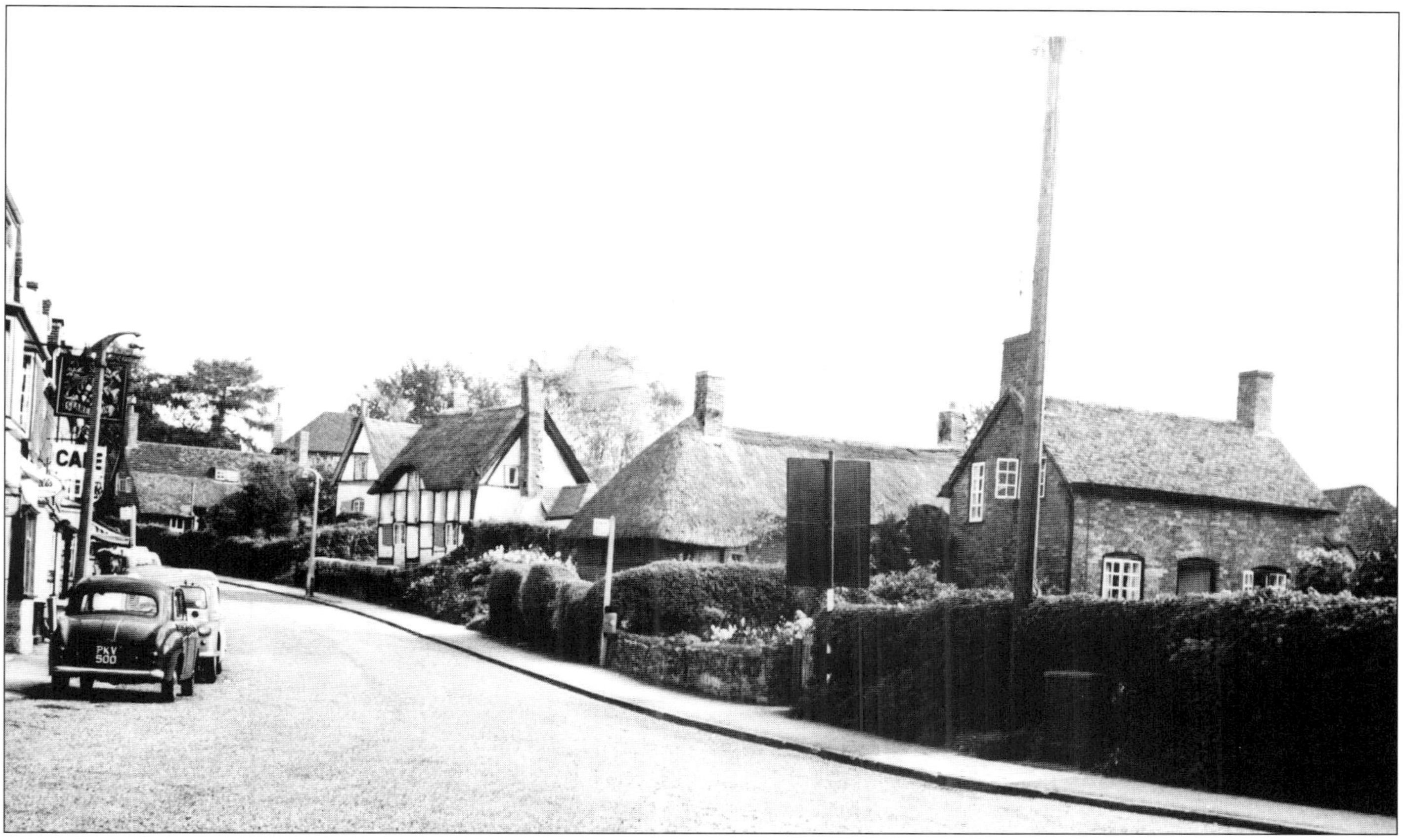

CASTLE STREET, *c.*1960. K5310

Apart from bus stops, street lamps and motor cars, little else seems to have changed for perhaps half a century or more.

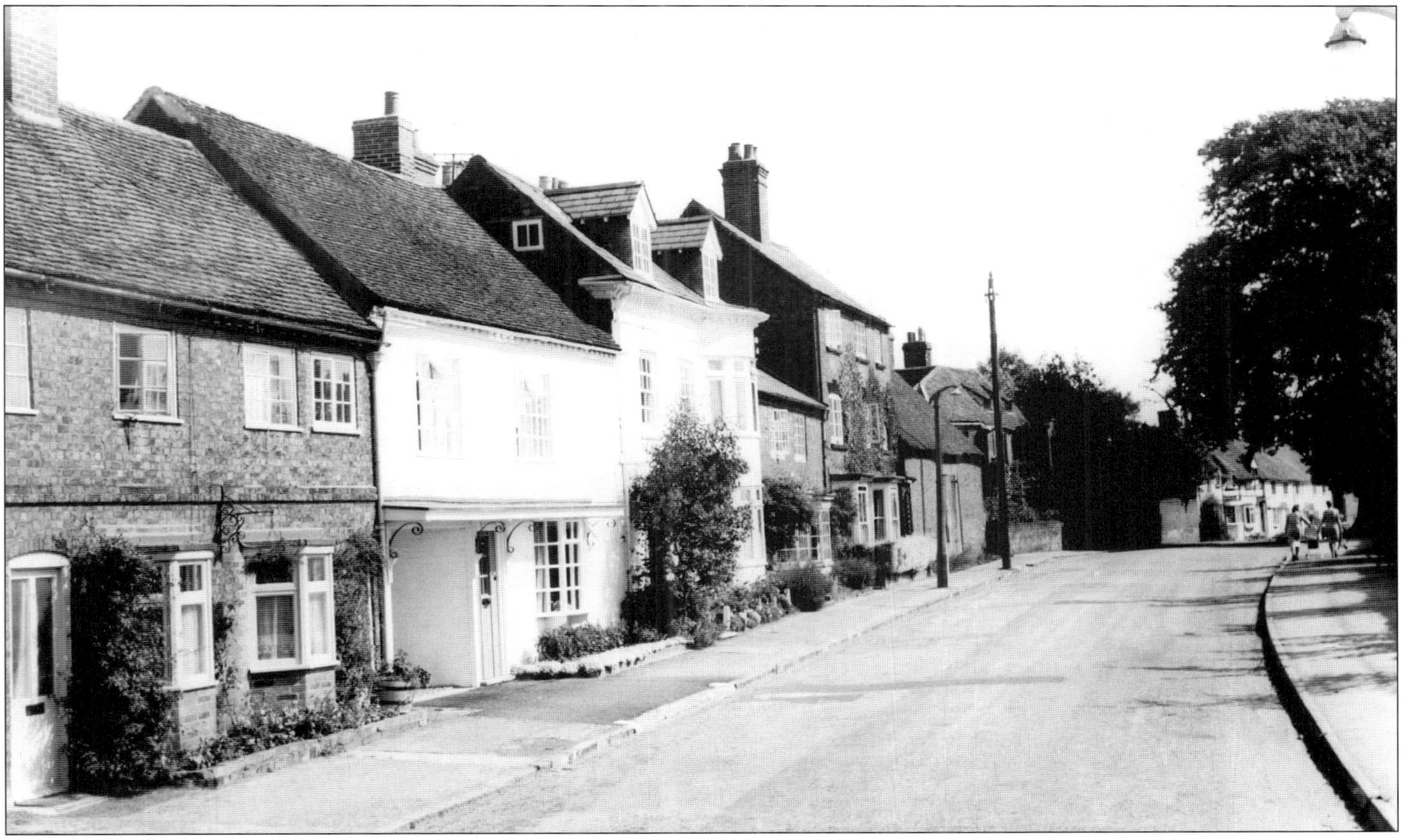

CASTLE HILL, *c.*1960. K5048

Kenilworth was still lit by gas lamps in the 1920s. During the winter months the lamplighter would turn on the lamps using a long pole. One end of the pole was pushed through a little window in the lamp and hooked onto the mantle chain. The chain was pulled and the mantle ignited. On windy nights the council sent workers out to inspect the lamps and make sure they were still lit.

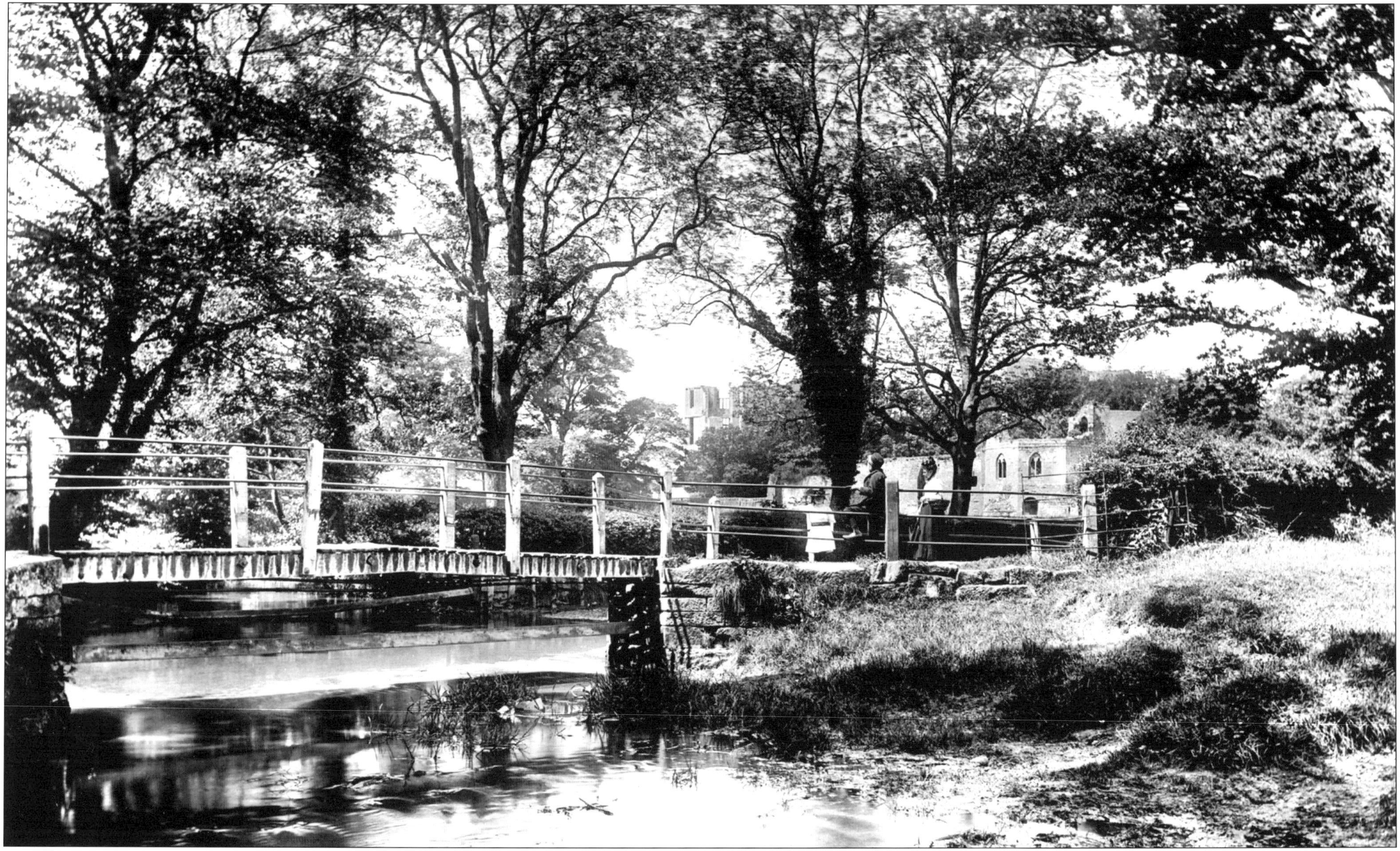

KENILWORTH CASTLE FROM BELOW THE FOOTBRIDGE, 1892. 30941

It was John of Gaunt who set about transforming Kenilworth from a Norman fortress to a Gothic palace. Work began around 1389, with only the keep being retained. The entire inner ward was rebuilt and included a great hall, private apartments, kitchens and store rooms.

CHAPTER 5

WARWICK & WARWICK CASTLE

The earliest fortifications at Warwick were thrown up in AD 915 by Ethelfleda of Mercia. The ditch and palisade defences were placed round the town itself, Warwick at this time being little more than a frontier town next to the Danelaw. Ethelfleda joined with her brother Edward the Elder to reconquer English territory held by the Danes. In AD 917 she took Derby and the following year captured Leicester.

Henry de Newburgh built a large wooden motte and bailey on the site of the present castle, and before his death in 1123 he might well have begun to replace the wood with stone. During the Barons' War, Warwick Castle was sacked and all but destroyed by forces loyal to Simon de Montfort. In 1268 the earldom passed to the Beauchamp family who set about the task of rebuilding.

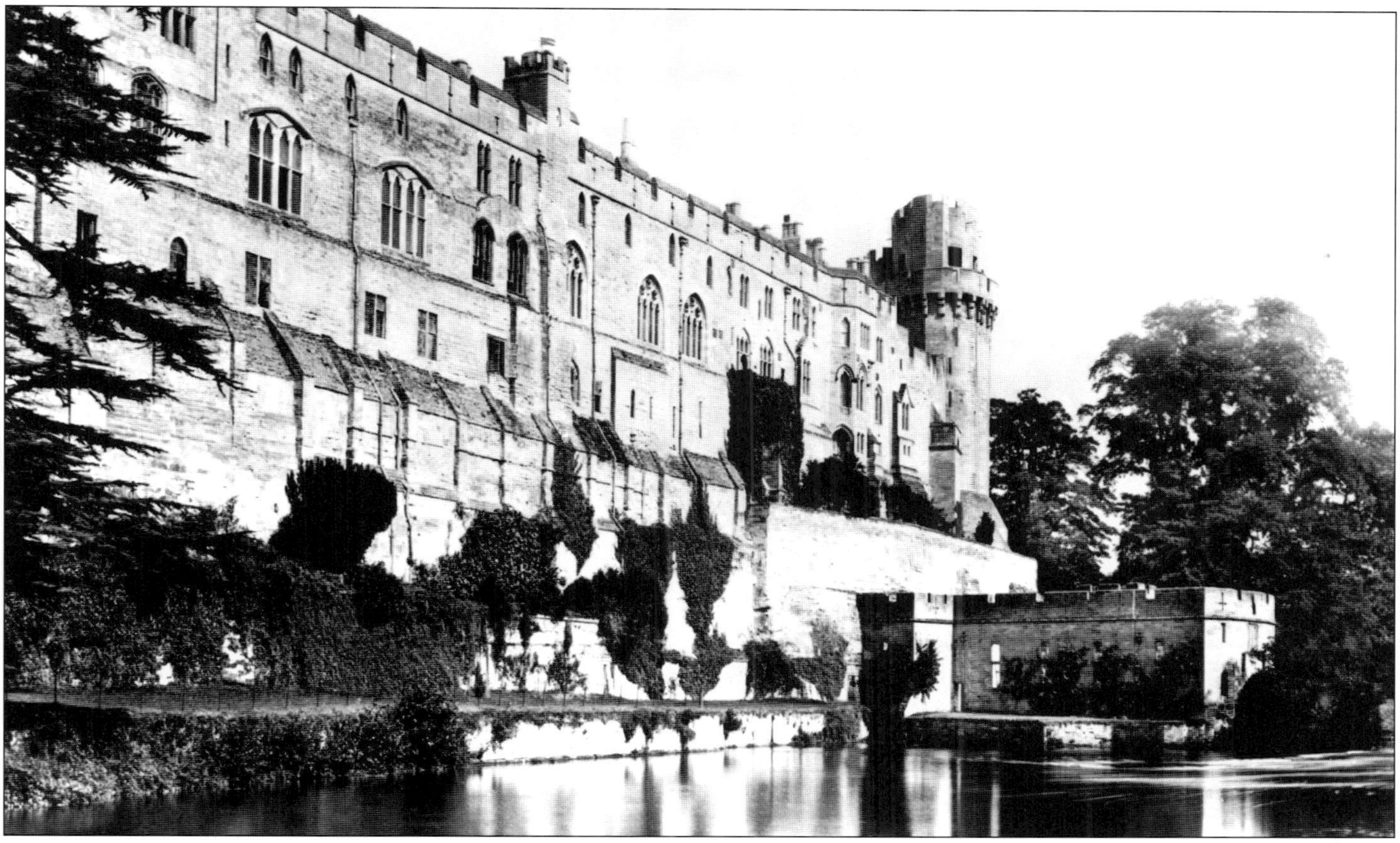

WARWICK CASTLE, 1886. 17039

The domestic buildings of Warwick Castle are situated on the southern side of the fortress overlooking the river. The roof of the Great Hall and several other rooms were restored at considerable cost after being seriously damaged by fire in 1871.

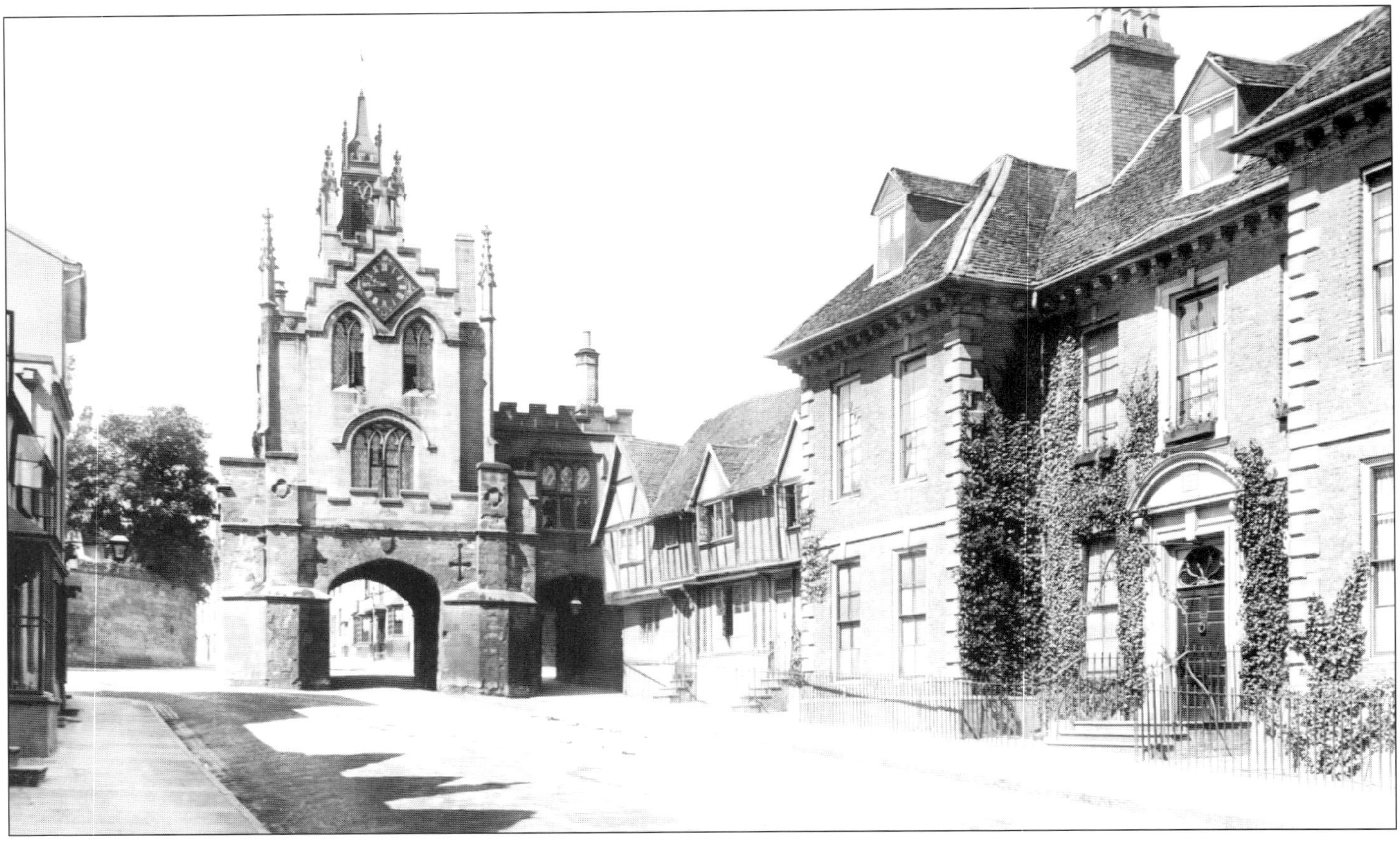

THE EAST GATE AND LANDOR HOUSE, 1892. 31029

Walter Savage Landor was a poet and essayist who lived 1775-1864. Among his works are *Imaginary Conversations*, *The Crimean Heroes*, *Around the Child*, *A Foreign Ruler* and *The Last Fruit Off an Old Tree*. He was also expelled from Rugby School.

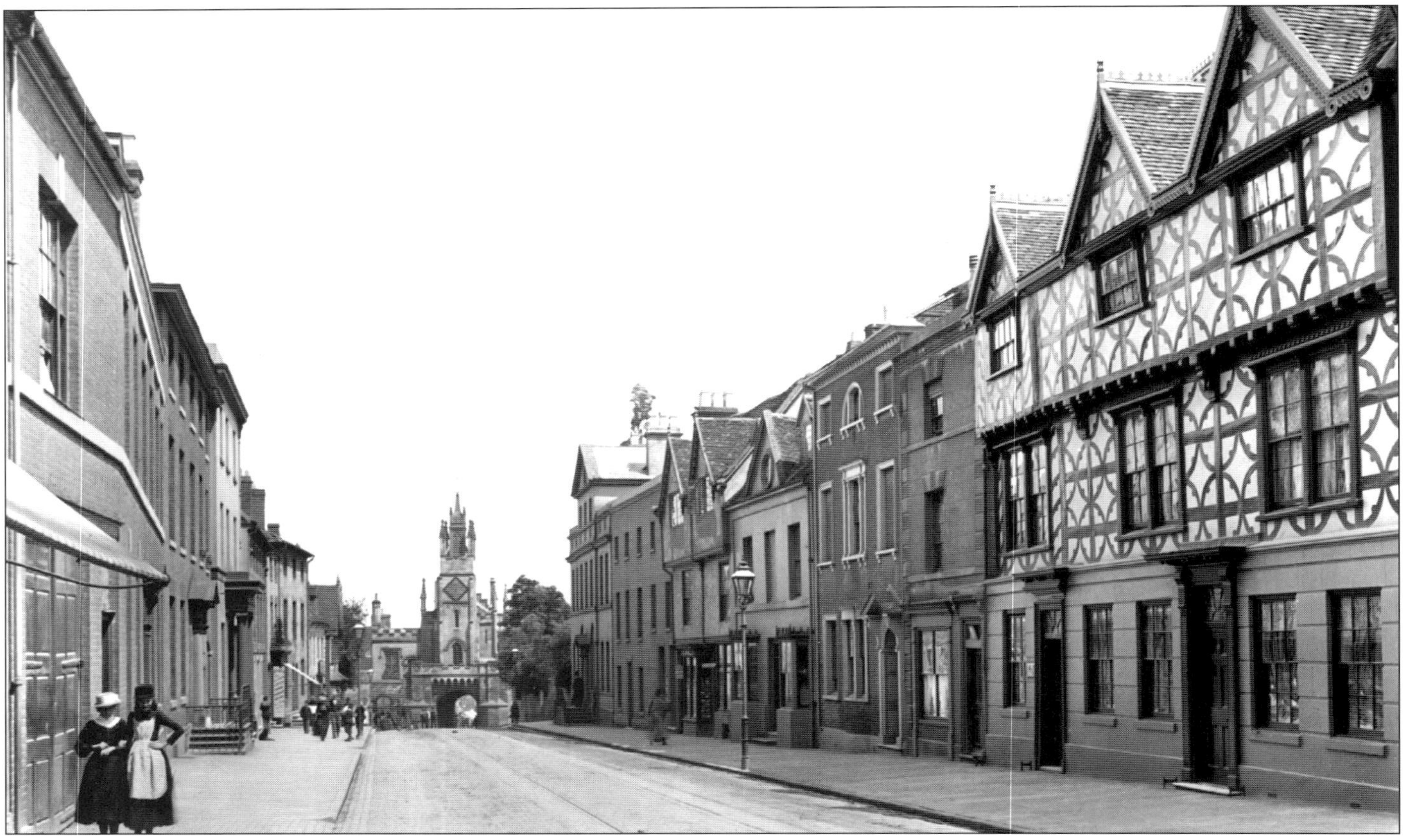

VIEW TOWARD THE EAST GATE, 1892. 31030

Though probably the least spoilt all the English county towns, little survives of pre-1694 Warwick. In that year much of the town centre was destroyed by fire.

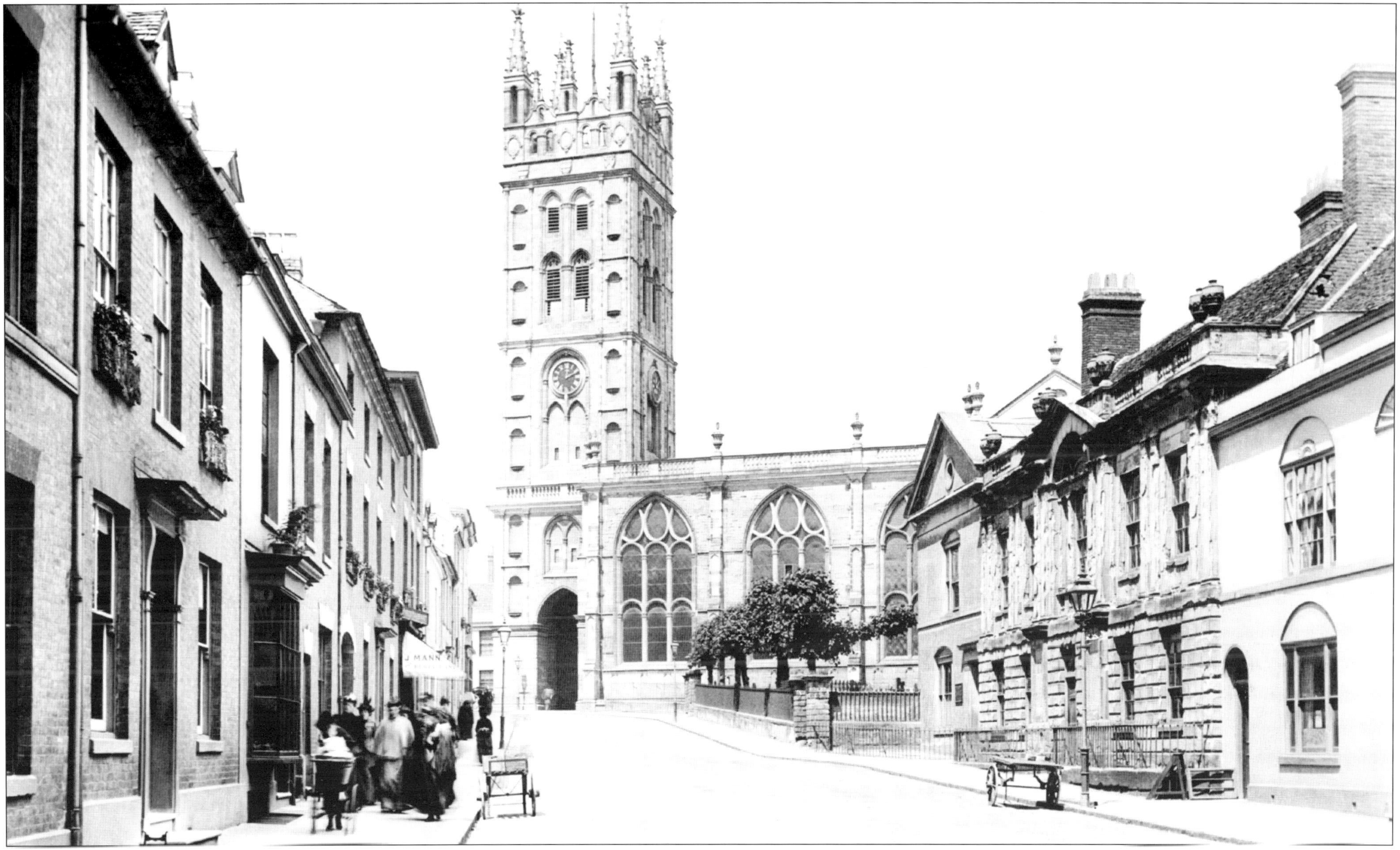

ST MARY'S CHURCH, 1892. 31015

In 1694 St Mary's was partly destroyed by fire. The choir, chapter house and Beauchamp Chapel escaped destruction and by 1704 a new nave and a Gothic tower had been built.

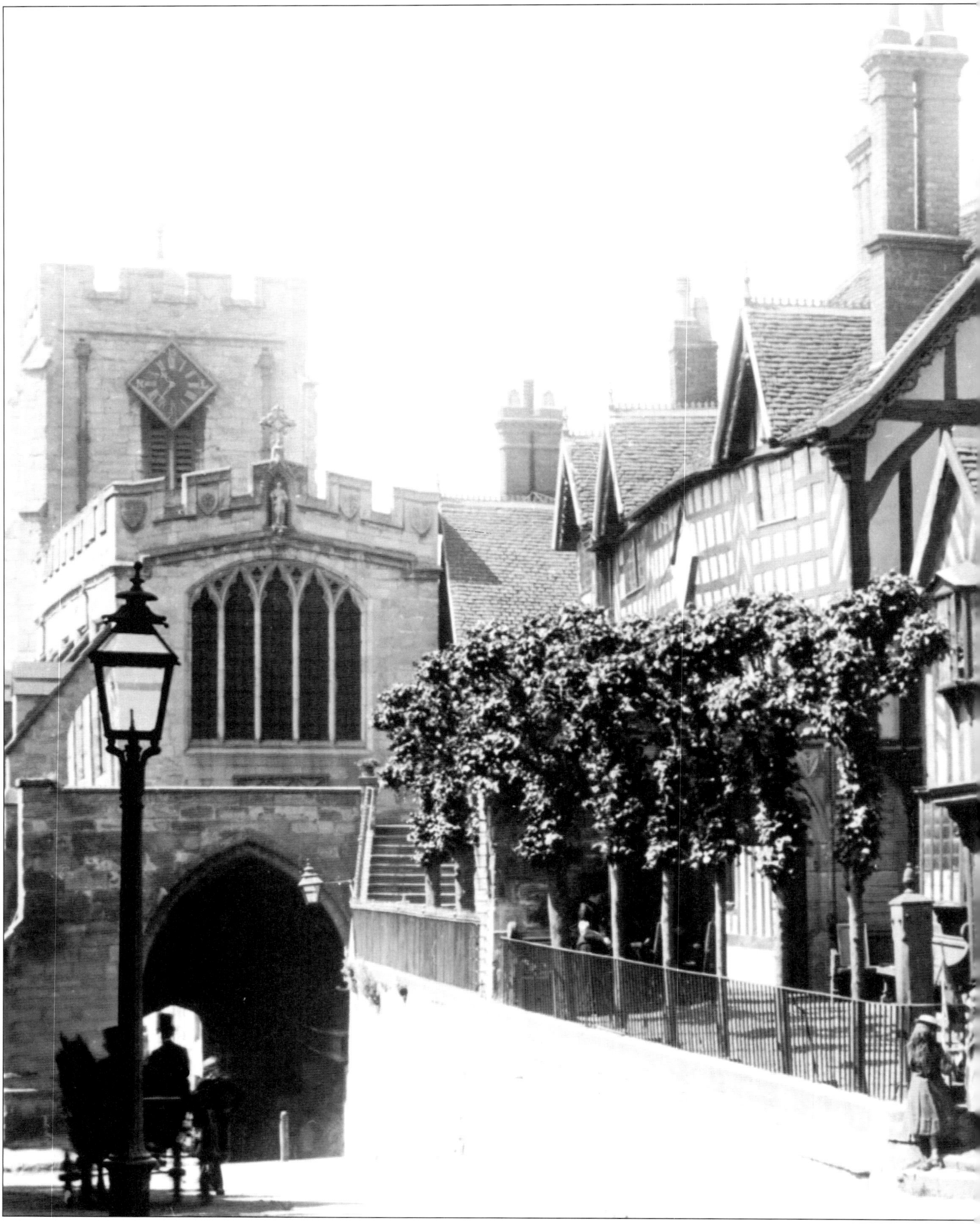

West Gate, 1892.
Standing beneath St James' Chapel is the West Gate, a part of the town's twelfth-century fortifications. The half-timbered buildings are Lord Leycester's Hospital, an almshouse founded by Robert Dudley, Earl of Leicester.

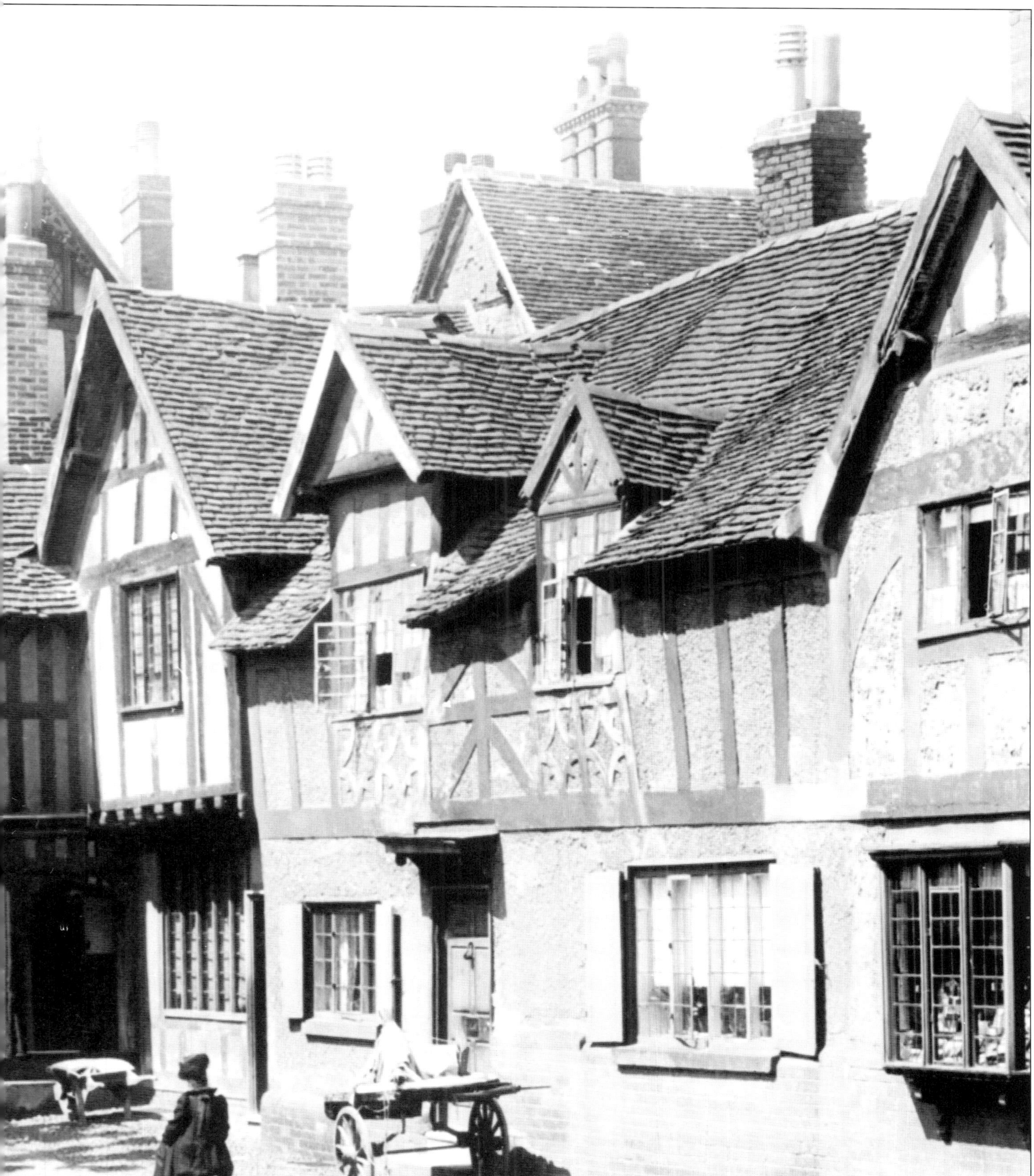

31022

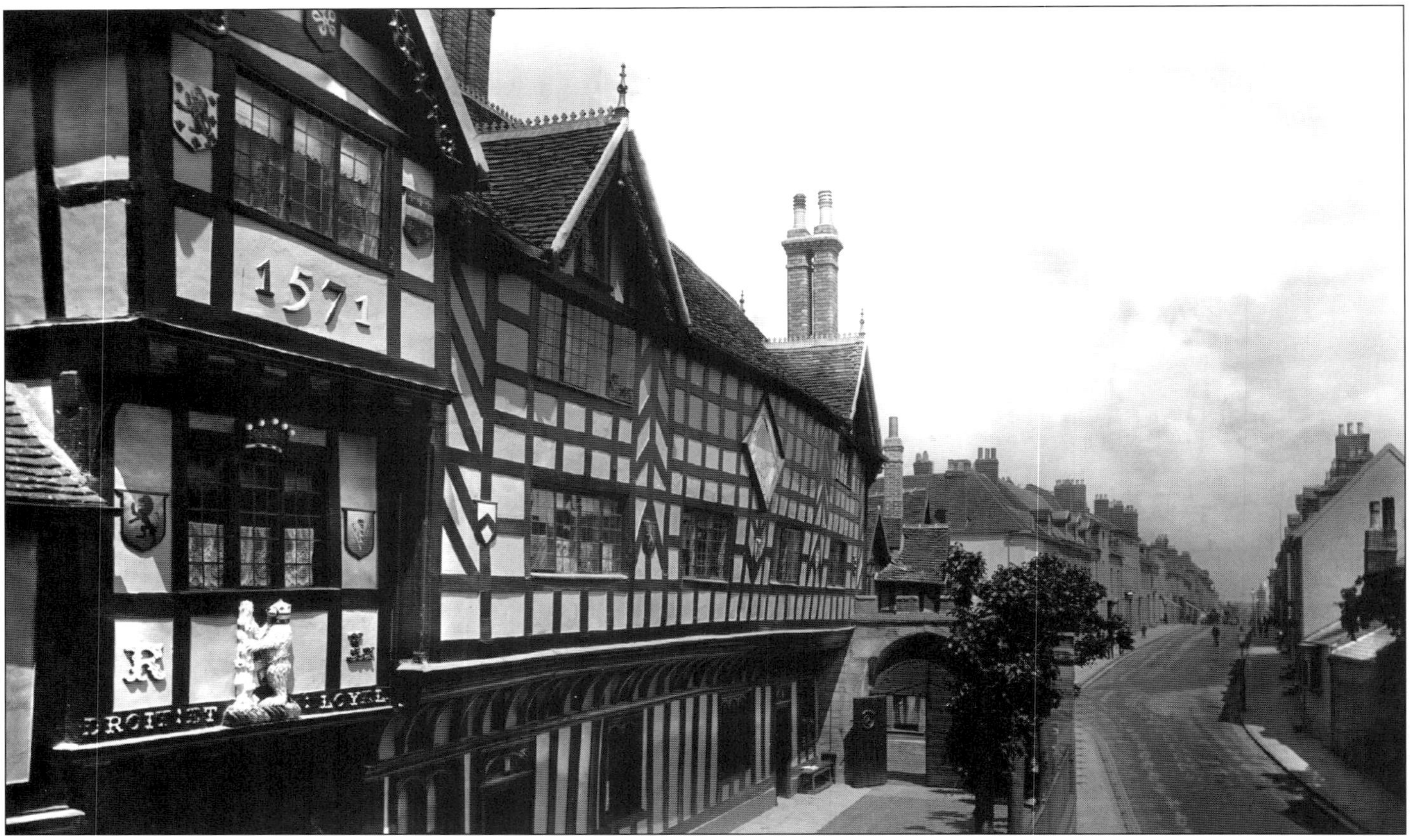

HIGH STREET, 1892. 31023

Looking from Lord Leycester's Hospital along the high street. Built in 1571 the hospital provided accommodation for 12 poor brothers, former soldiers who had seen service with the family. They were required to wear a blue gown and the silver badge of the Bear and Ragged Staff of the Warwick earldom.

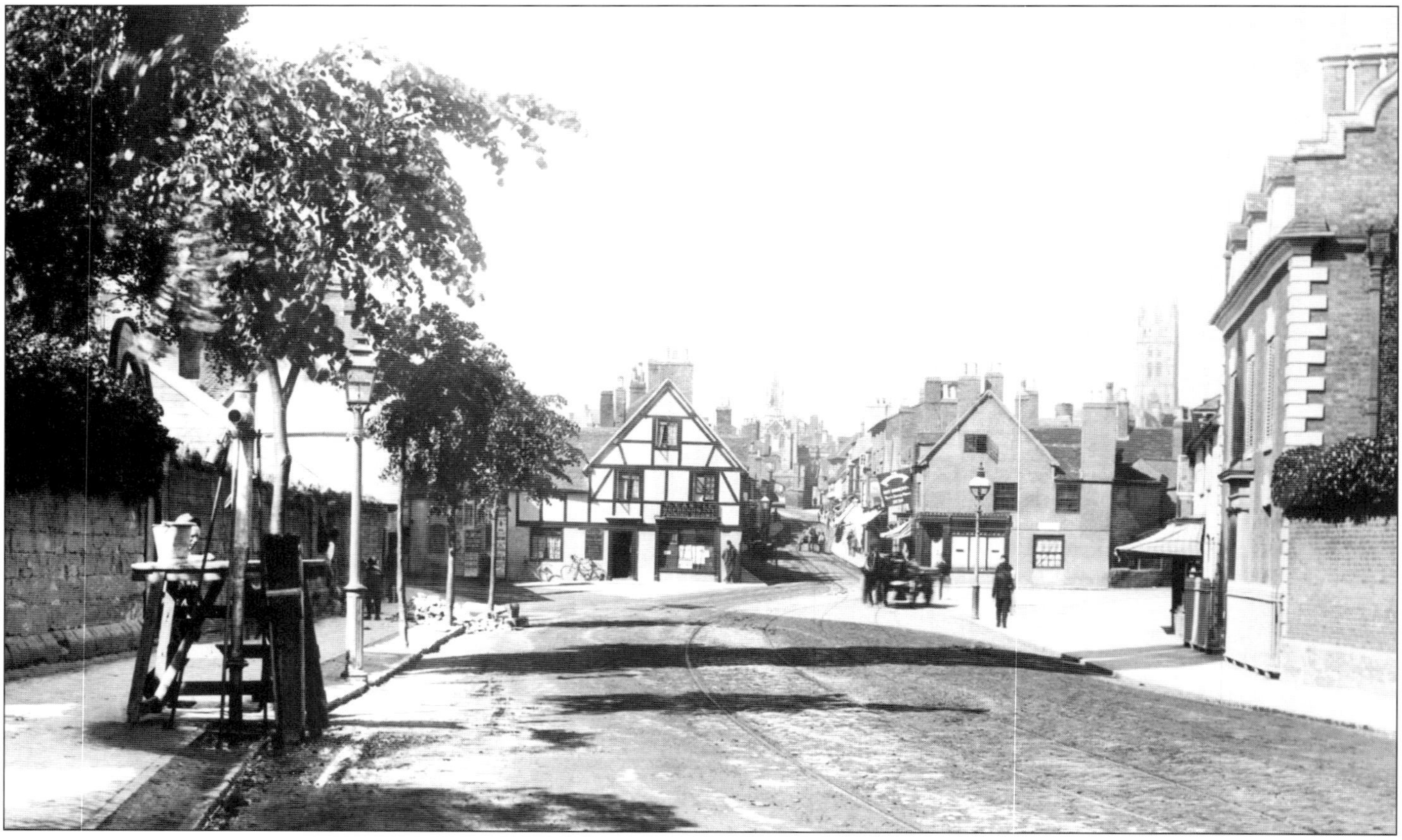

ST JOHN'S STREET, 1892. 31031

Following the death of Ambrose Dudley in 1589, Warwick Castle was once again in the hands of the Crown. James I awarded it to Sir Fulke Greville, who was also given the title of Baron Brooke of Beauchamp Court. However, for over 150 years the castle and the earldom were separate, the title having been awarded to Robert, Lord Rich. When the last of the male Richs died in 1759 the title quickly came to the Grevilles.

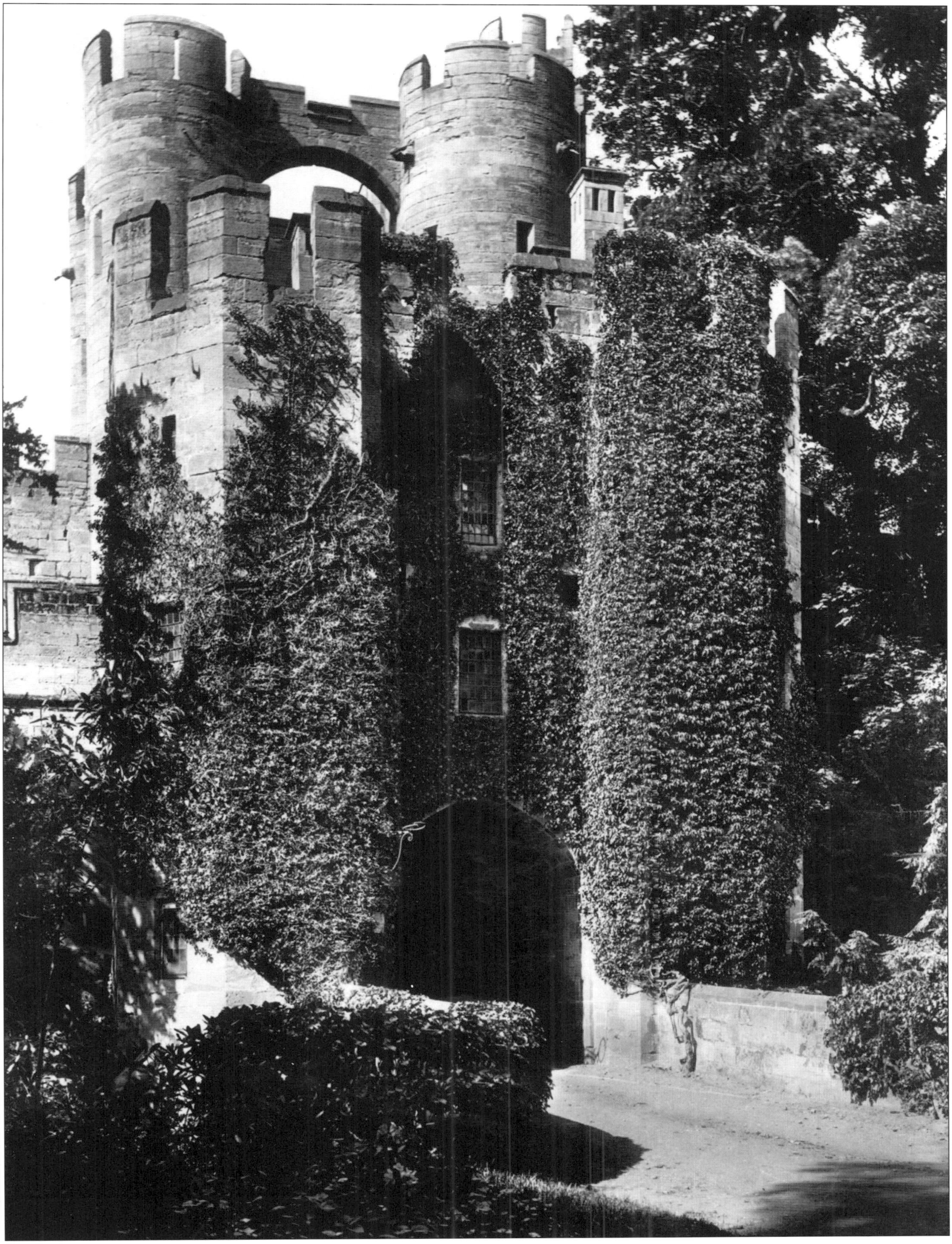

THE CASTLE GATEHOUSE, 1892. 31007

The great gatehouse sits astride the curtain wall between Caesar's Tower and Guy's Tower.

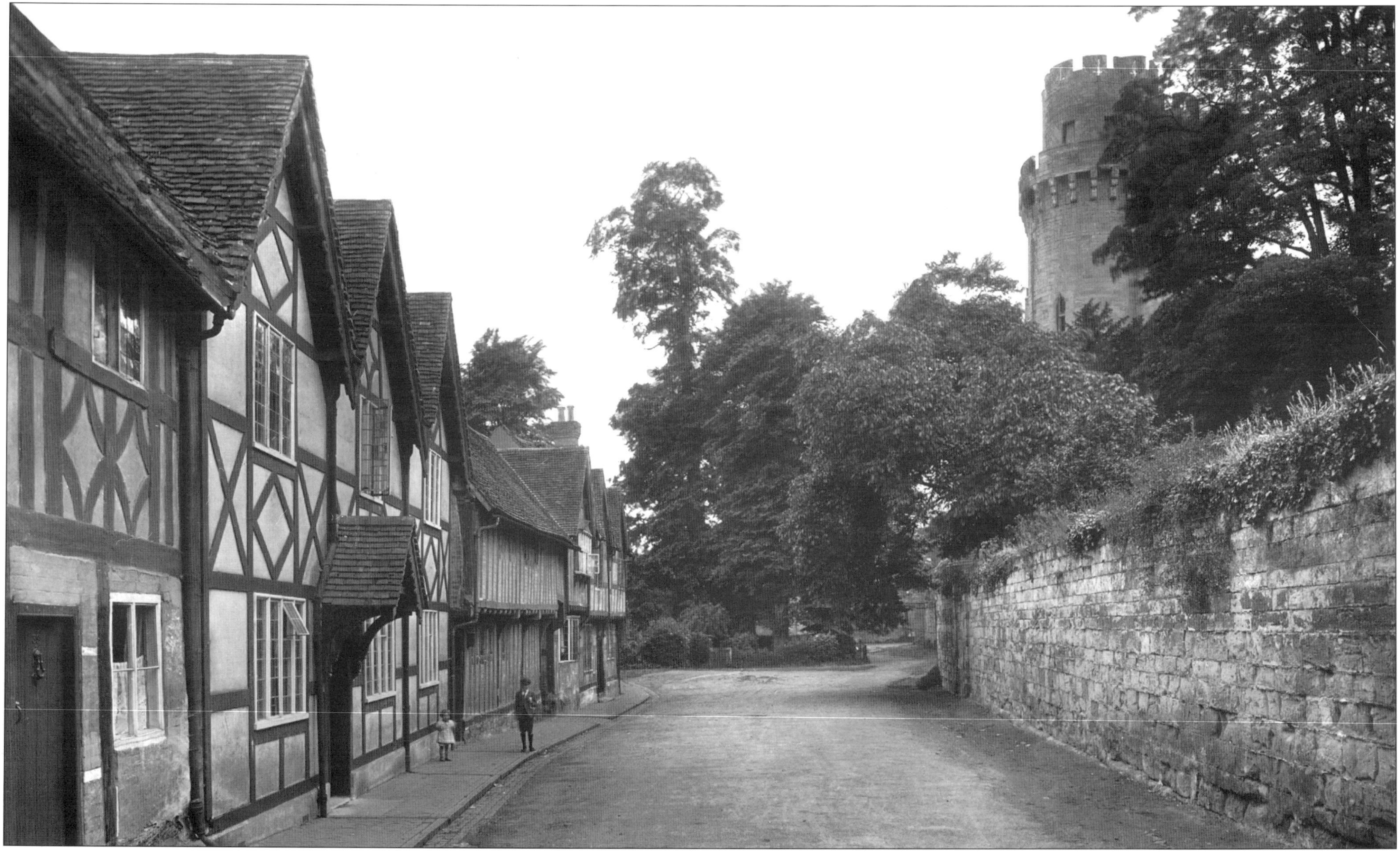

MILL STREET, 1922. 72351

On the right is Caesar's Tower, which rises to a height of 147 ft. It was built by Thomas Beauchamp.

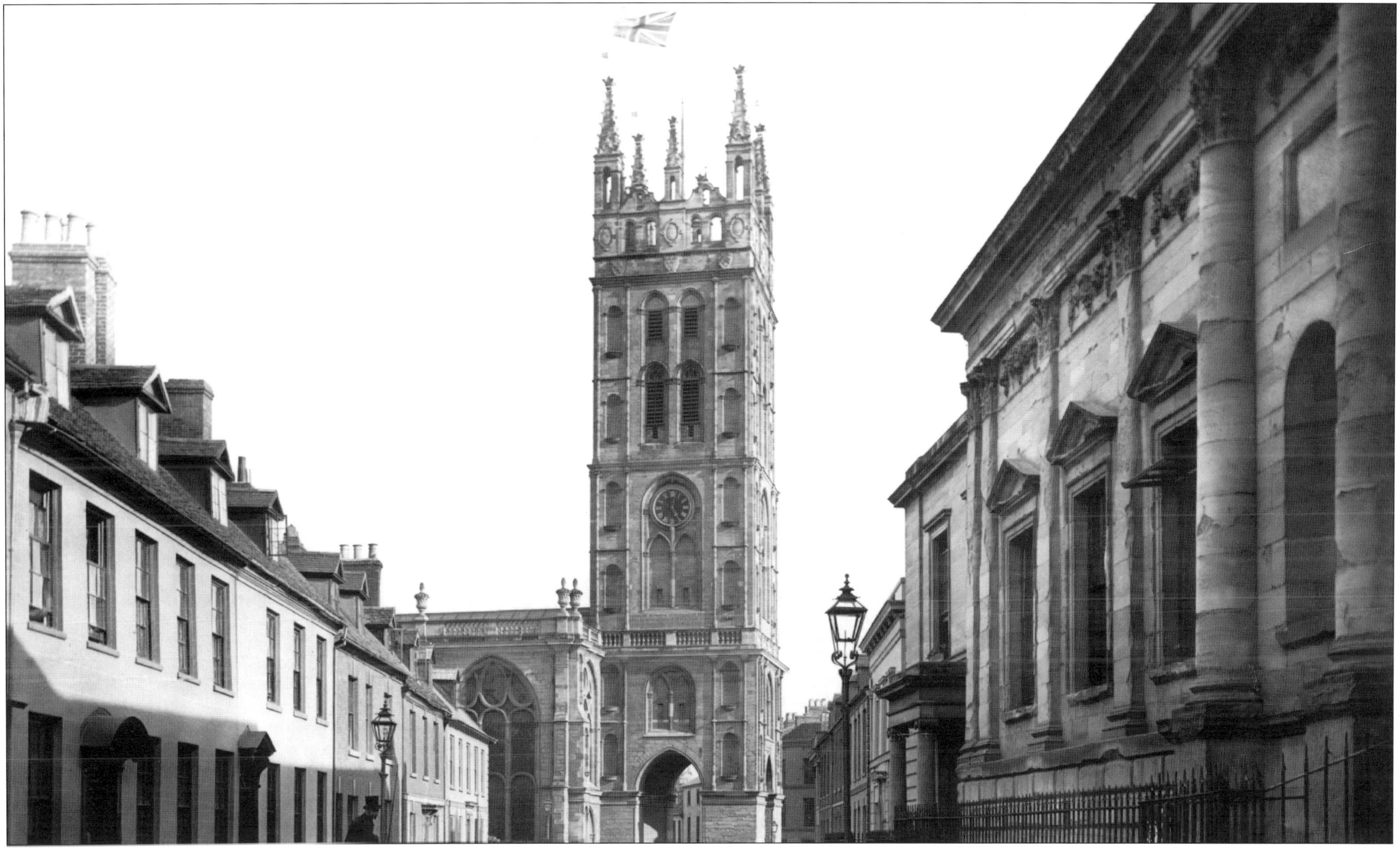

ST MARY'S CHURCH, 1892. 31016

At the time this photograph was taken it cost 2*d* to go up the tower. The Beauchamp Chapel was built as directed in the will of Richard Beauchamp, fourteenth Earl of Warwick. His tomb has a cage-like structure over it, which at one time supported a velvet or brocade canopy. In the chapter house is the tomb of Fulke Greville, Lord Brooke.

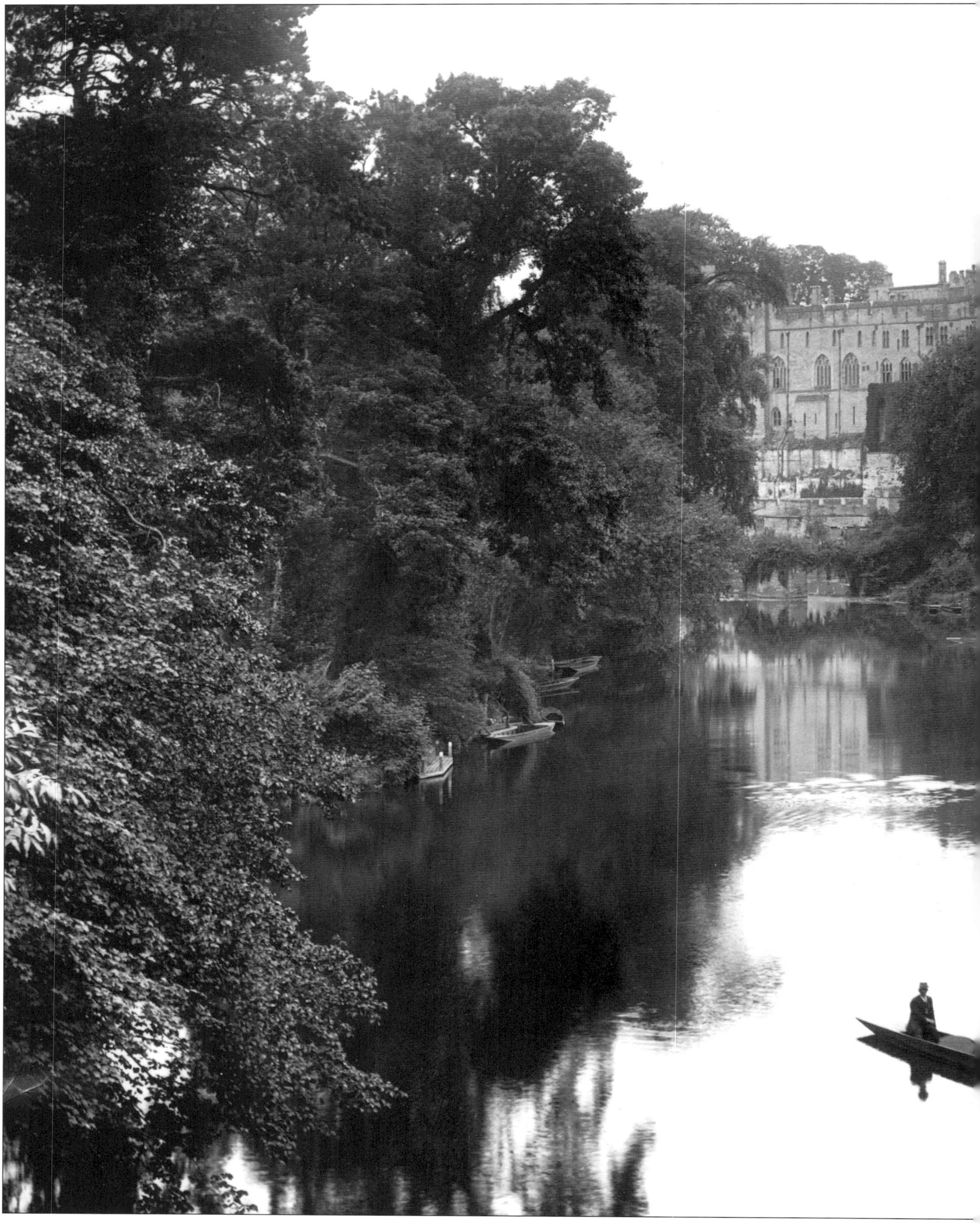

Caesar's Tower and Guy's Tower, 1922.

These were built to provide additional accommodation for visitors, and militarily they are of limited use. On each floor there is a suite of rooms comprising of a sitting-room, bedroom and toilet. There are guardrooms on the top floors and only here are there arrow-loops in the tower walls.

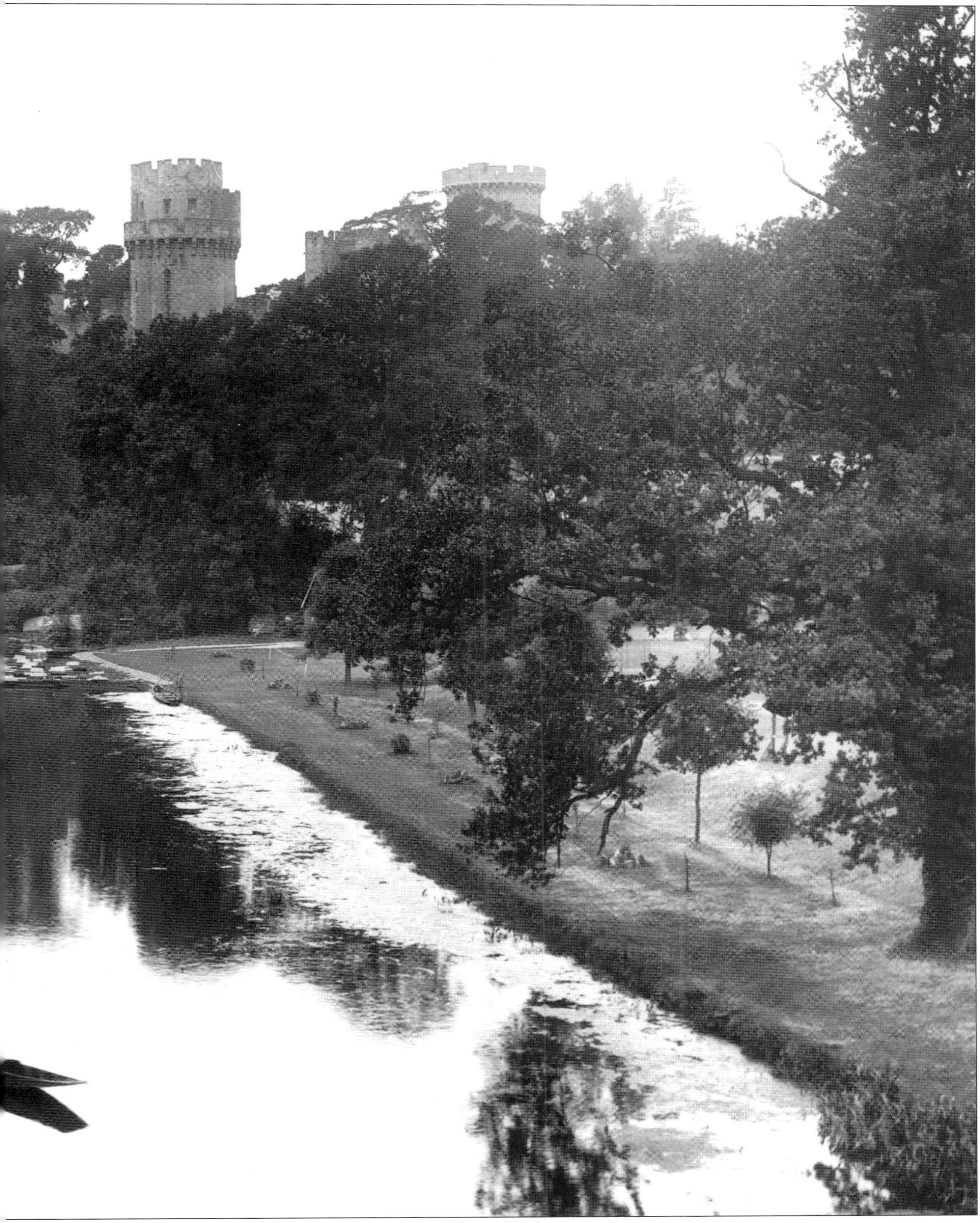

72366

Chapter 6

STRATFORD-UPON-AVON

By the fourteenth century Stratford-upon-Avon was a prosperous market town noted for its annual Mop Fair, when farm workers and others would offer their services for the forthcoming year. These hiring fairs were common throughout England and in some areas lasted into the early years of the twentieth century.

Stratford's affairs were dominated by the Guild of the Holy Cross who was also responsible for some of the building work done on Holy Trinity Church. The guild's power was destroyed in 1547 when it was disbanded on the orders of Henry VIII. The town was then placed under the control of a bailiff; one holder of this office being none other than John Shakespeare, William's father. Without doubt it is the Shakespeare connection that has played an important part in the modern prosperity of Stratford; the town is now England's premier tourist attraction outside London.

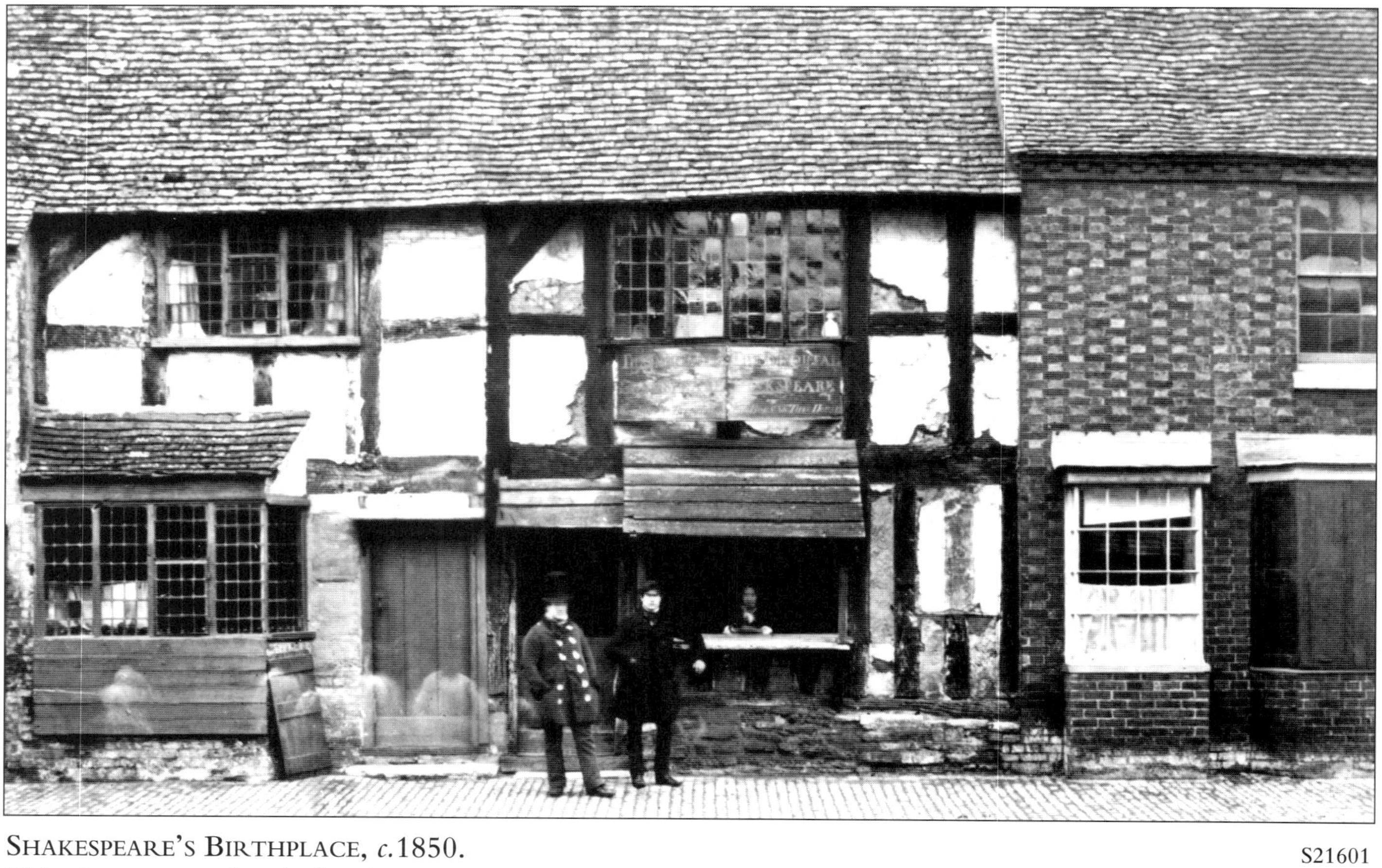

SHAKESPEARE'S BIRTHPLACE, *c.*1850. S21601

This picture was taken before its restoration in 1857. The house had undergone a number of incarnations since the Bard's day, but the timber framework, floors and some of the internal walls are as they were in the sixteenth century.

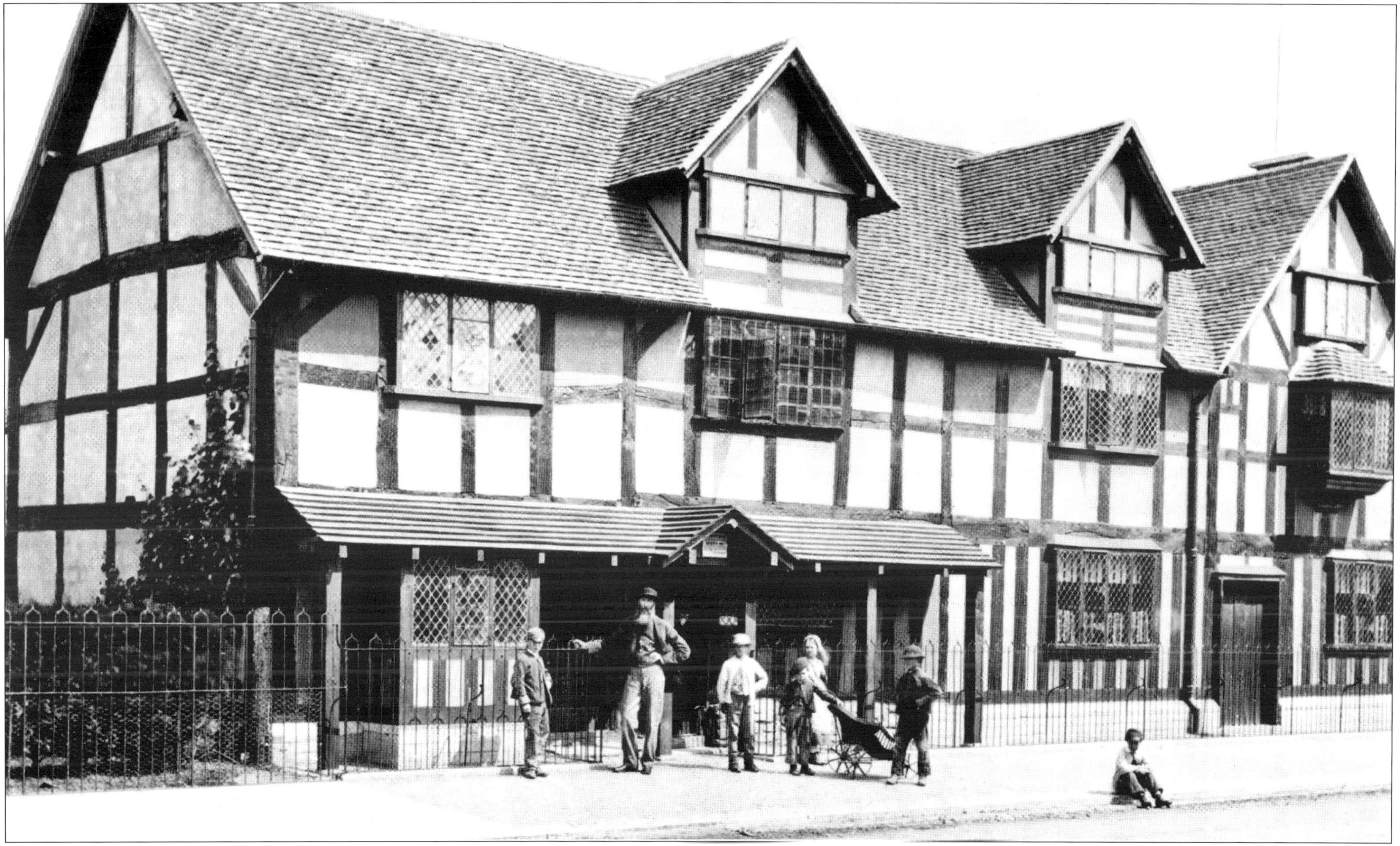

SHAKESPEARE'S BIRTHPLACE, 1861. S21602

The walls were, and to some extent still are, covered with the signatures of visitors, though a great many have been whitewashed over. Some visitors even scratched their names on the window panes. Among the signatures are those of Sir Walter Scott, Thomas Carlyle, Robert Browning and William Makepeace Thackery.

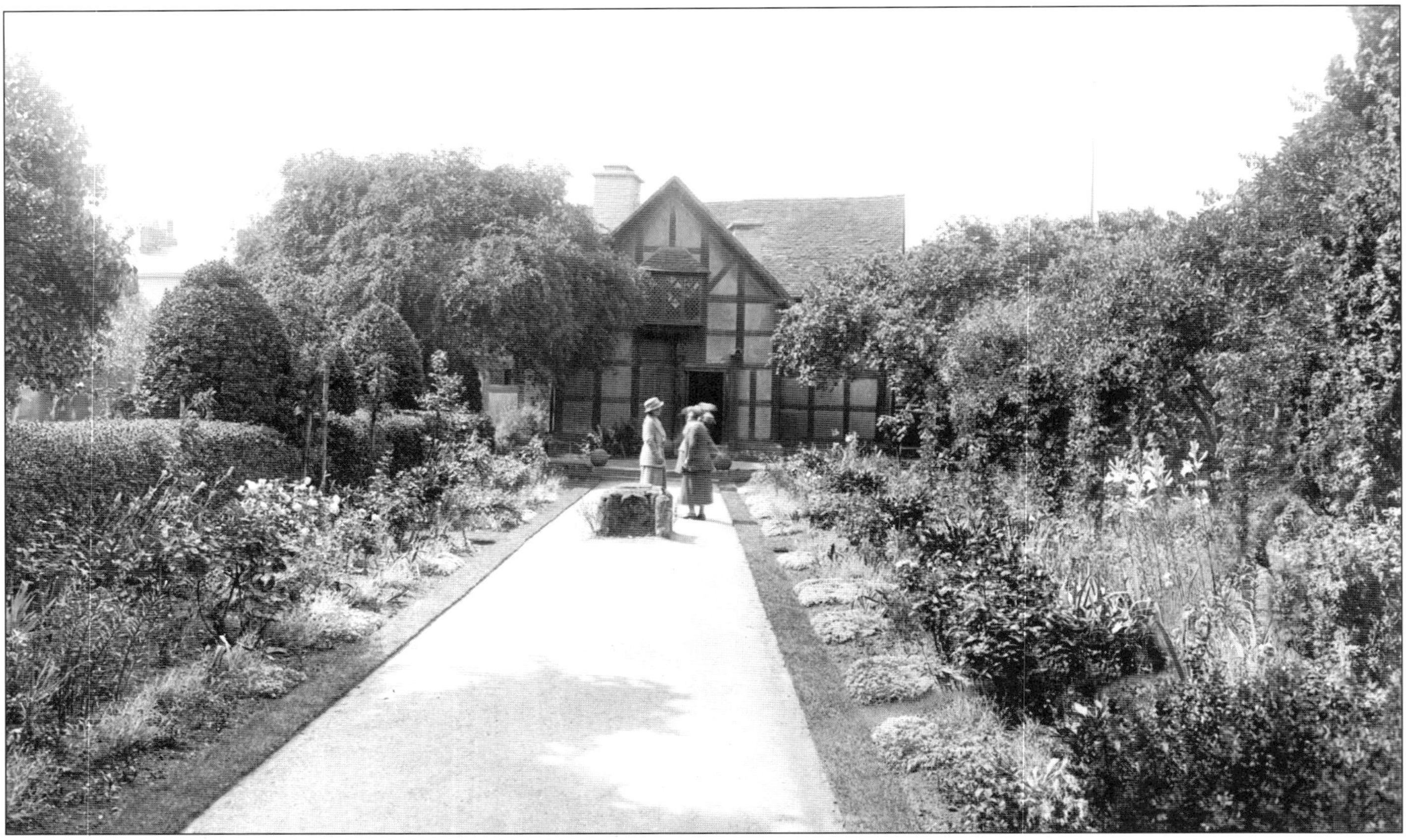

SHAKESPEARE'S BIRTHPLACE, 1922. 72387

The restoration was directed at putting the house into a representation of what it might have looked like in 1564. The garden was planted out with trees and flowers mentioned in the Bard's works.

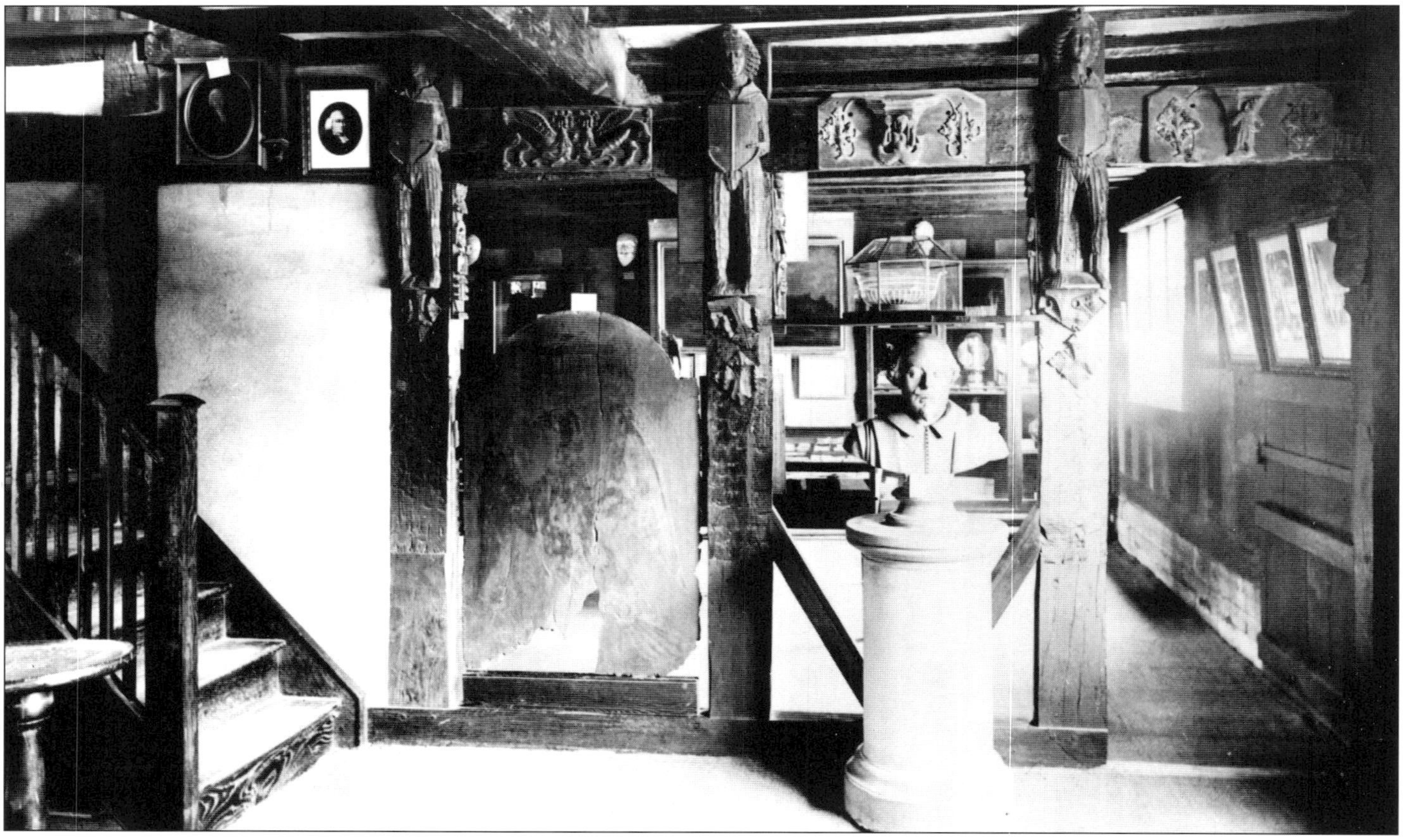

SHAKESPEARE'S BIRTHPLACE, 1892. 31063

The house was really two houses: one for the family, the other where John Shakespeare worked as a glover and wool merchant. In later years the family home became a butcher's shop, and the other part became an inn.

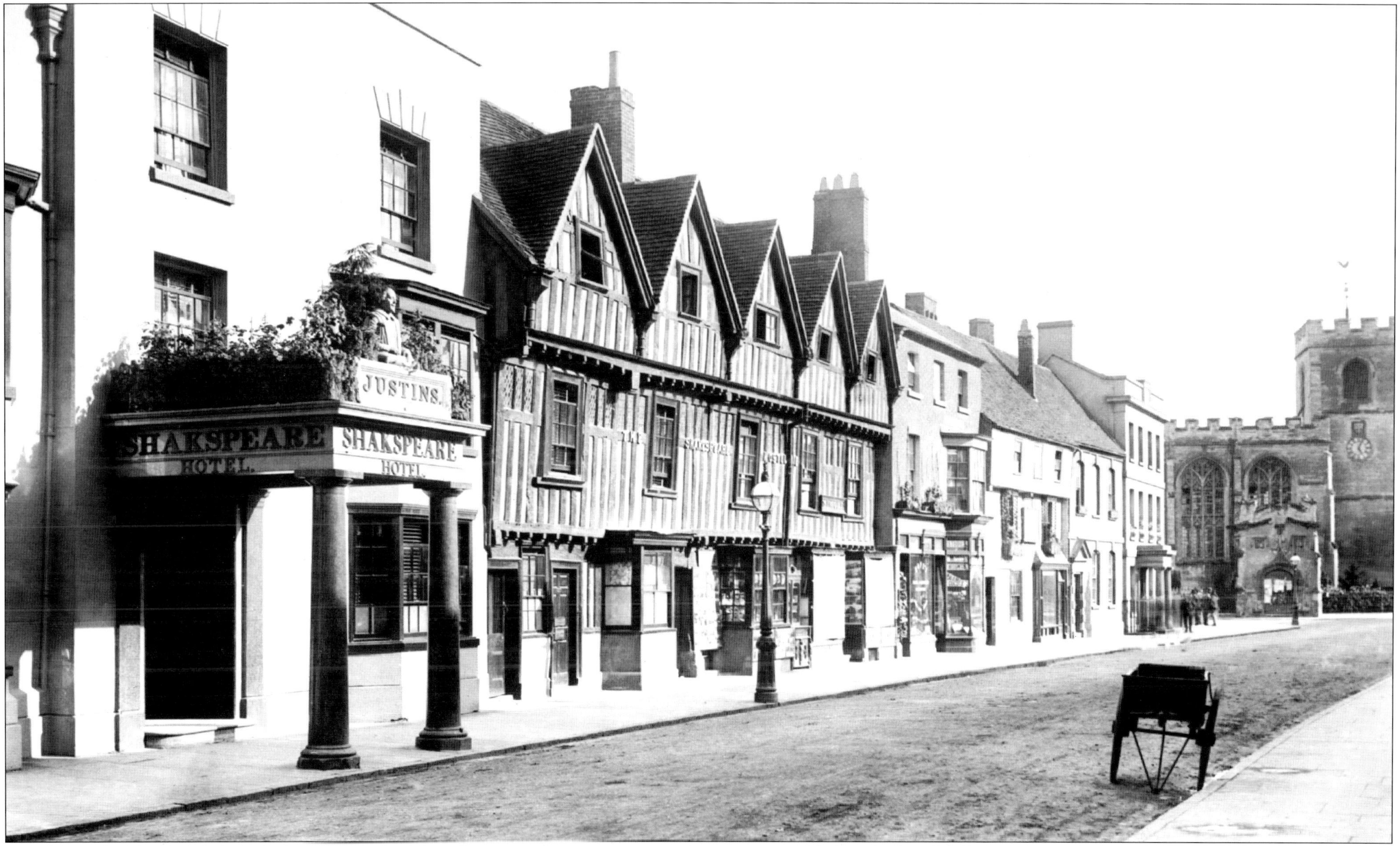

THE SHAKESPEARE HOTEL, 1892. 31071

The Shakespeare Hotel in 1892 had rooms named after the Bard's plays. It cost 4*s* 6*d* a night to stay here, with dinner costing between 4-5*s*. The Red Horse and the Golden Lion were slightly cheaper.

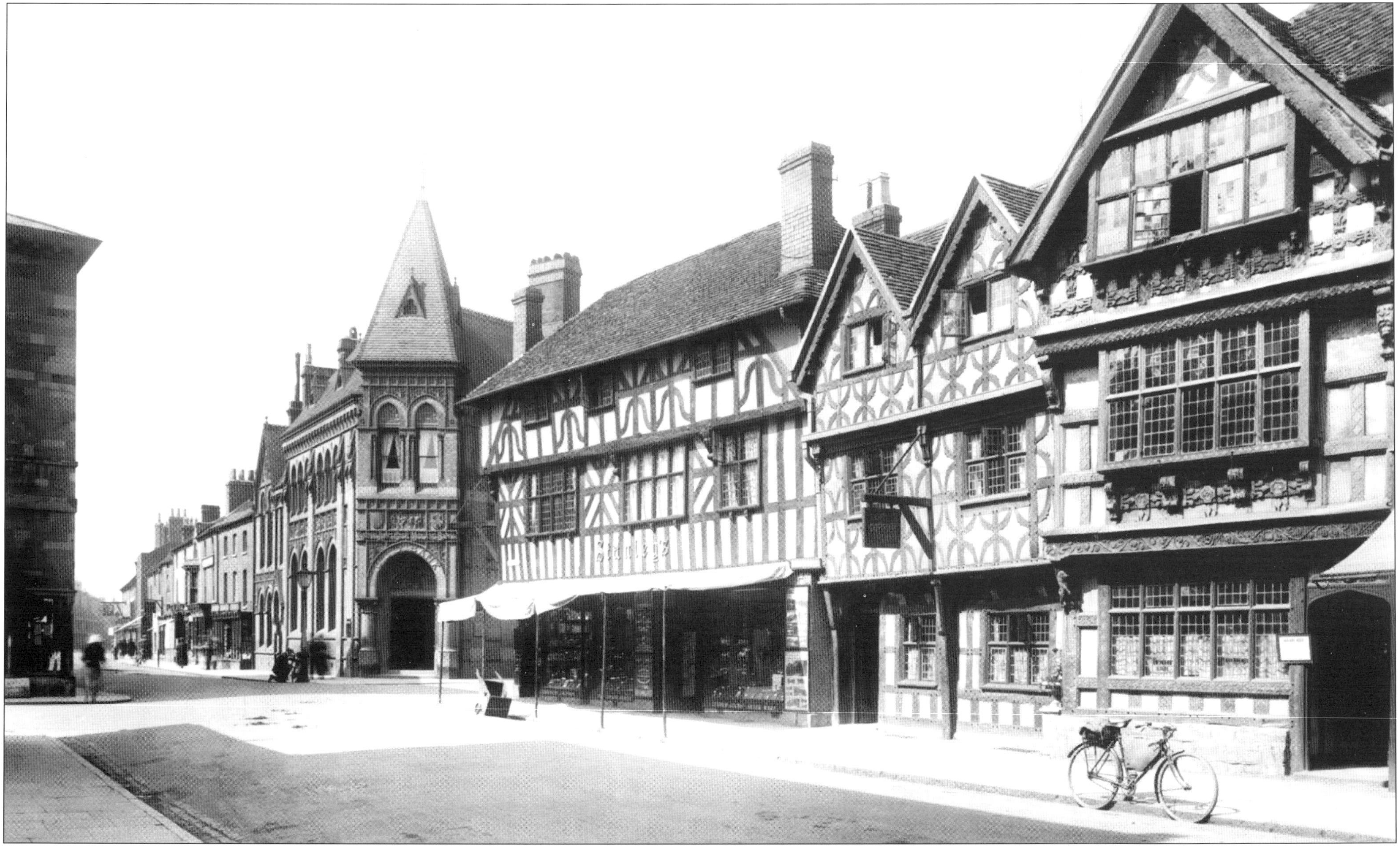

HARVARD HOUSE, 1922. 72383

The house is situated in the high street and was completed in 1596 for Thomas Rogers. Rogers' daughter married Robert Harvard and it was their son who founded Harvard University.

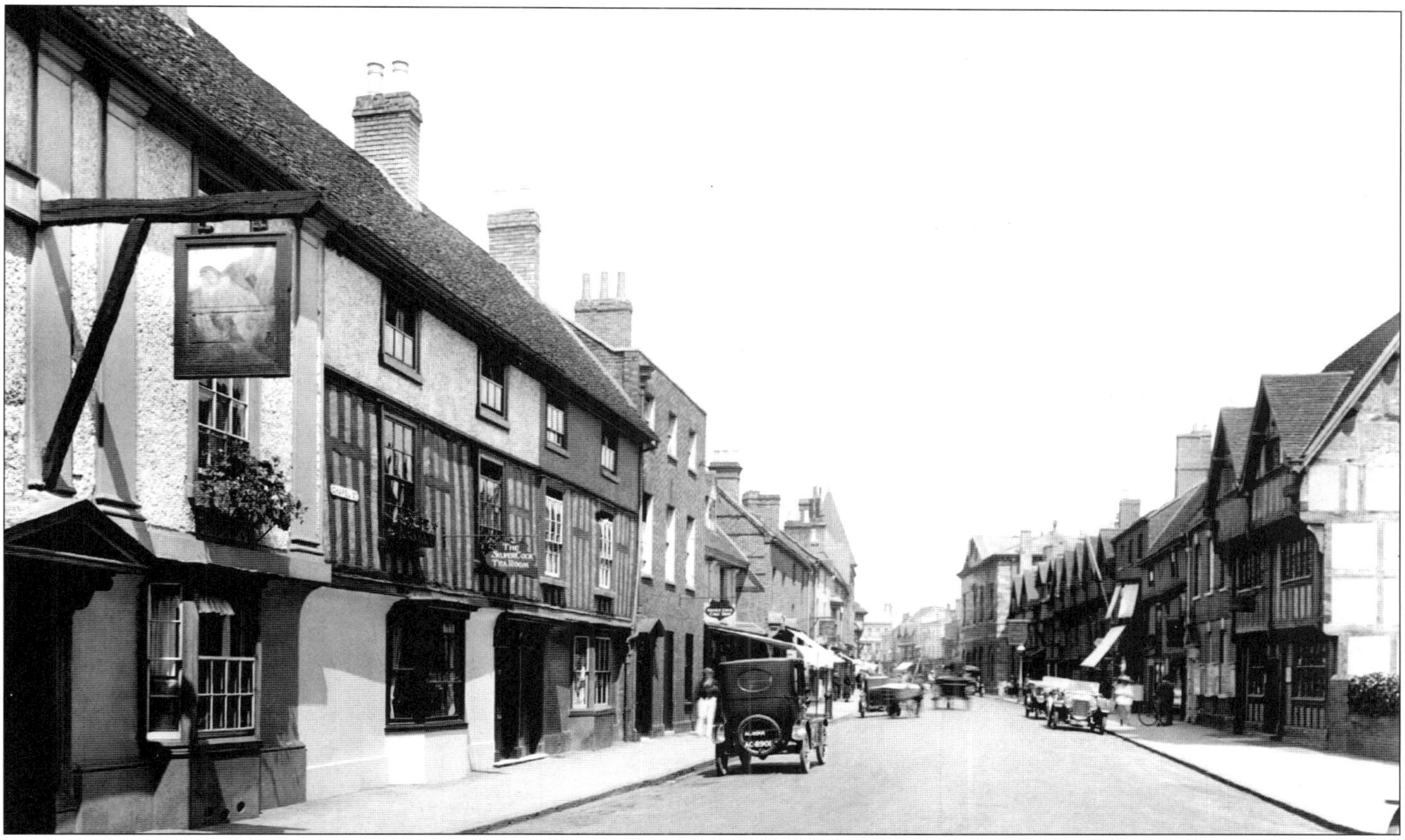

CHAPEL STREET, 1922. 72379

A continuation of Church Street, Chapel Street leads on to the high street. At the corner with Sheep Street stands the town hall which dates from 1767 and on this building is a statue of the Bard presented by David Garrick. Garrick was the driving force behind the establishment of the annual Shakespeare Festival, the first of which was held in 1789.

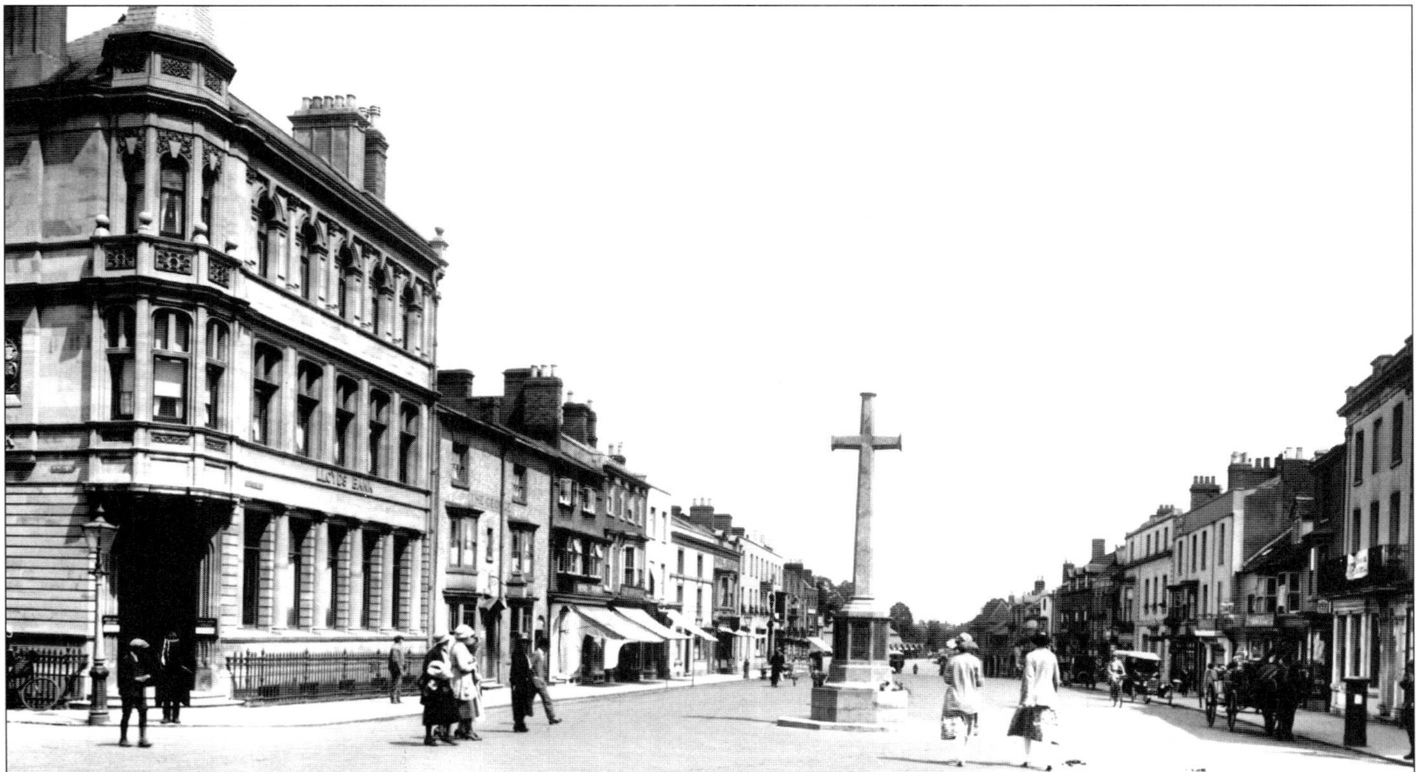

BRIDGE STREET, 1922. 72381

The Red Horse Hotel is where Washington Irving penned his paper on the town. Bridge Street leads on to Wood Street where there is a fountain and a clock tower presented to the town in 1888 by an American visitor.

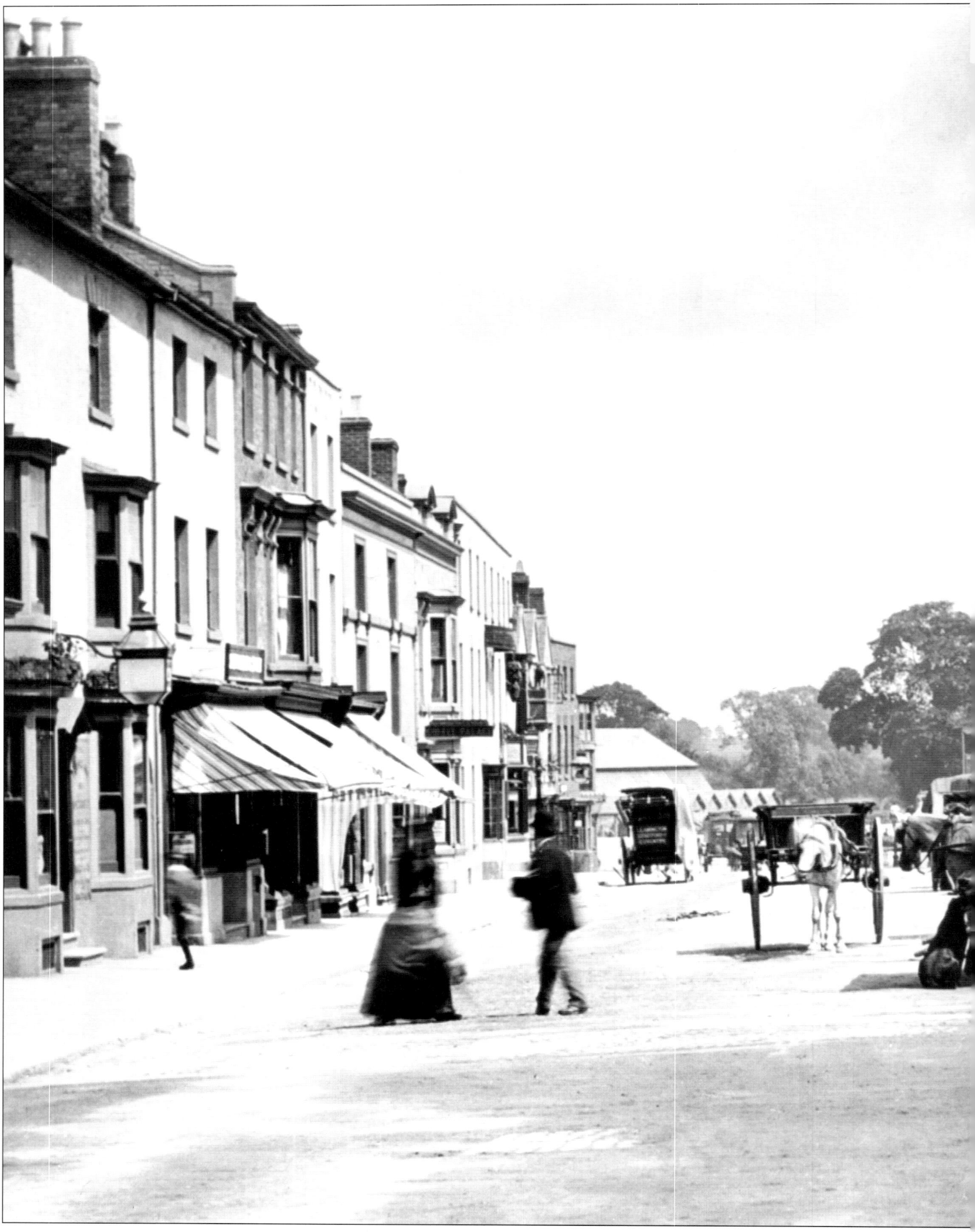

THE MARKET PLACE, 1892.
Stratford once boasted two temperance hotels: McNeille's and the Fountain. In 1838 the South Midland Temperance Association embraced a large number of towns, including Stratford-upon-Avon. One of the movement's organisers was Thomas Cook, founder of the famous travel agents.

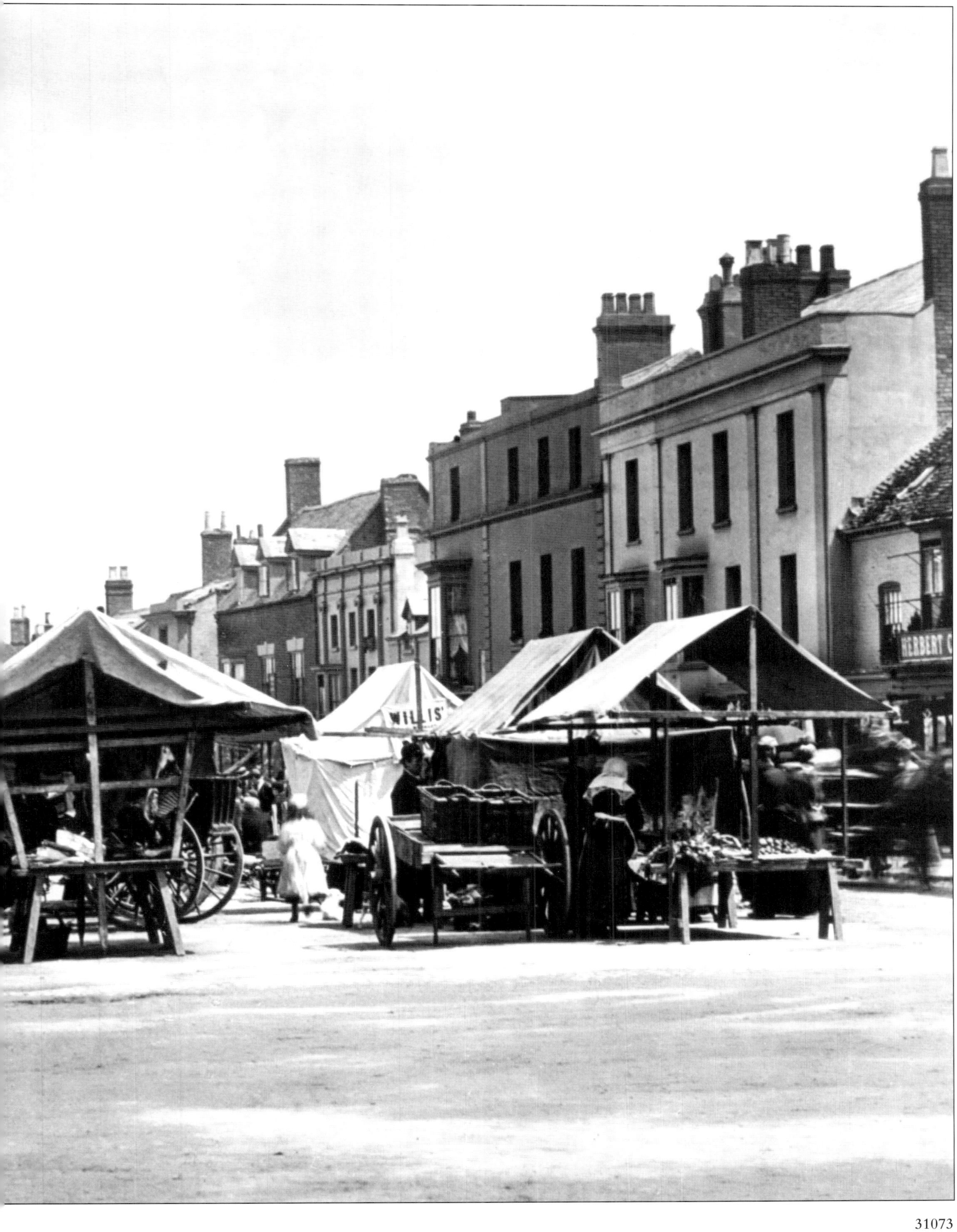

31073

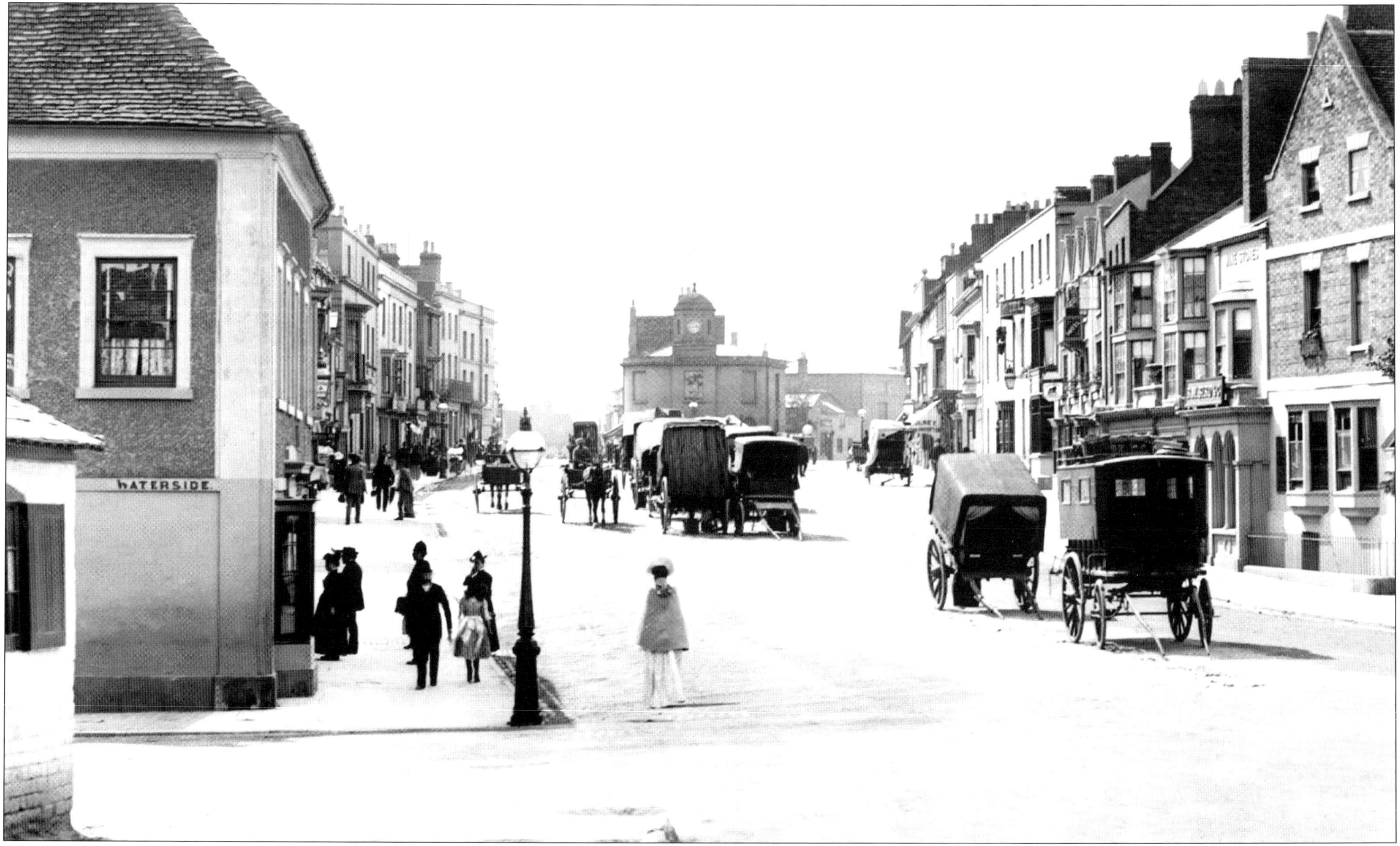

THE MARKET PLACE, 1892. 31075
Another view of the Market Place, but this time from the opposite direction. The first grant for a weekly market was given by King John in 1196.

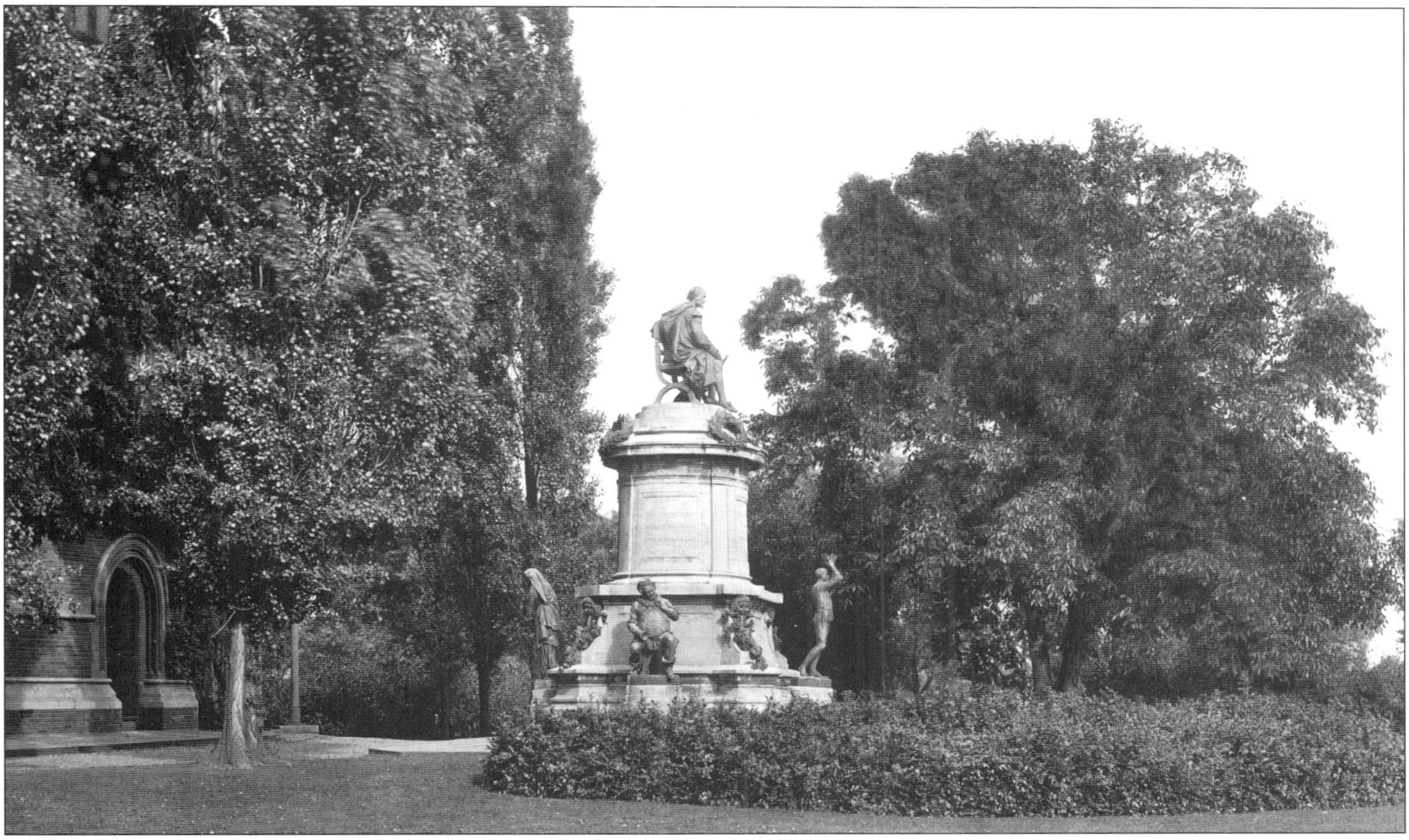

SHAKESPEARE'S MONUMENT, 1922. 72389

It was presented to the town in 1888 by the sculptor Lord Ronald Gower. Around the base are characters from various plays. Prince Hal represents history; Falstaff, comedy; Lady Macbeth, tragedy; Hamlet, philosophy.

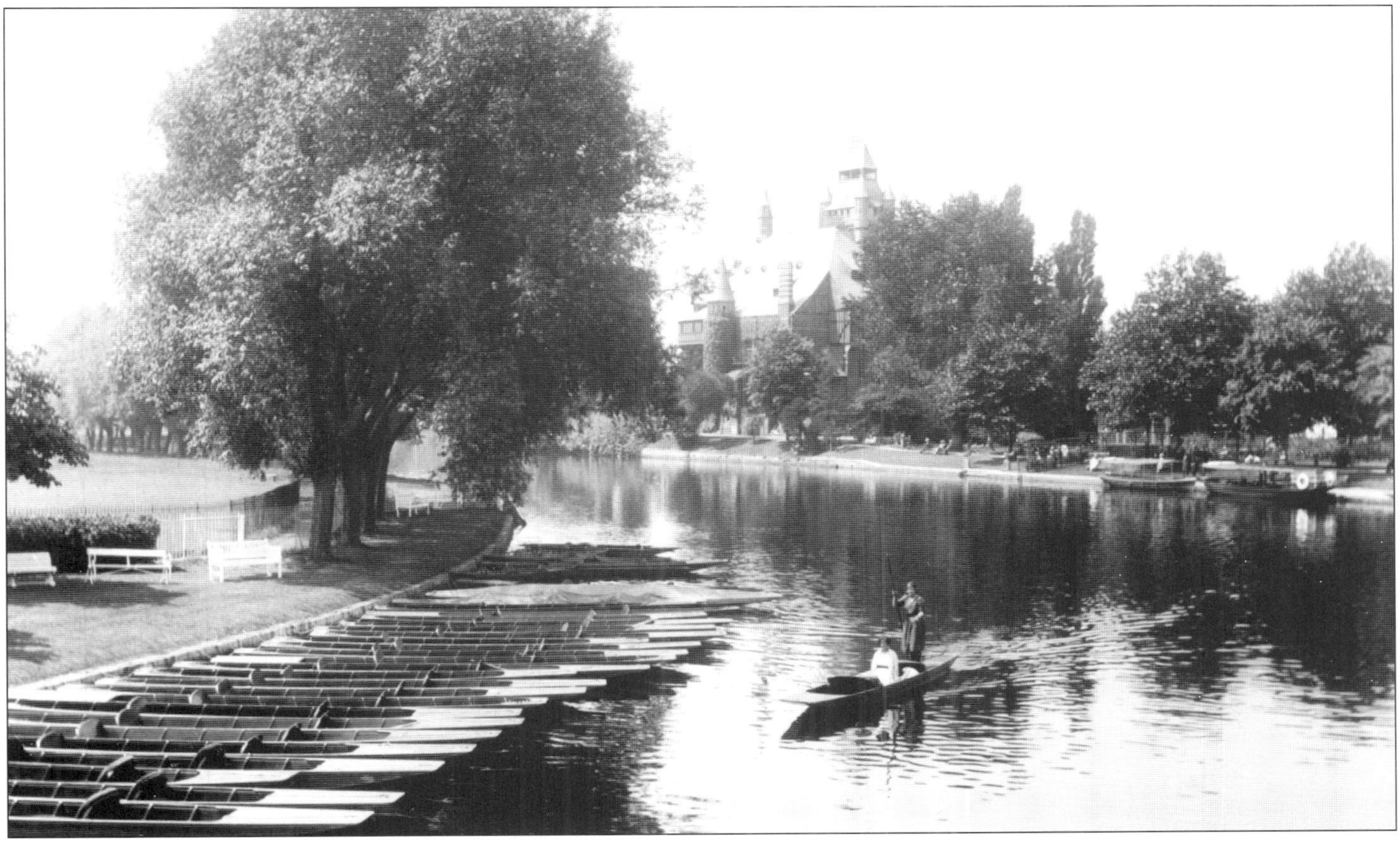

SHAKESPEARE MEMORIAL BUILDING, 1922. 72393

Here the Memorial Building is viewed from the river. As well as a theatre, there was a library of rare Shakespearian books and the view from the tower was highly recommended. The theatre burned down in 1926, plays then having to be performed in a local cinema.

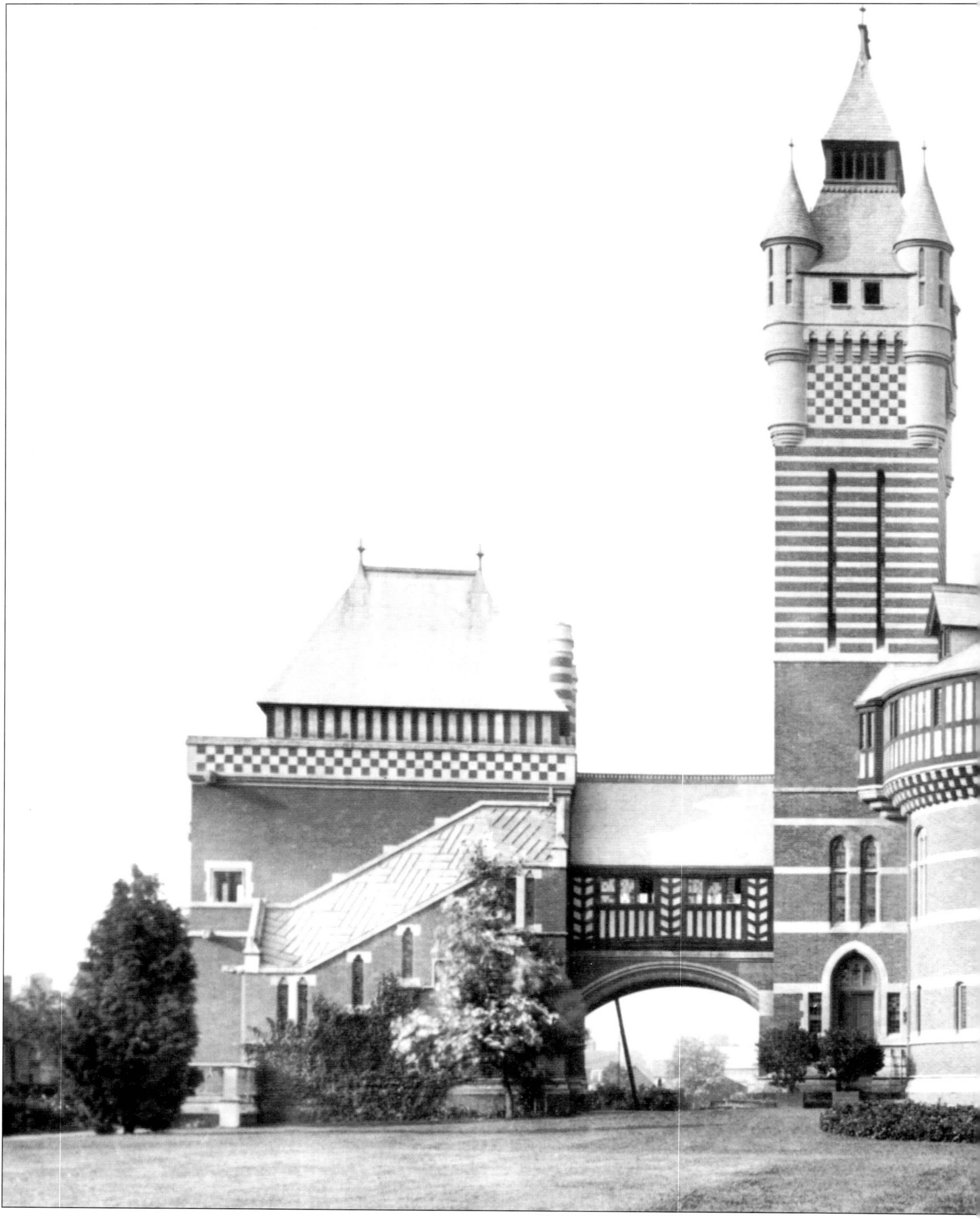

SHAKESPEARE MEMORIAL BUILDING, 1892.

Looking like a refugee from Disneyworld, or something dreamed up by mad King Ludwig of Bavaria, the Shakespeare Memorial Building was erected in 1879. Built out of red brick and stone, it was completely at odds with its surroundings.

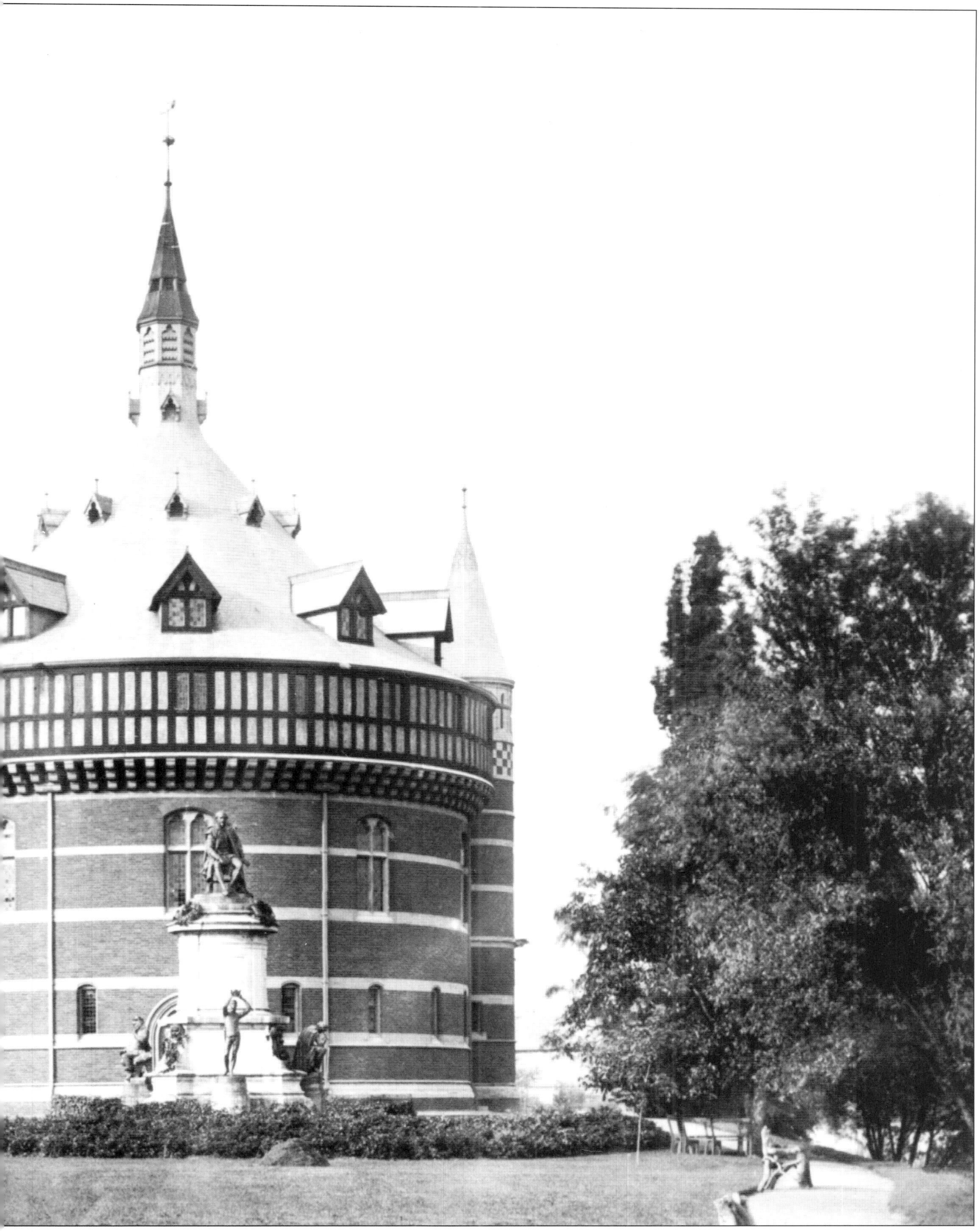

31056

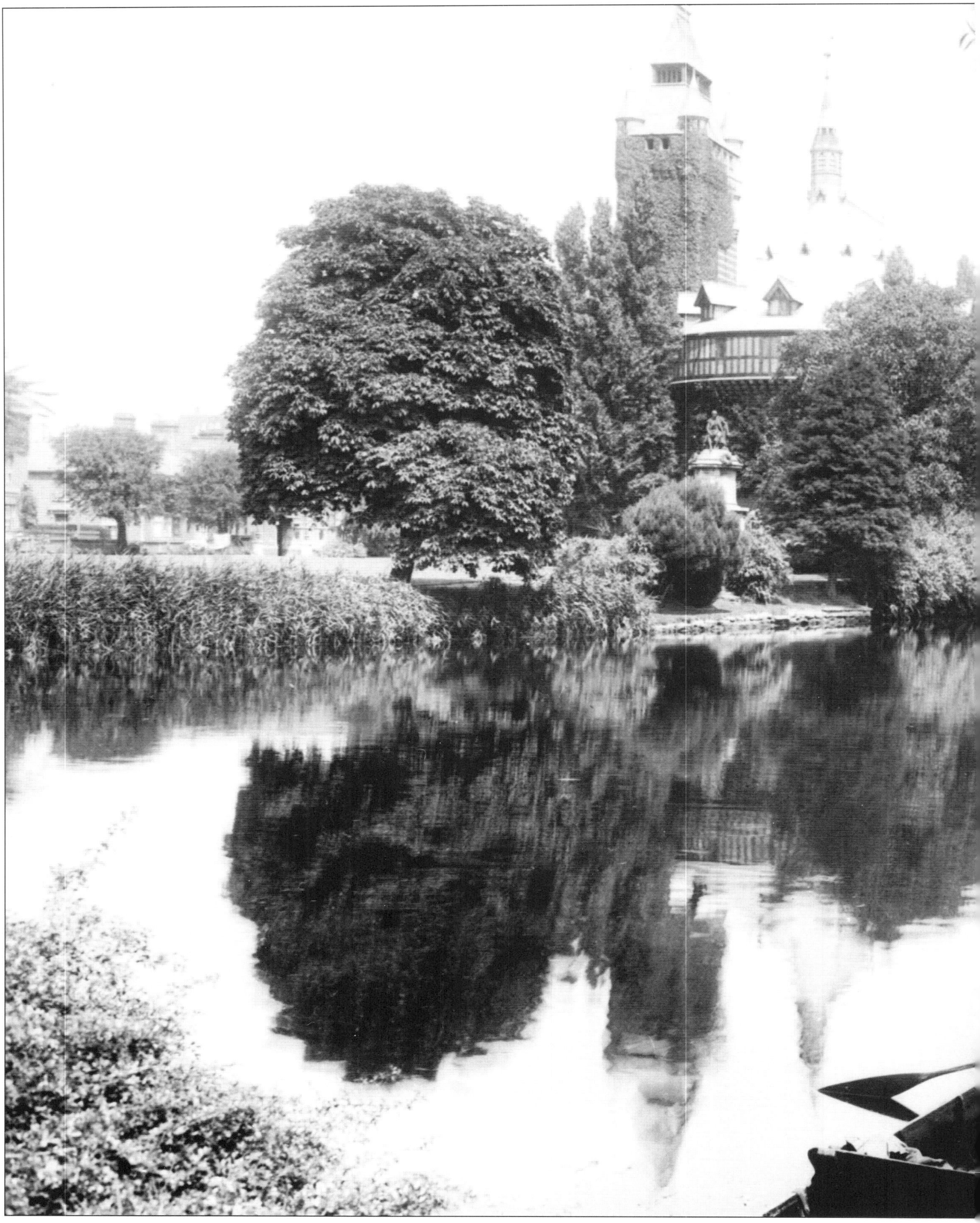

STRATFORD-UPON-AVON CANAL, 1922.

By the late-1780s the ever-expanding canal network looked set to by-pass Stratford. Business interests in the town realised they had to do something and a canal was authorised by an Act of Parliament in 1793. The canal would link up with the Worcester & Birmingham Canal at King's Norton. Due to protracted negotiations and financial

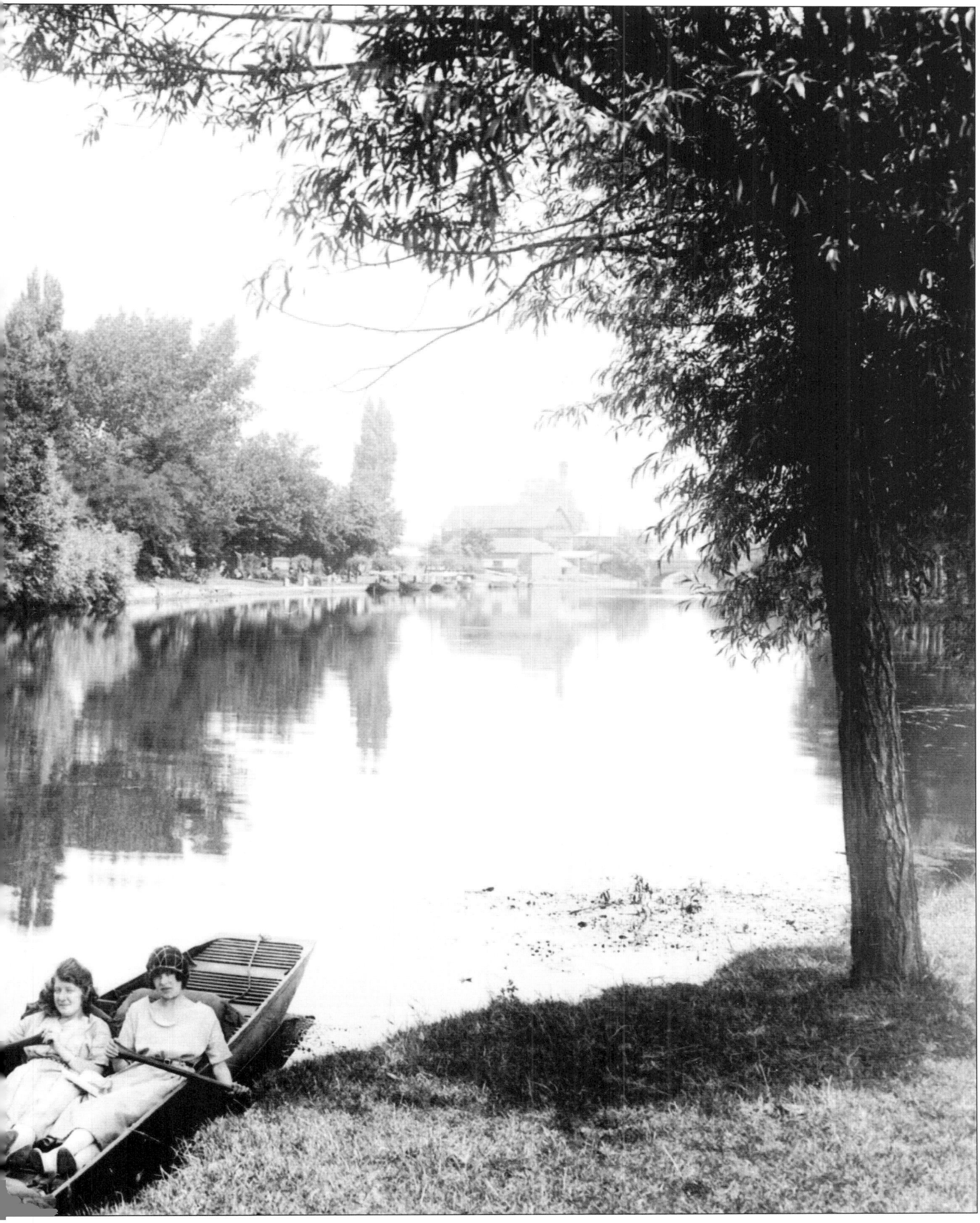

72392

problems the route had to be revised on several occasions. It did not open throughout until 1815 but this included a junction with the River Avon. The Avon was navigable as far as Tewksbury where it joined the Severn. The Memorial Building was erected just a few yards from the canal basin.

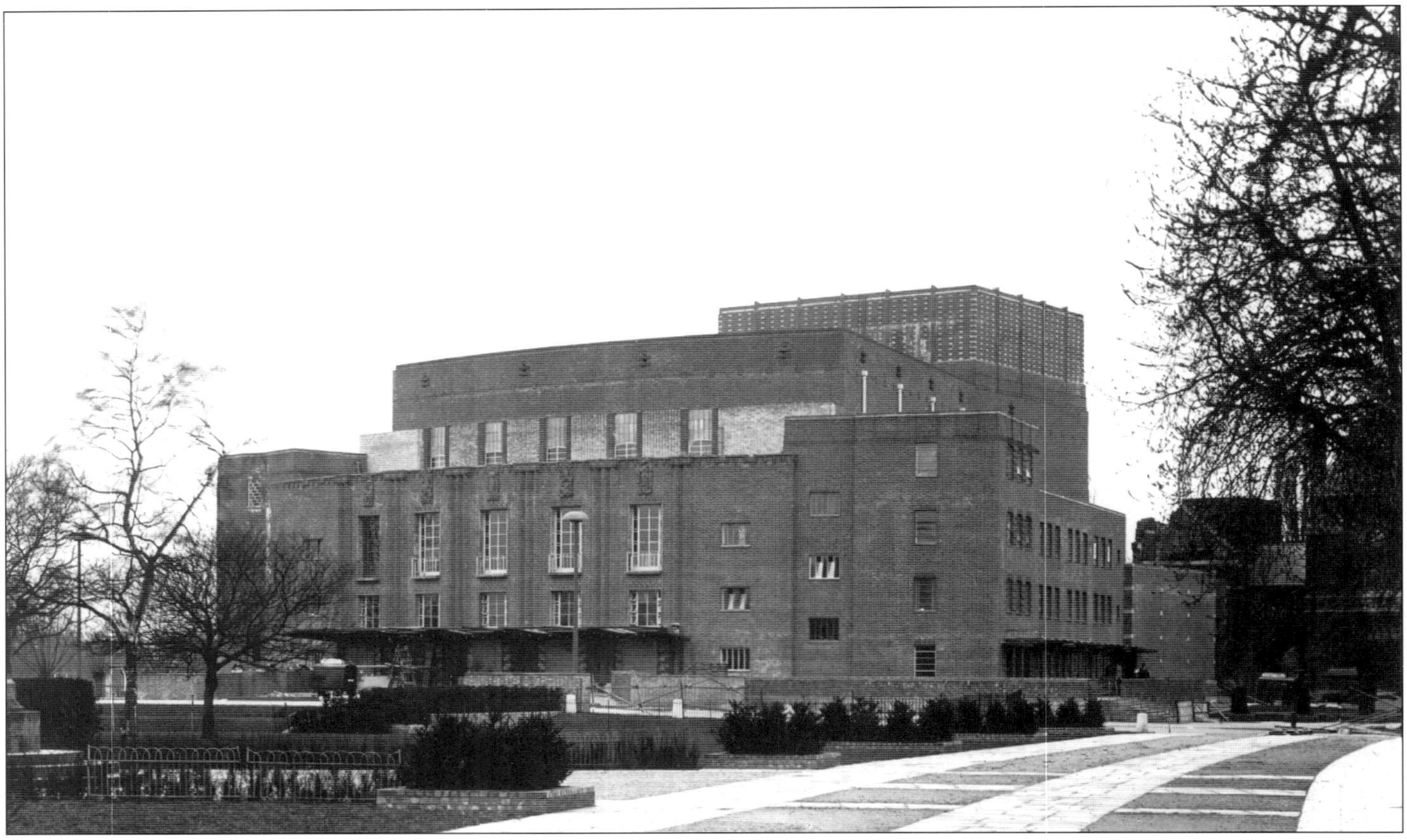

SHAKESPEARE MEMORIAL THEATRE, 1922. 72392B

The design for a new Shakespeare Memorial Theatre was thrown open to competition, the winning entry being submitted by Elizabeth Scott, great-niece of Sir Gilbert Scott. The new theatre opened in 1932.

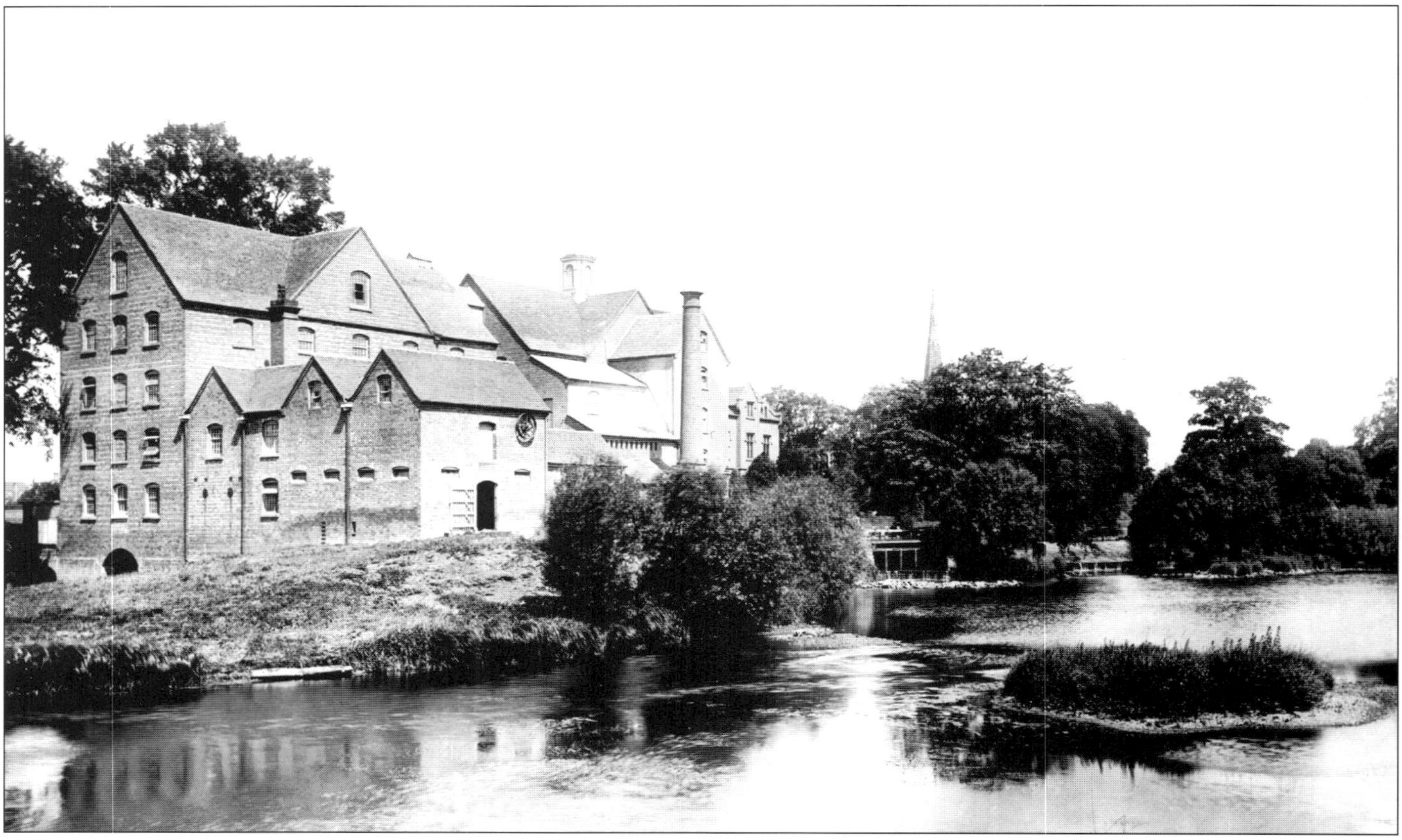

LUCY'S MILL, 1892. 31080

The Lucy Family had lived at Charlcote Hall since the twelfth century. It was in their Deer Park that Shakespeare is said to have been arrested for poaching.

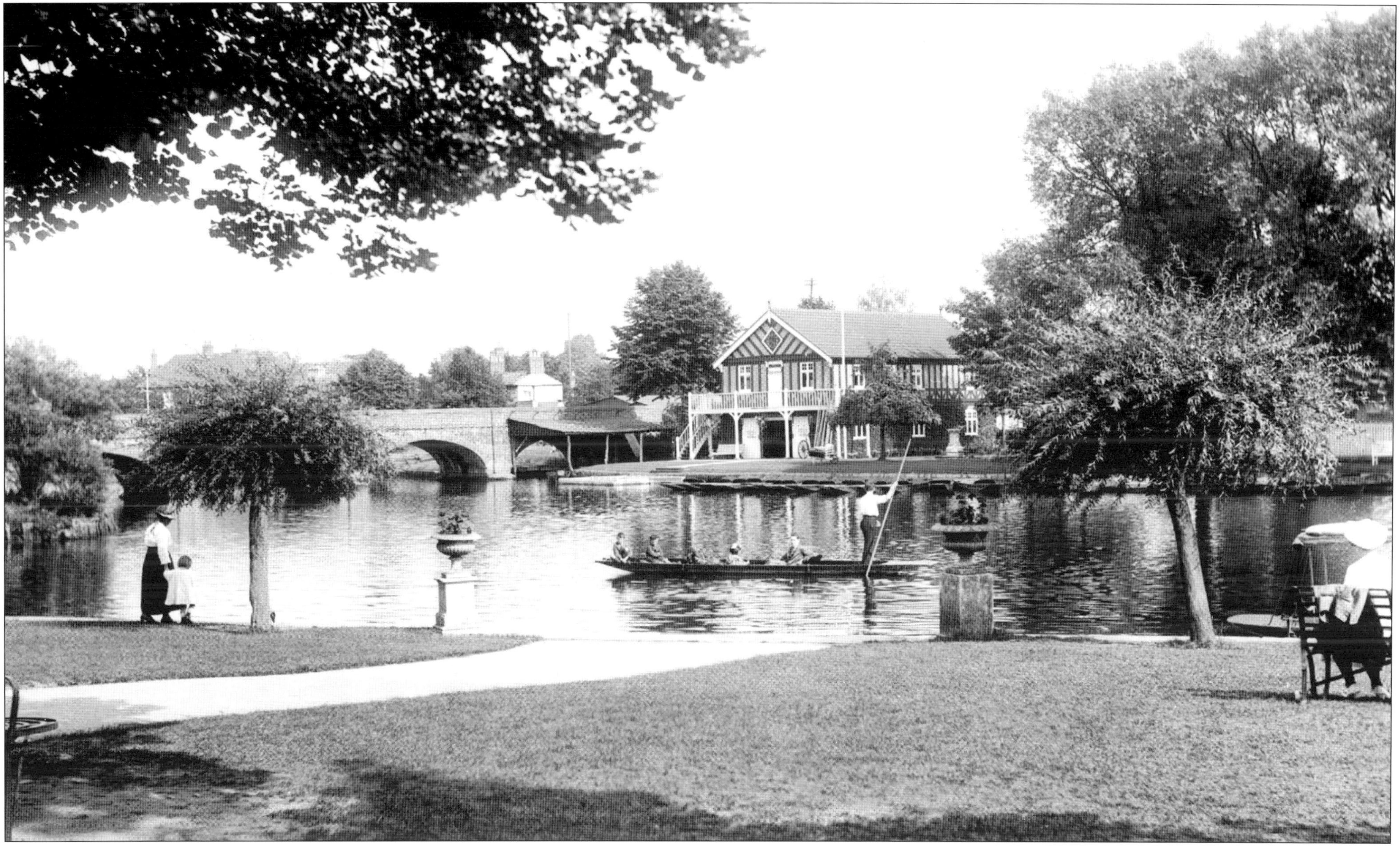

BOATHOUSE, STRATFORD-UPON-AVON, 1922. 72397

The annual Regatta, held in June, attracts crews from all parts of the United Kingdom. Boats can be hired at the Swan's Nest Boathouse and at Clopton Bridge.

Chapter 7

BIDFORD-ON-AVON

Bidford-on-Avon is one of eight villages satirically described in a rhyme attributed to William Shakespeare and penned after a heavy drinking session. The Bard and his cronies had a drinking bout with the Bidford Sippers and lost. Too sloshed to make it back to Stratford, they slept the night under a crab-apple tree. The following morning some of the Stratford drinkers wanted to go back to Bidford and carry on from where they had left off. It is said that the Bard would have none of it and wanted to go home. The rhyme attributed to him goes: *Piping Pepworth, Dancing Marston, Haunted Hillborough, Hungary Grafton, Dodging Exhall, Papist Wixford, Beggarly Broom, Drunken Bidford.*

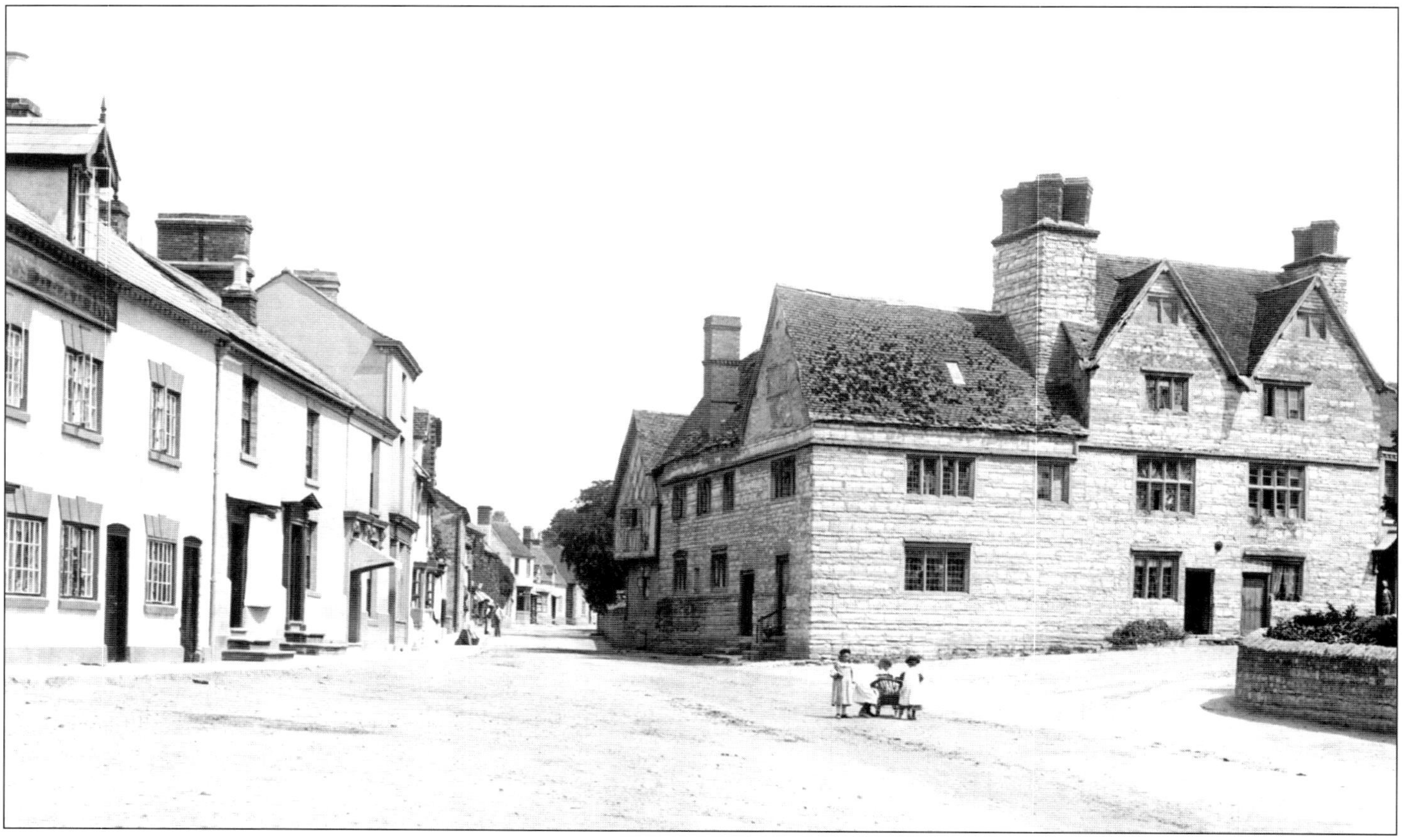

Ye Olde Falcon Inn, 1899. 44133

This is where Shakespeare and his friends met their match at the hands of the Bidford Sippers. The doggerel ends *Beggarly Broom and Drunken Bidford.*

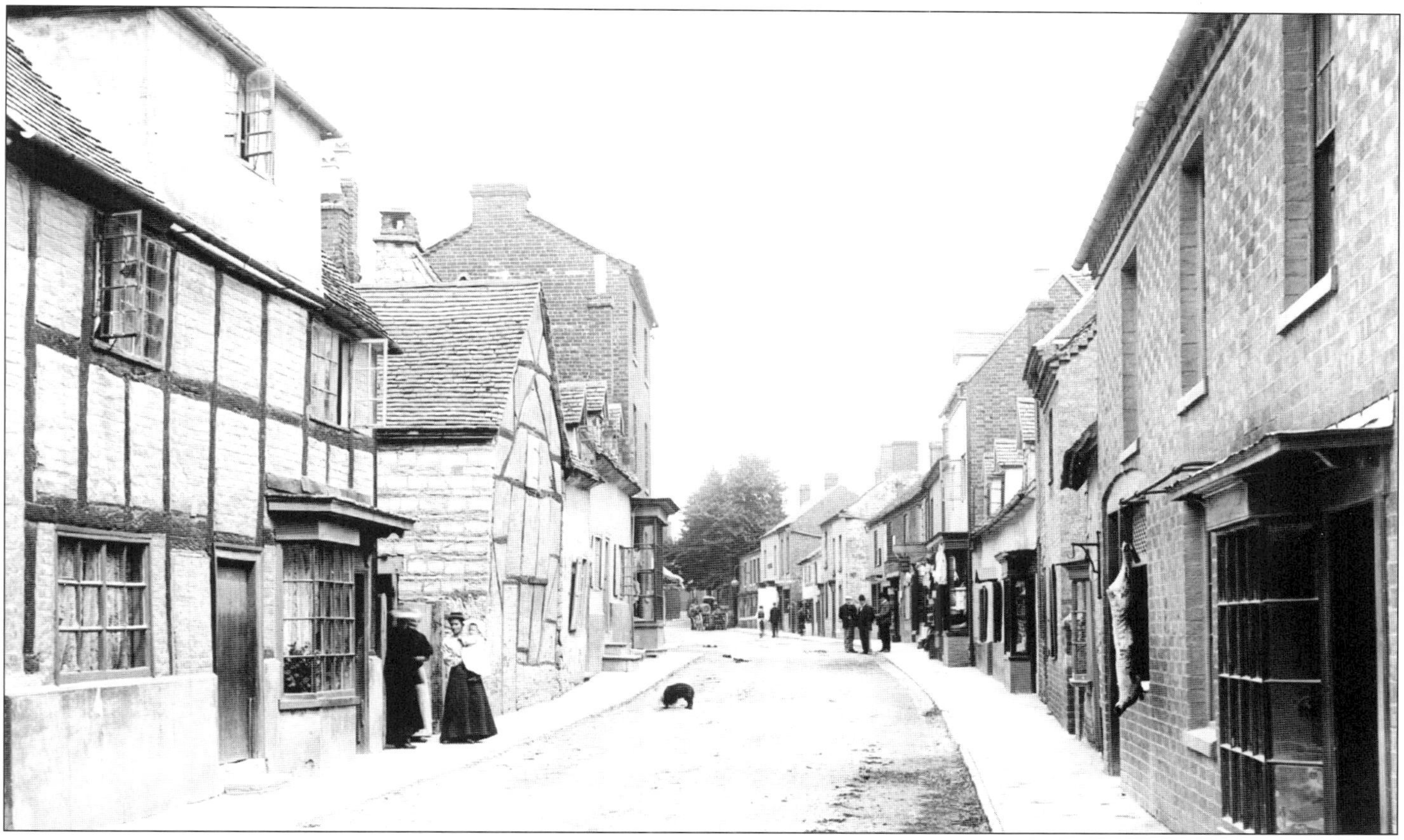

THE HIGH STREET, 1899. 44132

Bidford became famous in 1922 when a Saxon burial ground was discovered containing 200 graves, including those of warriors buried with their weapons.

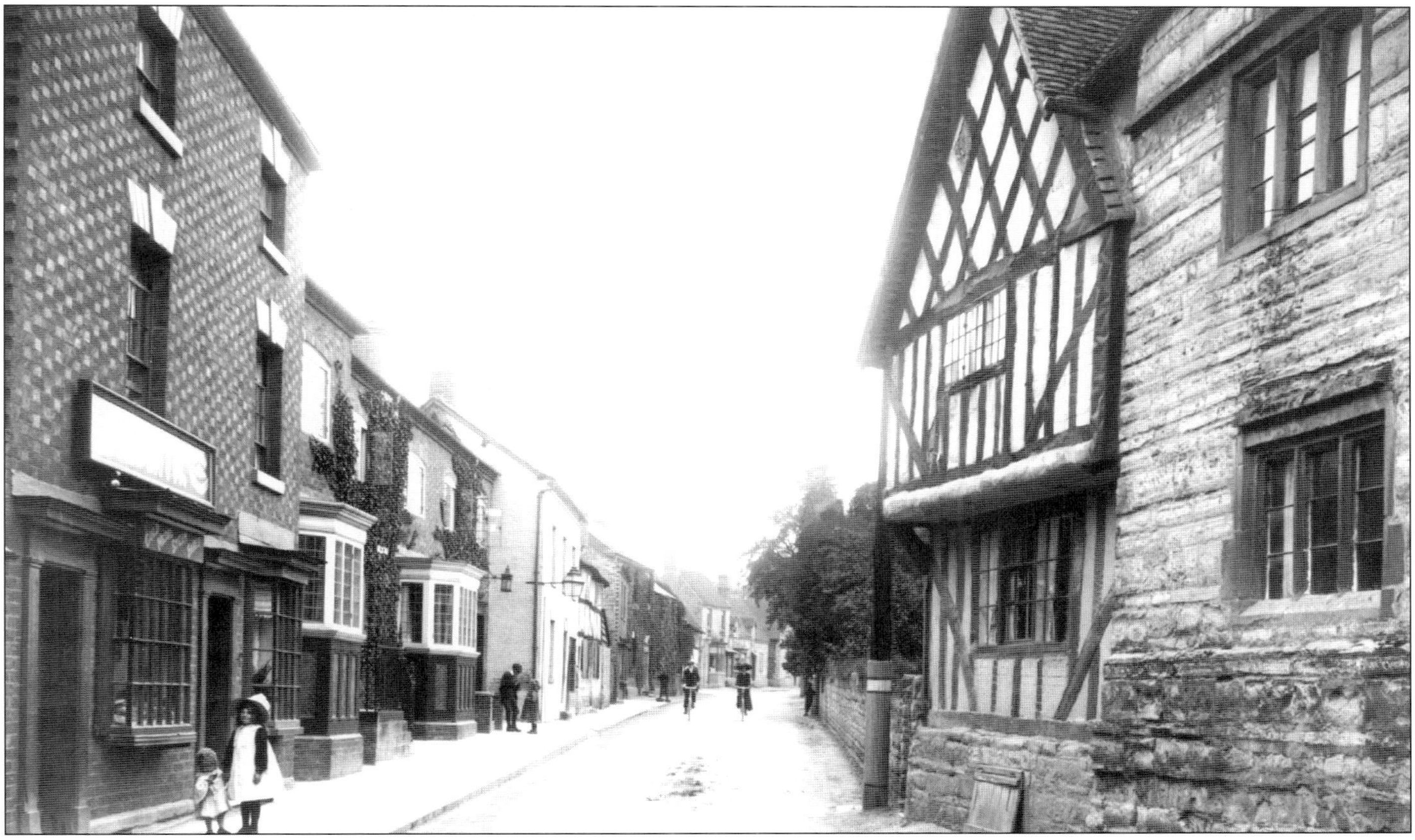

THE HIGH STREET, *c.*1910. 62642

The High Street still retains some fifteenth and sixteenth-century buildings.

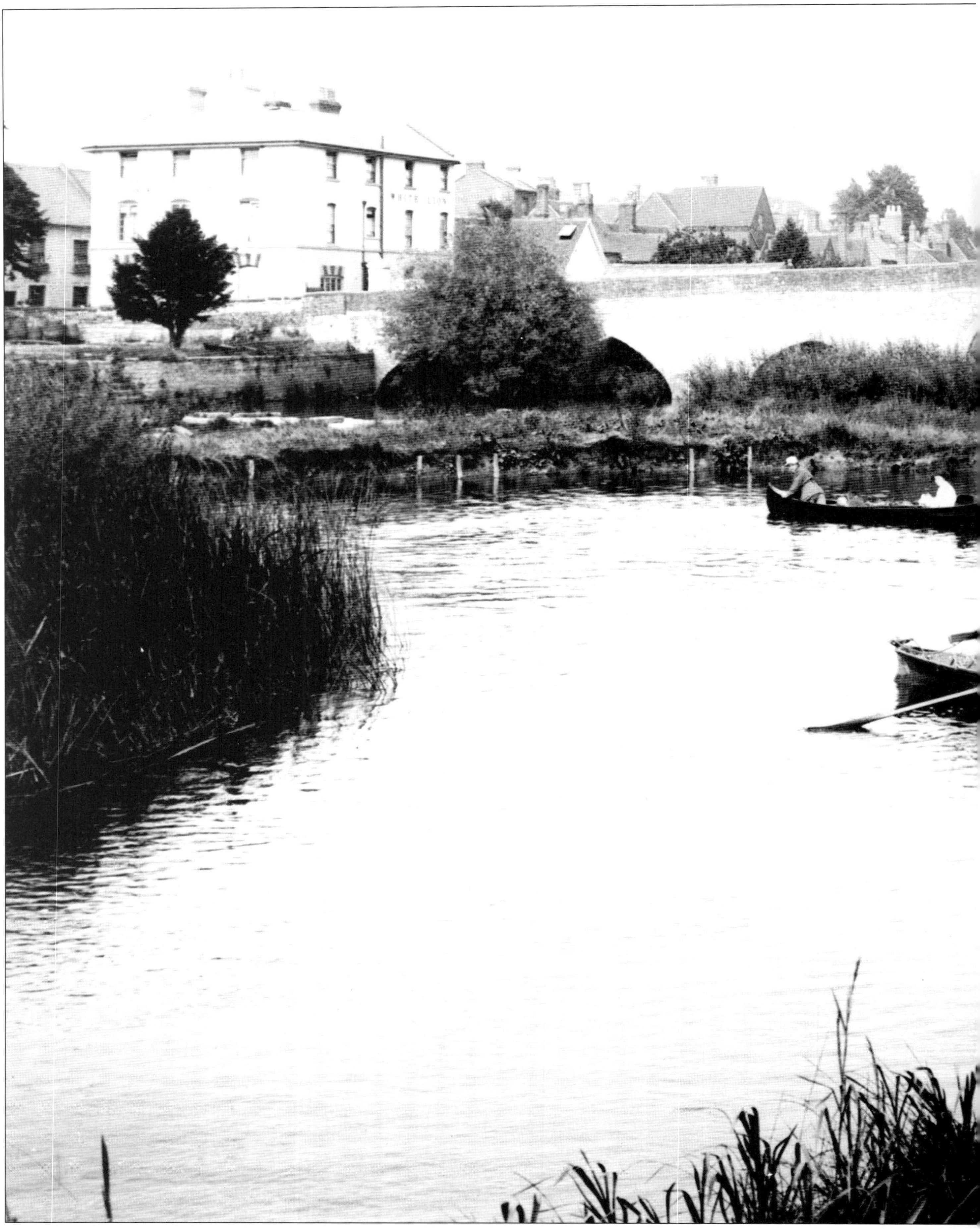

BRIDGE OVER THE AVON, 1910.
Noted for its irregular arches, the bridge dates mainly from the fifteenth century but some parts are thought to be much older.

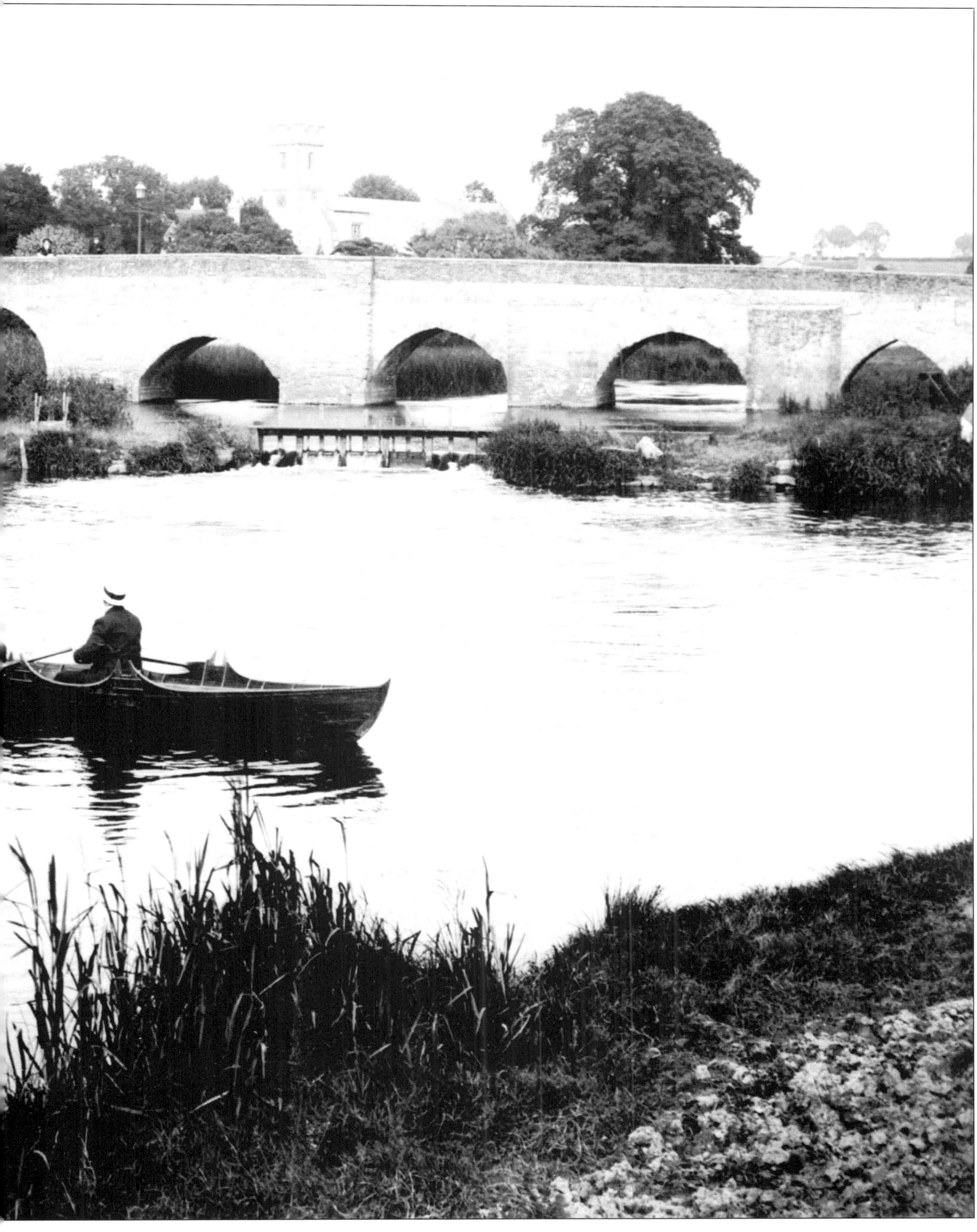

62637

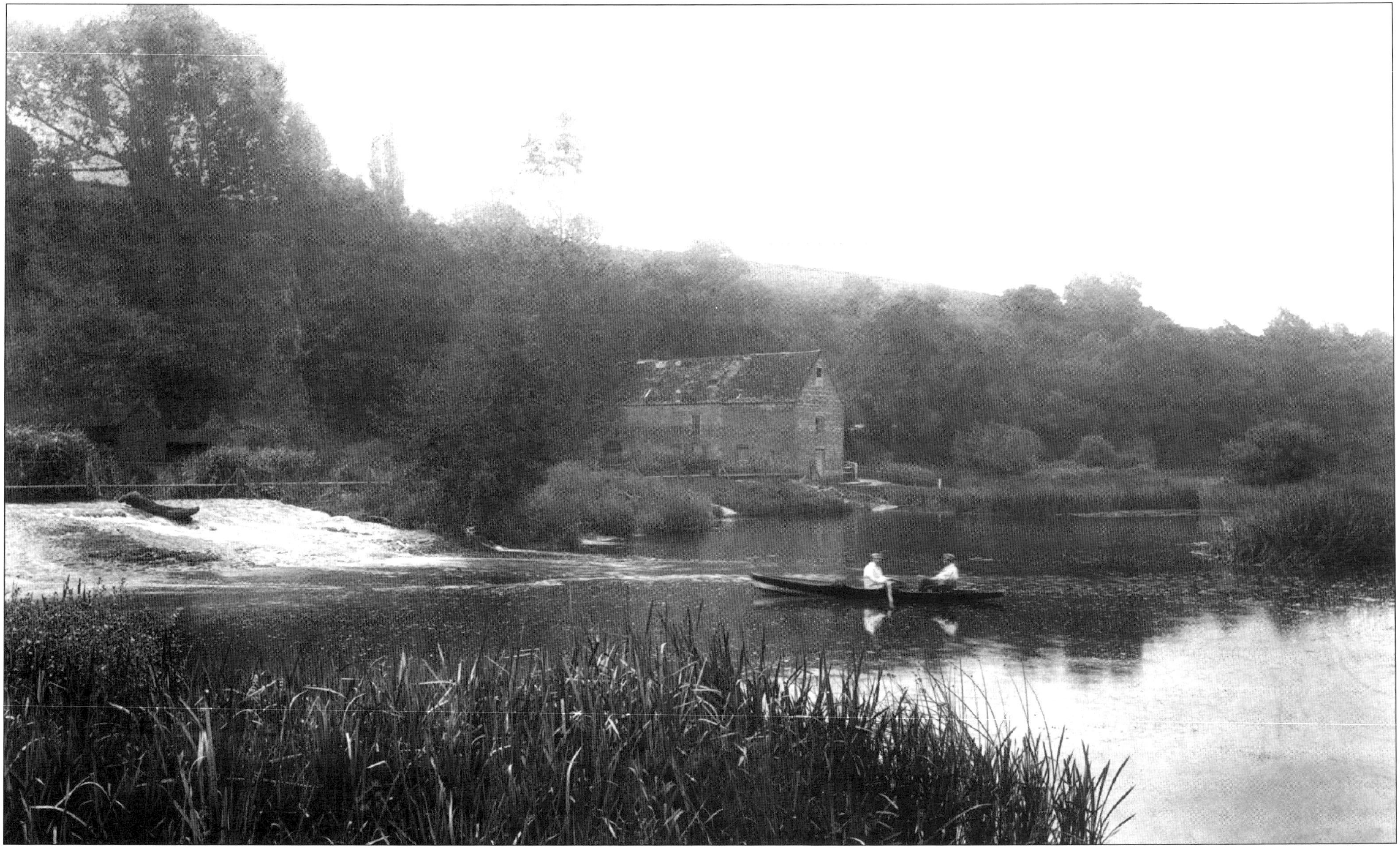

BOATING ON THE AVON, 1910. 47335
The building in this view of the river Avon is Cleeve Mill.

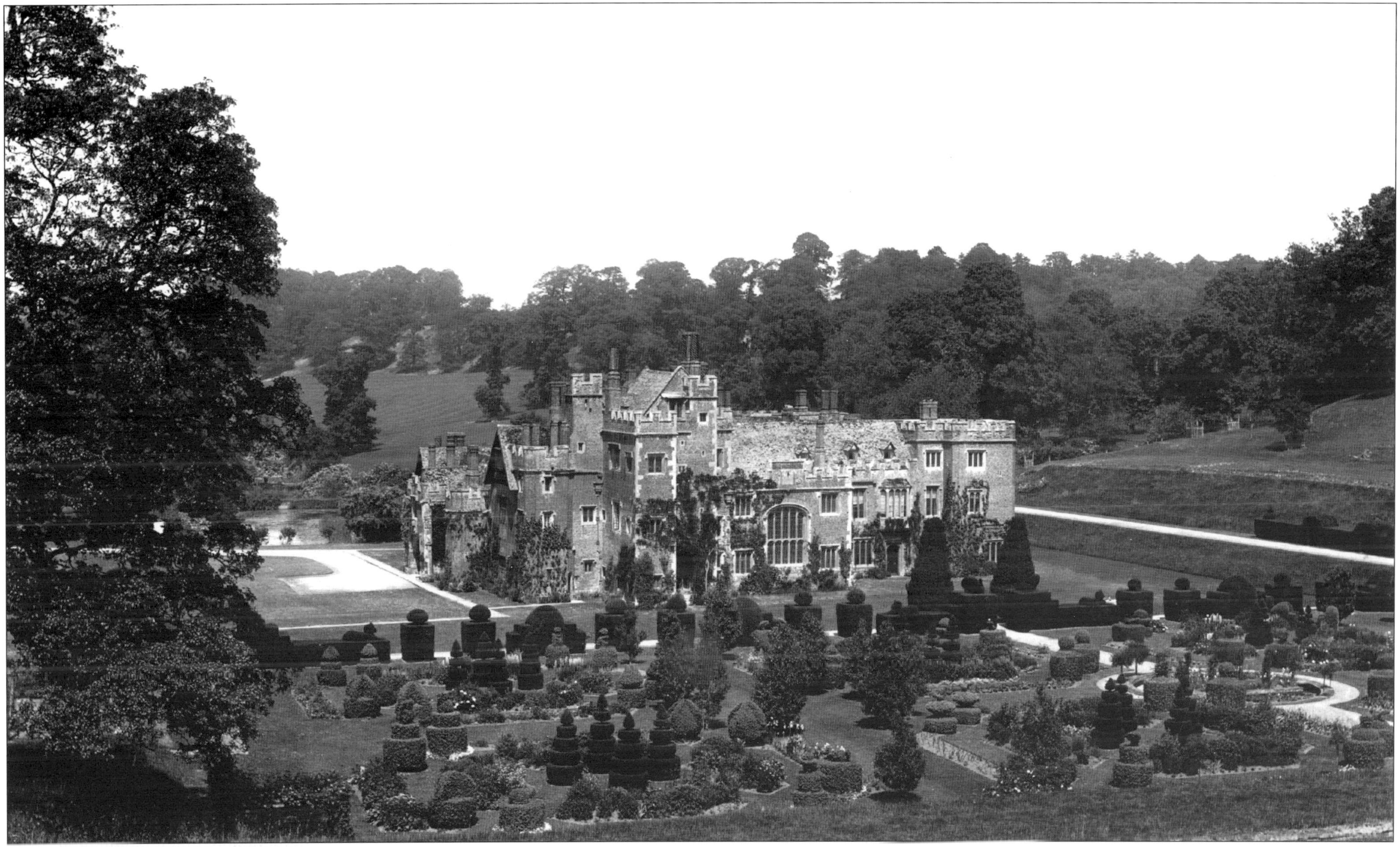

COMPTON WYNYATES HOUSE, 1922. 72096

Built between 1480 and 1520 on the site of a Norman manor house, much of the stone came from the ruined Fulbrook Castle, which had been given to William de Compton by Henry VIII.

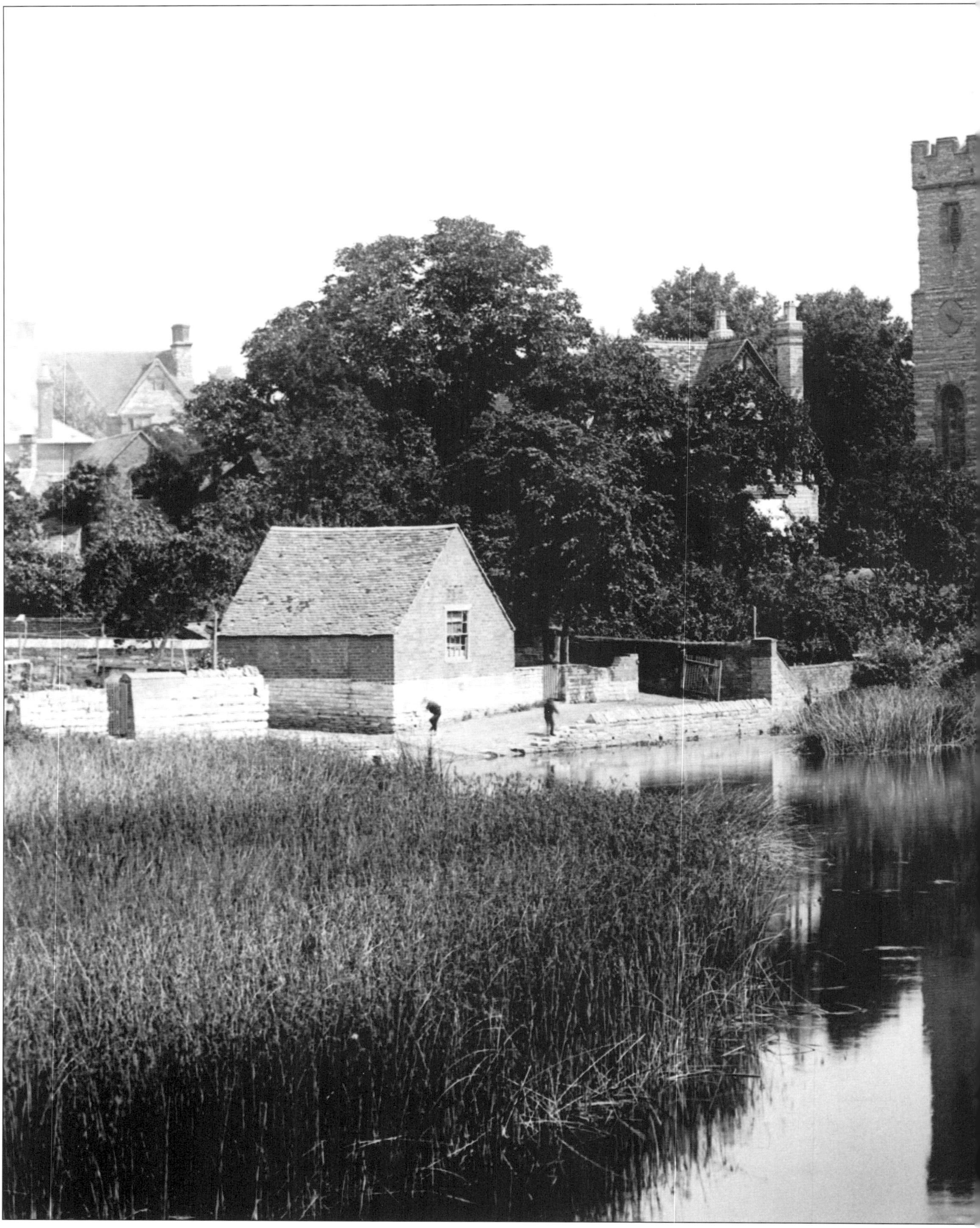

St Laurence Church, 1899.
The parish church with its medieval tower was one of hundreds of churches to suffer from the Victorian predilection for restoring ancient buildings extremely badly. The church suffered twice: once in 1835 and again in 1889.

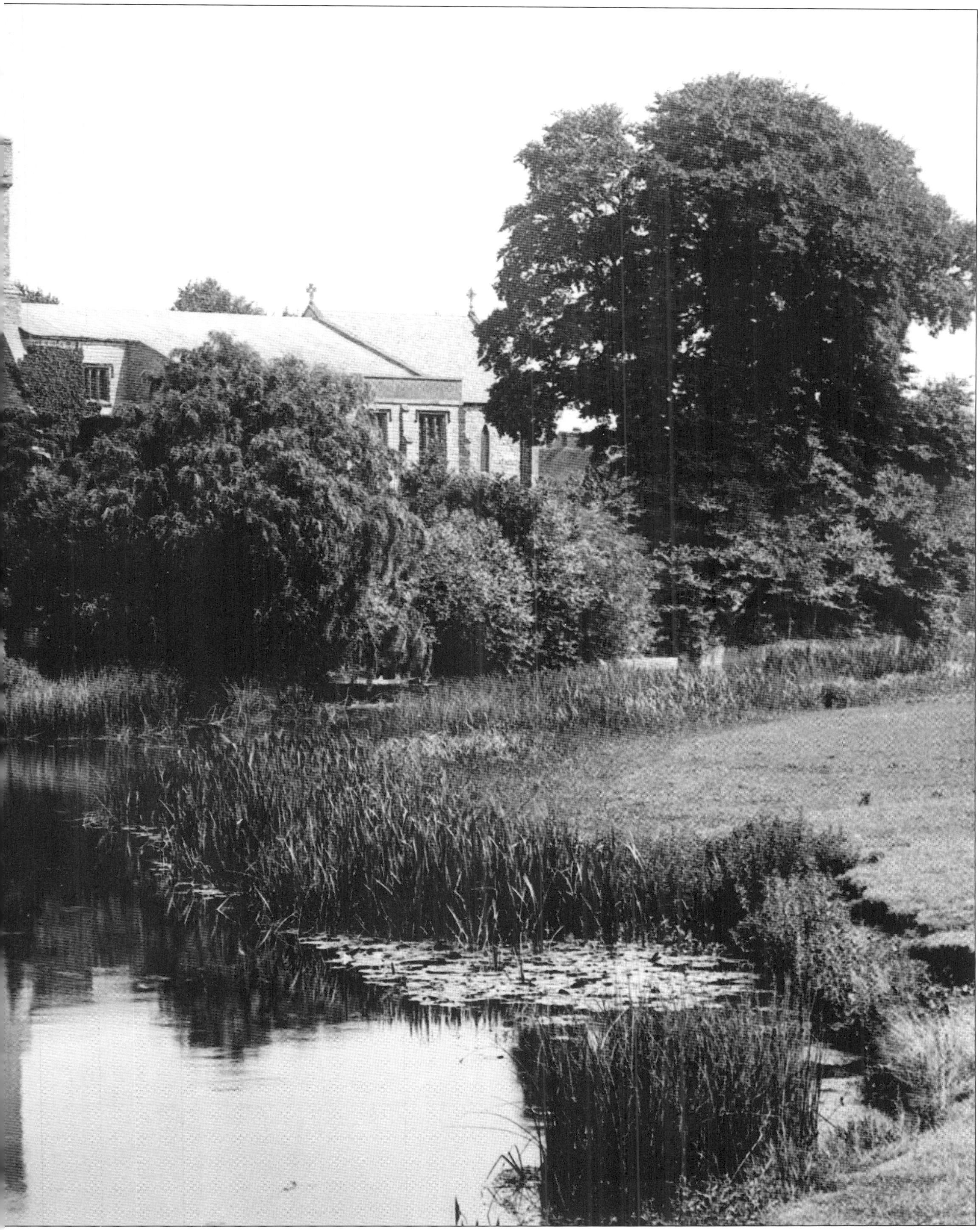

44130

Chapter 8

AROUND THE COUNTY

Polesworth

Like the nearby village of Alvecote, Polesworth was once a mining area. Construction of the Coventry Canal began in the late 1760s, the objective being to link industrial Coventry with the coalfield around Bedworth and to open a navigation to the Grand Trunk (Trent & Mersey) Canal.

Atherstone

The village of Atherstone straddles the old Roman road of Watling Street and lies about five miles south-east of Bosworth field where Richard III was defeated and killed in 1485. On the eve of the battle, Henry of Lancaster stayed at the Three Tuns Inn, Atherstone and the following morning took the sacrament at the local church of an Augustinian friary.

Arbury Hall

Situated three miles west of Nuneaton, Arbury Hall stands in 300 acres of parkland; the home of the Newdegate family since the sixteenth century. The hall was built as a Tudor manor house, but was extensively rebuilt in the Gothic Revival style during the eighteenth century by Sir Roger Newdiegate.

Guy's Cliffe

Guy's Cliffe is between Kenilworth and Warwick. The legend is that in the tenth century, Earl Guy had not only killed the Danish giant Colbrand, he had also slain the Dun Cow, killed dragons and even strangled a wild boar with his bare hands. Guy then decided to give up his Rambo lifestyle, living the life of a hermit in the cave now named after him.

Henley-in-Arden

The market town of Henley-in-Arden is noted for having a high street almost a mile long. The town's first charter was granted in the reign of Henry VI and the Court Leet continues one of its ancient functions with the annual election of the High Bailiff.

Shottery

The village of Shottery, just one mile from Stratford is where Shakespeare chose to do his courting. Anne Hathaway was the eldest of three daughters of John Hathaway, a farmer. She was eight years older than William, who was only eighteen when they married.

Broom

Situated to the south of Alcester on the Midland Railway line running between Evesham and Barnt Green, Broom railway station was once a busy place during the summer. It was the interchange for a cross-country route linking up with the Midland main line from Rugby to Bedford by way of Stratford-upon-Avon.

Edge Hill

On 23 October 1642 the King's army clashed with Parliamentary forces commanded by the Earl of Essex at Edge Hill. Essex had with him some 14,800 men, the King's forces numbered 14,300. The Parliamentarians had two things in their favour. Firstly, they were better armed and equipped because the magazines at Hull and the Tower of London were in Parliament's hands. Secondly, the locals around Edge Hill supported Parliament and provided the troops with food and drink. The Royalists on the other hand had to fend for themselves. The battle itself was an indecisive shambles; neither side could honestly claim a victory.

Alester

Alcester is situated eight miles west of Stratford-upon-Avon and the area is known to have been occupied in Roman times. The town was a staging post during the days of the stagecoach. Like Wetherby in Yorkshire, it lost considerable trade when the railways replaced the stagecoach as the principle form of long-distance travel. The town's principal industry was the manufacture of needles.

Shipston-on-Stour

Shipston-on-Stour is situated ten miles south south-east of Stratford and was once a centre for sheep and wool for the Vale of the Red Horse. Farmers and merchants came from miles around to do their business here, and there were enough of them to support several inns.

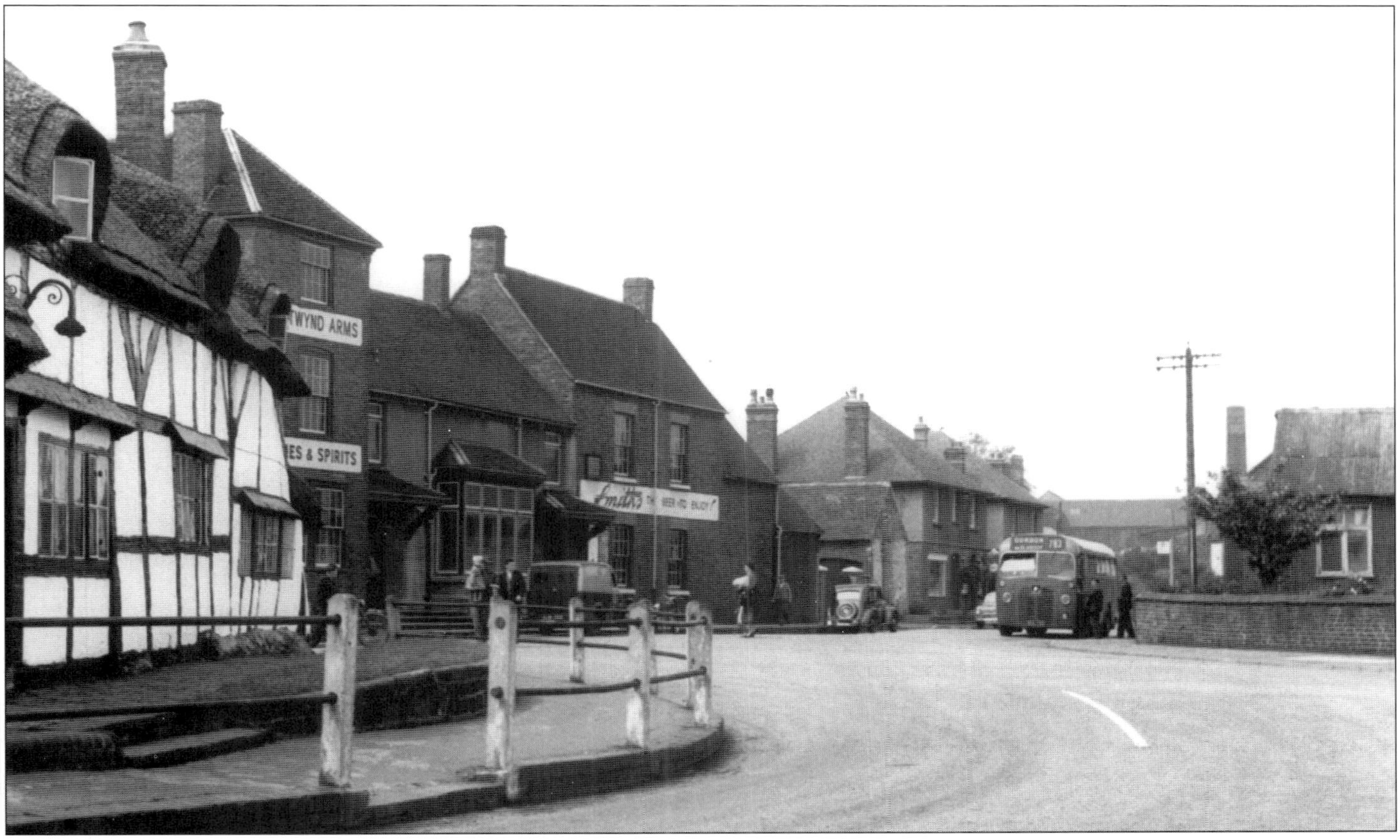

MARKET SQUARE, POLESWORTH, 1958. P64012

The parish church incorporates some of the remains of a tenth-century abbey, the most substantial part being the old gatehouse.

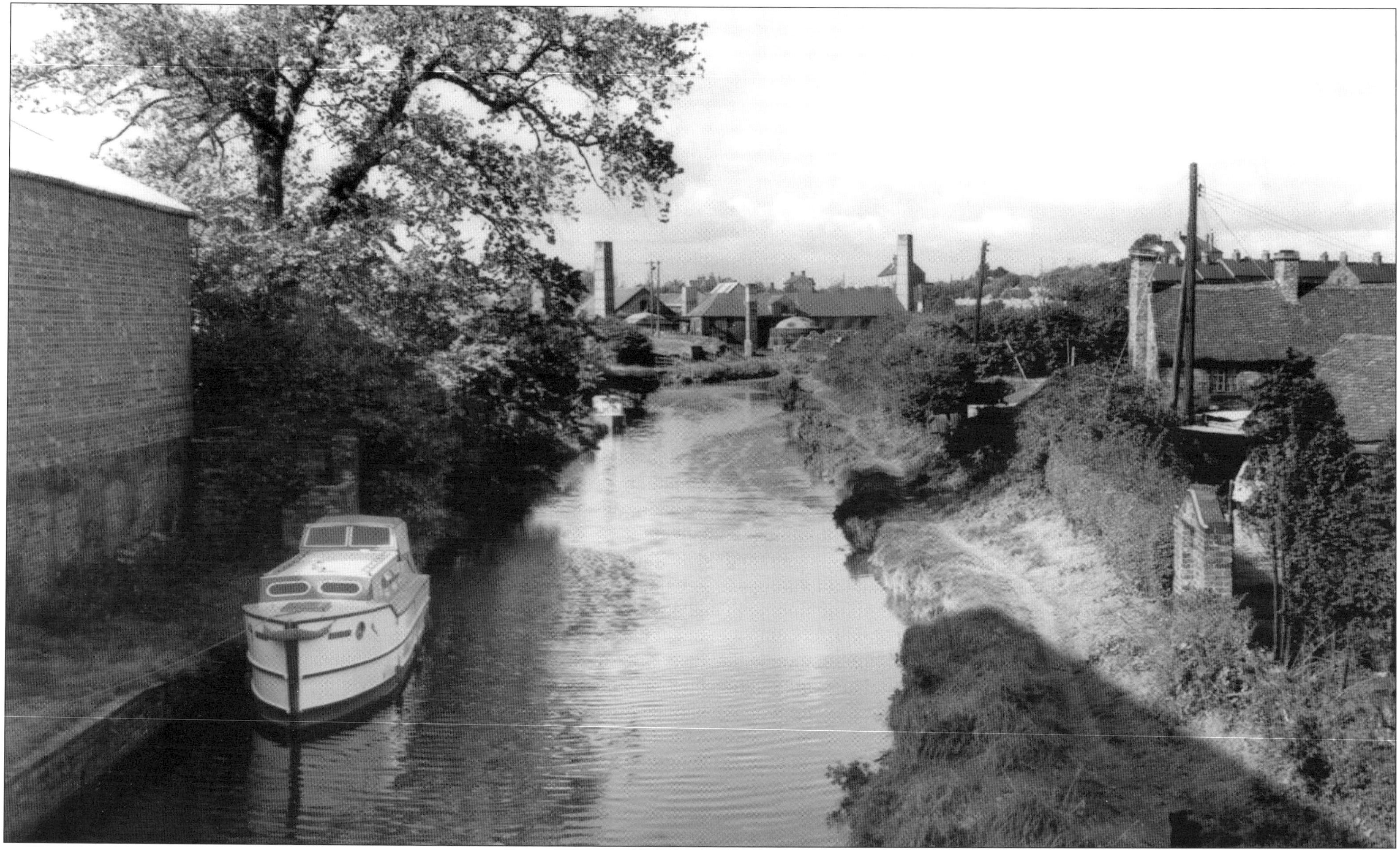

COVENTRY CANAL, POLESWORTH, 1963. P64016

The canal reached Atherstone in 1771, by which time all the authorised capital had been spent and James Brindley sacked. The canal eventually reached a junction with the Fazeley & Birmingham Canal in 1790. Despite the delays in completing the cut, it remained one of the most profitable of England's waterways, paying dividends up to 1947.

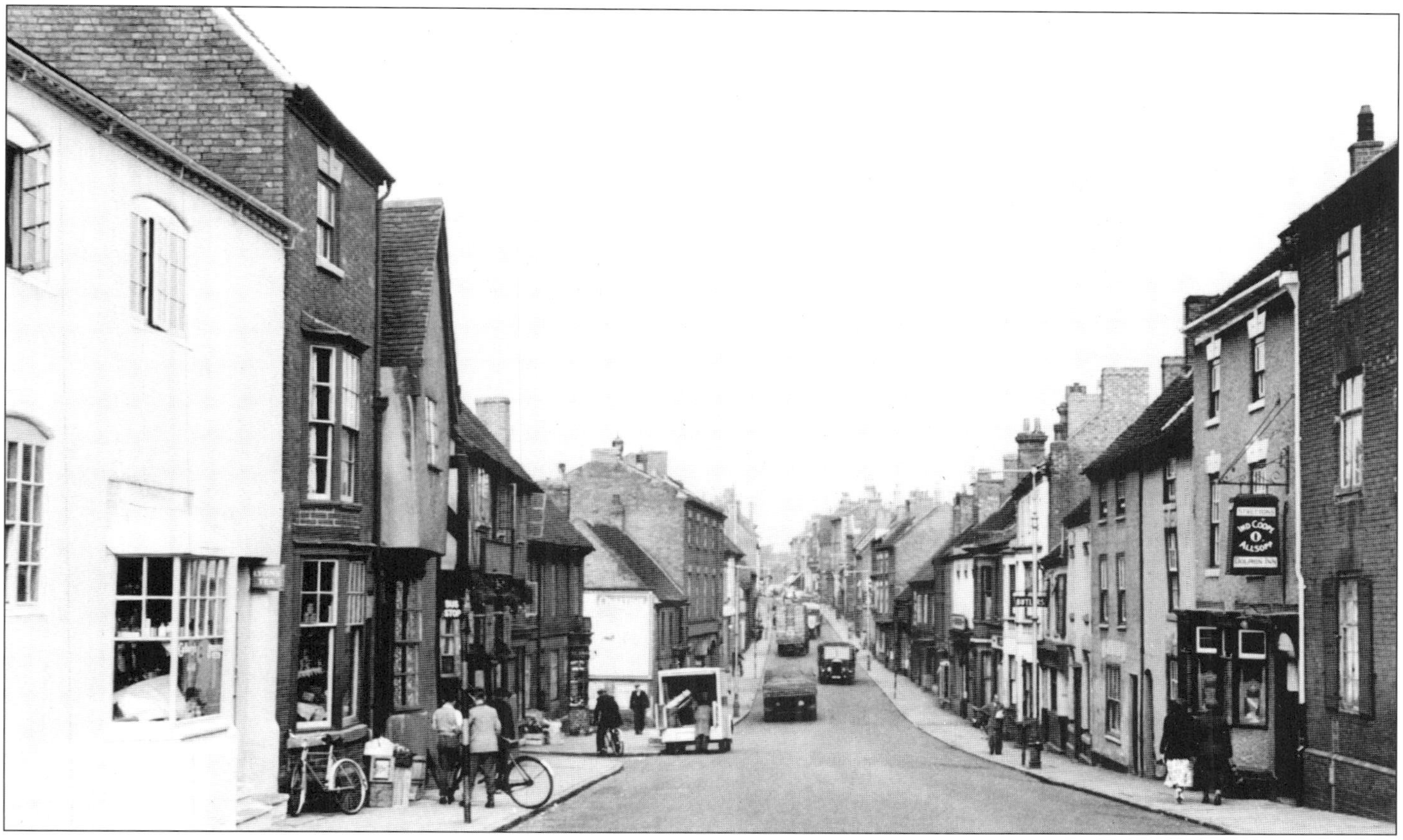

LONG STREET, ATHERSTONE, *c.*1955. A116004

Atherstone is one of only two places where the game of Shrovetide football is played; the other is Ashbourne in Derbyshire. In 1846 the game was finally banned from the streets of Derby, hence the expression a 'Derby game' when two local teams play one another.

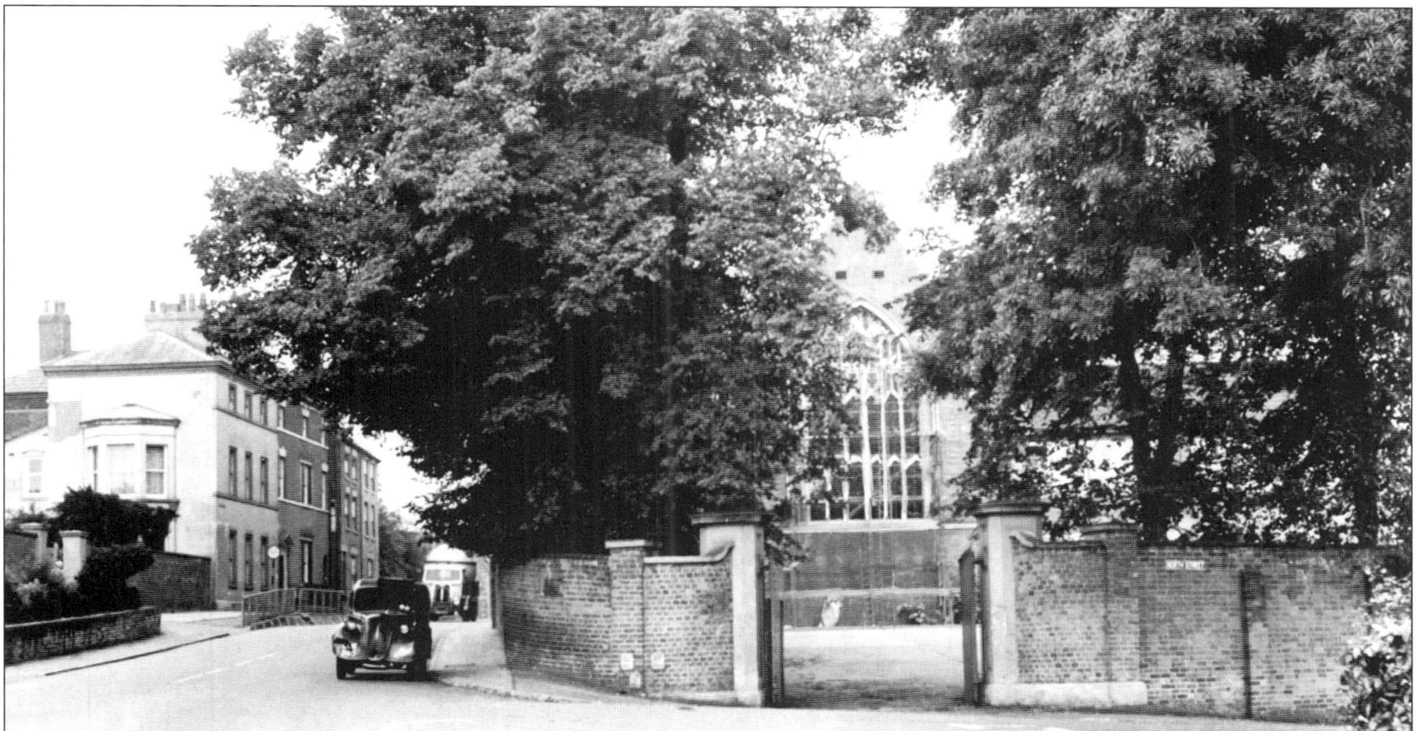

QUEEN ELIZABETH GRAMMAR SCHOOL, ATHERSTONE, *c.*1955. A116007

The school has a charter dating back to the sixteenth century.

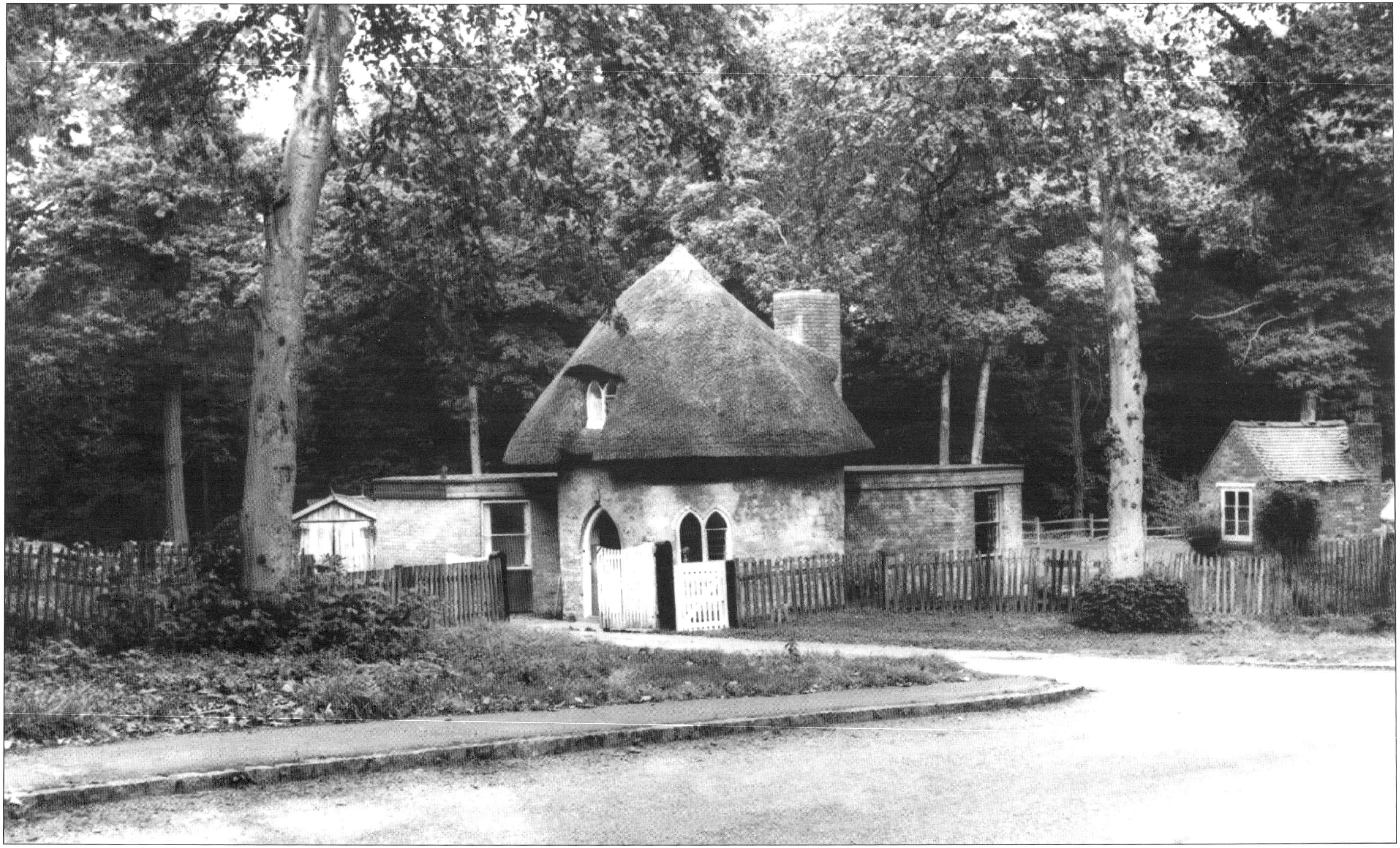

THE BEE HIVE, ATHERSTONE, *c*.1955. A116042

Another interesting building is the Red Lion, an old coaching inn outside of which is a milepost inscribed '100 miles London'. In 1906 a room at the Red Lion would set you back 2*s* 6*d*.

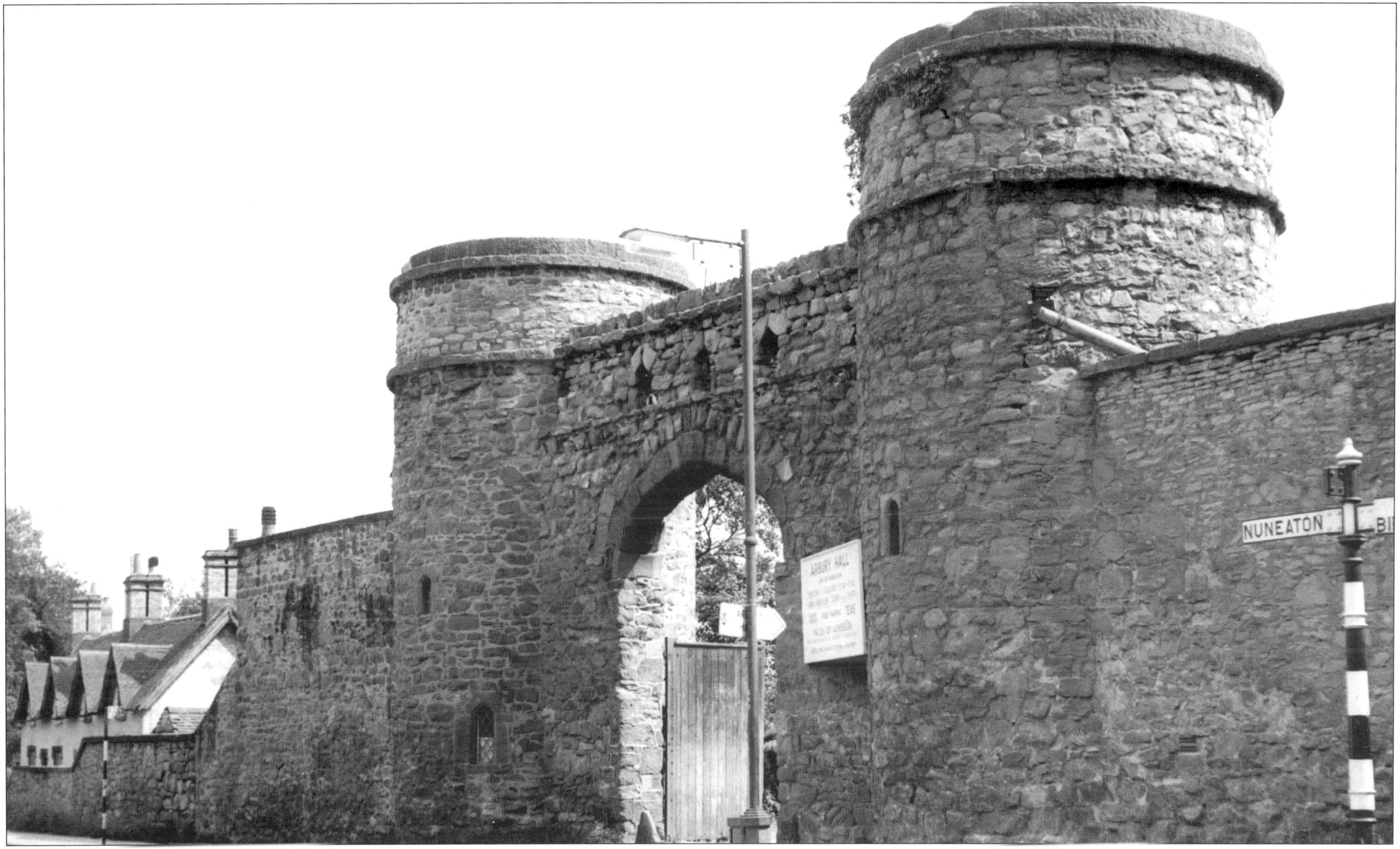

THE ROUND TOWERS OF ARBURY HALL, *c.*1960. N89031

The hall was Gothicized under the direction of Henry Keene, Henry Couchman and Saunderson Miller, who were responsible for both the exterior and interior decor. During the Second World War German prisoners were interned at Arbury.

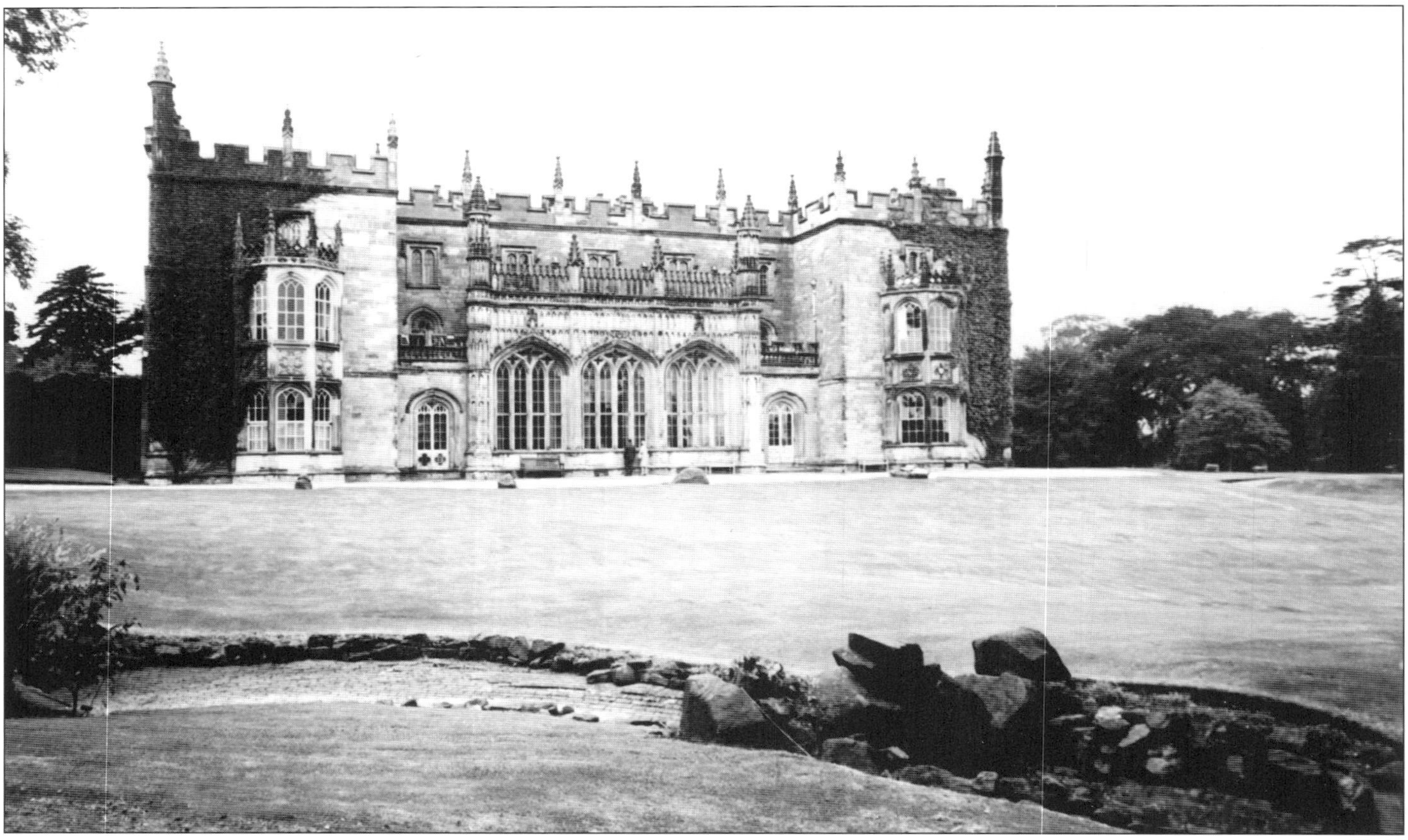

ARBURY HALL, *c.*1960. N89119

Considered to be one of the finest Gothic Revival houses in England. Arbury is built on the site of an Augustinian monastery demolished during the reign of Elizabeth I.

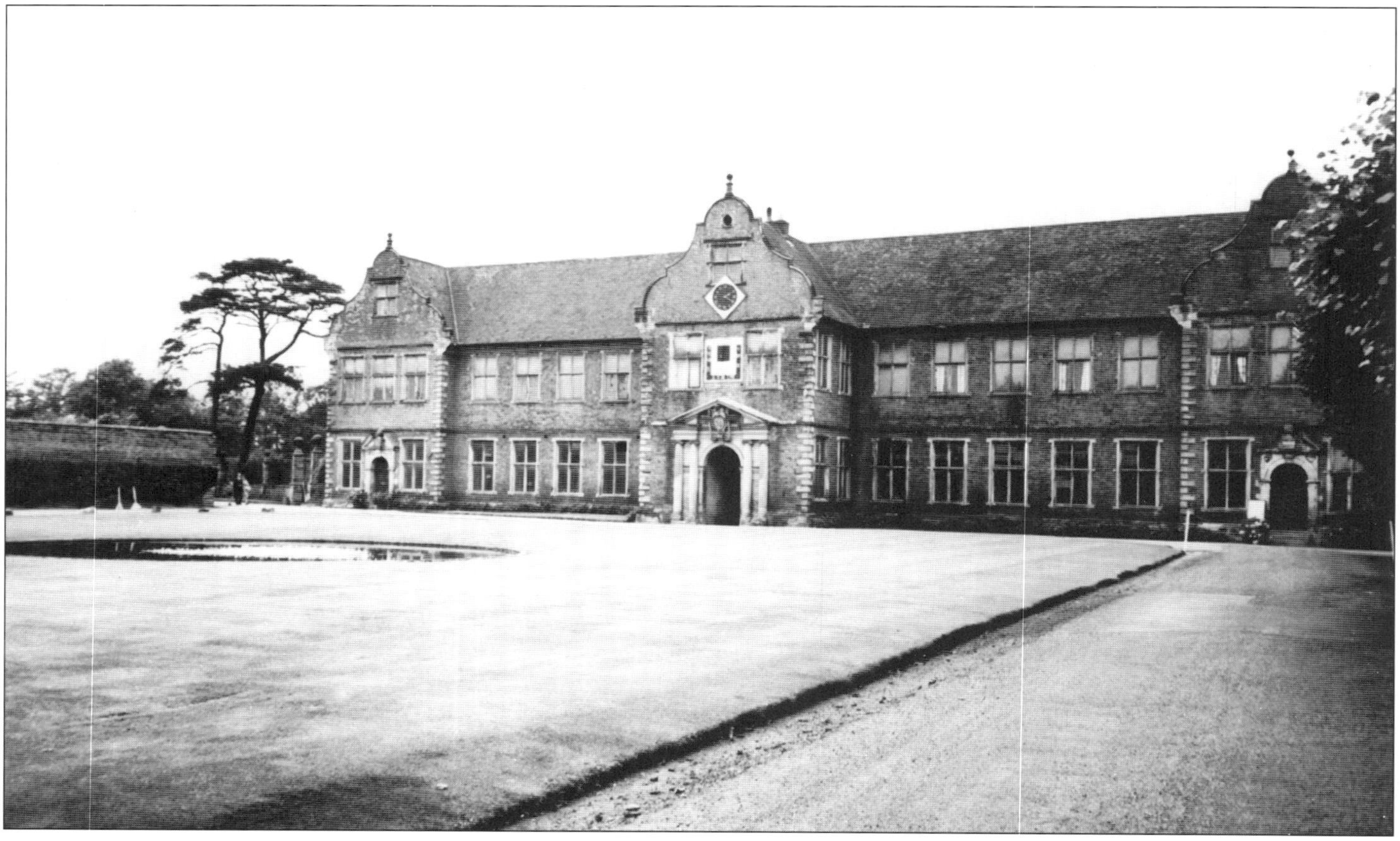

THE STABLES AT ARBURY, *c.*1965. N89118

A few hundred yards from the hall stands South Farm where Mary Ann Evans was born in 1819. Mary is better known to us as the writer George Eliot and as such wrote about the rural and industrialised Midlands.

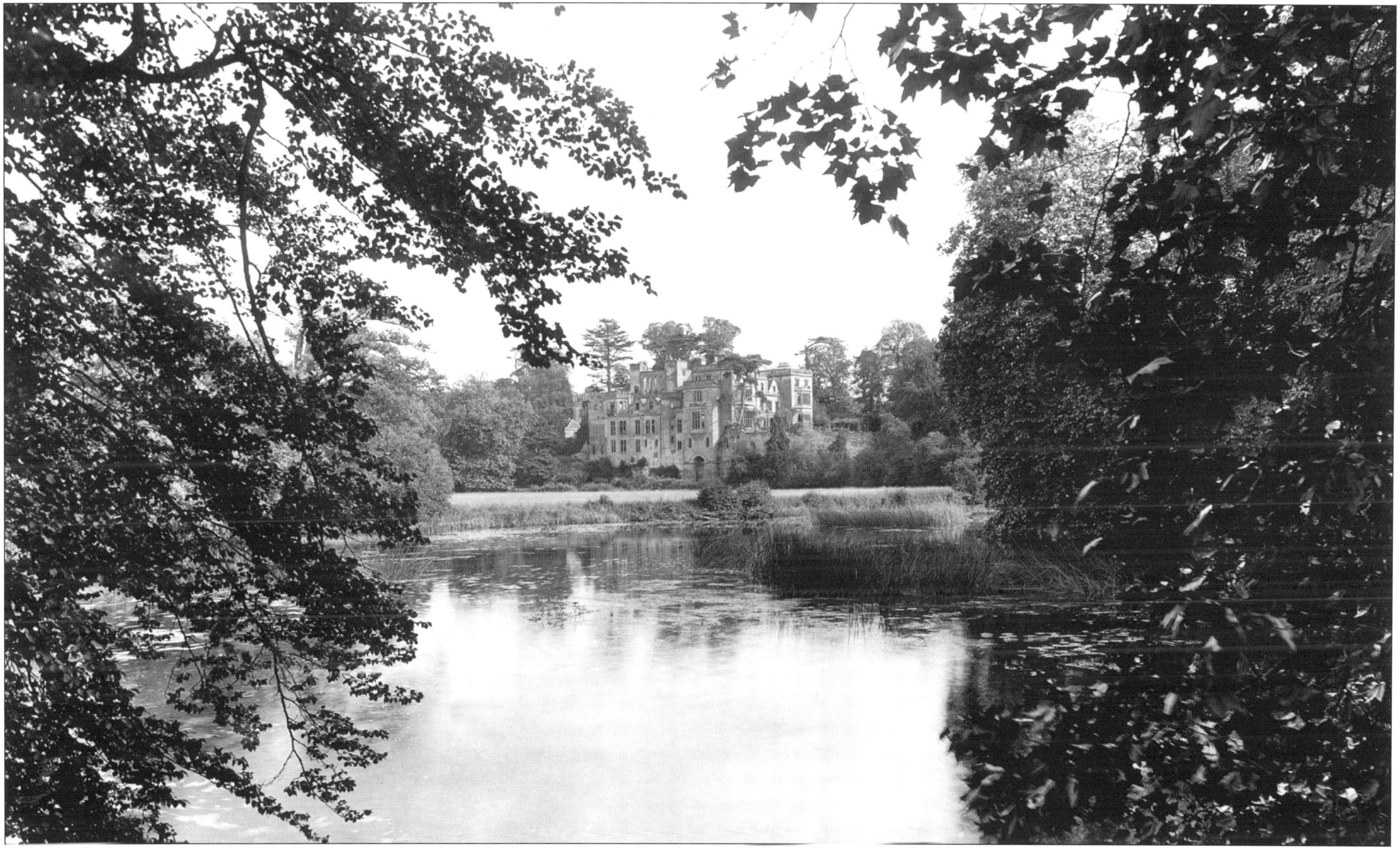

GUY'S CLIFFE HOUSE, 1922. 72370

Nearby on the summit of Blacklow Hill is a monument to Piers Gaveston, the favourite of Edward II. The arrogant son of a Gascon knight, he had the effrontery to call Guy, Earl of Warwick 'the black hound of Arden'. He was executed by the barons in 1312.

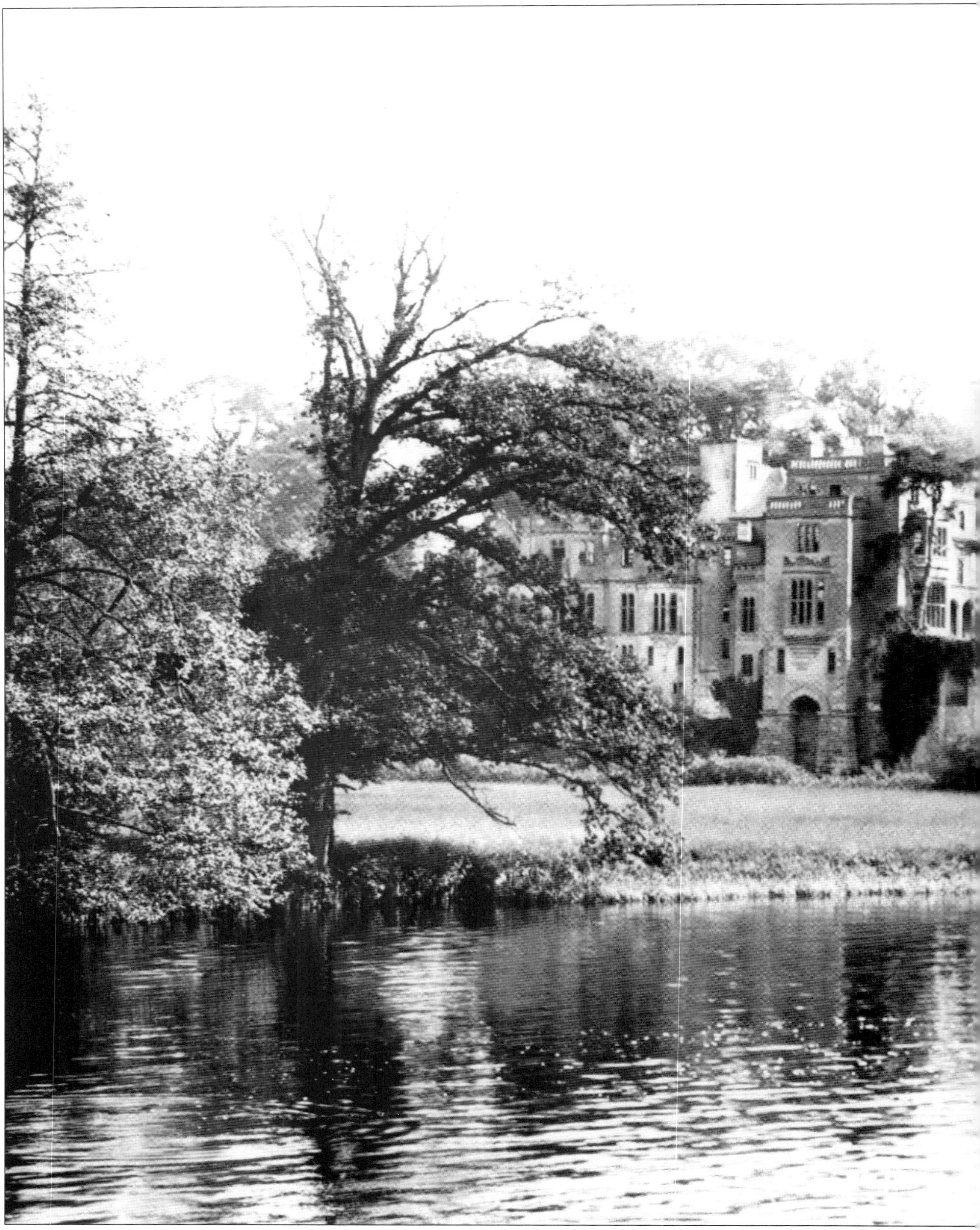

Guy's Cliffe House, 1892.
The house was built in 1751 by Samuel Greathead on the site of an Elizabethan mansion. In the 1920s domestic staff at Guy's Cliffe worked a six-and-a-half-day week. They were expected to attend church every Sunday, even if it was their half day off.

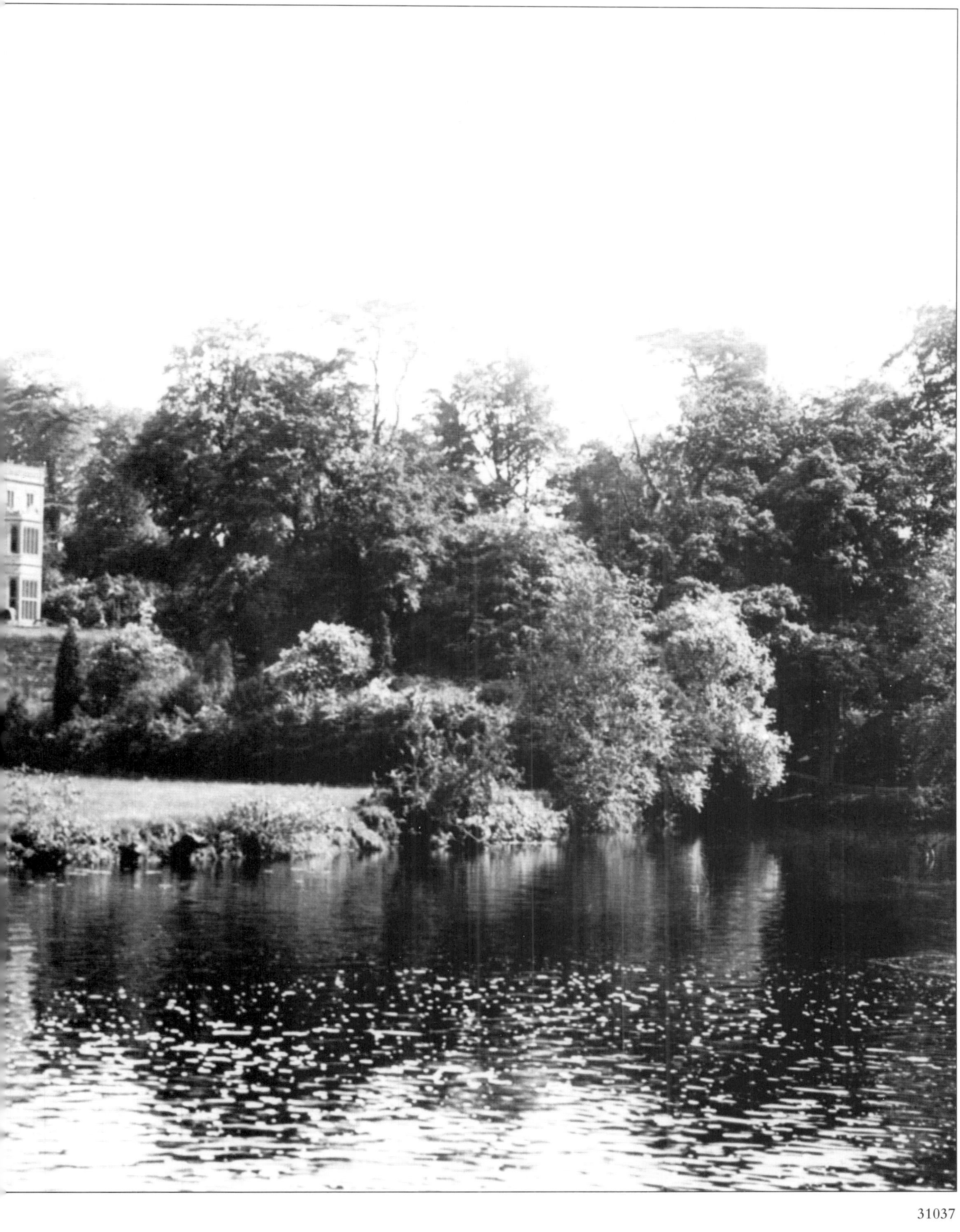

31037

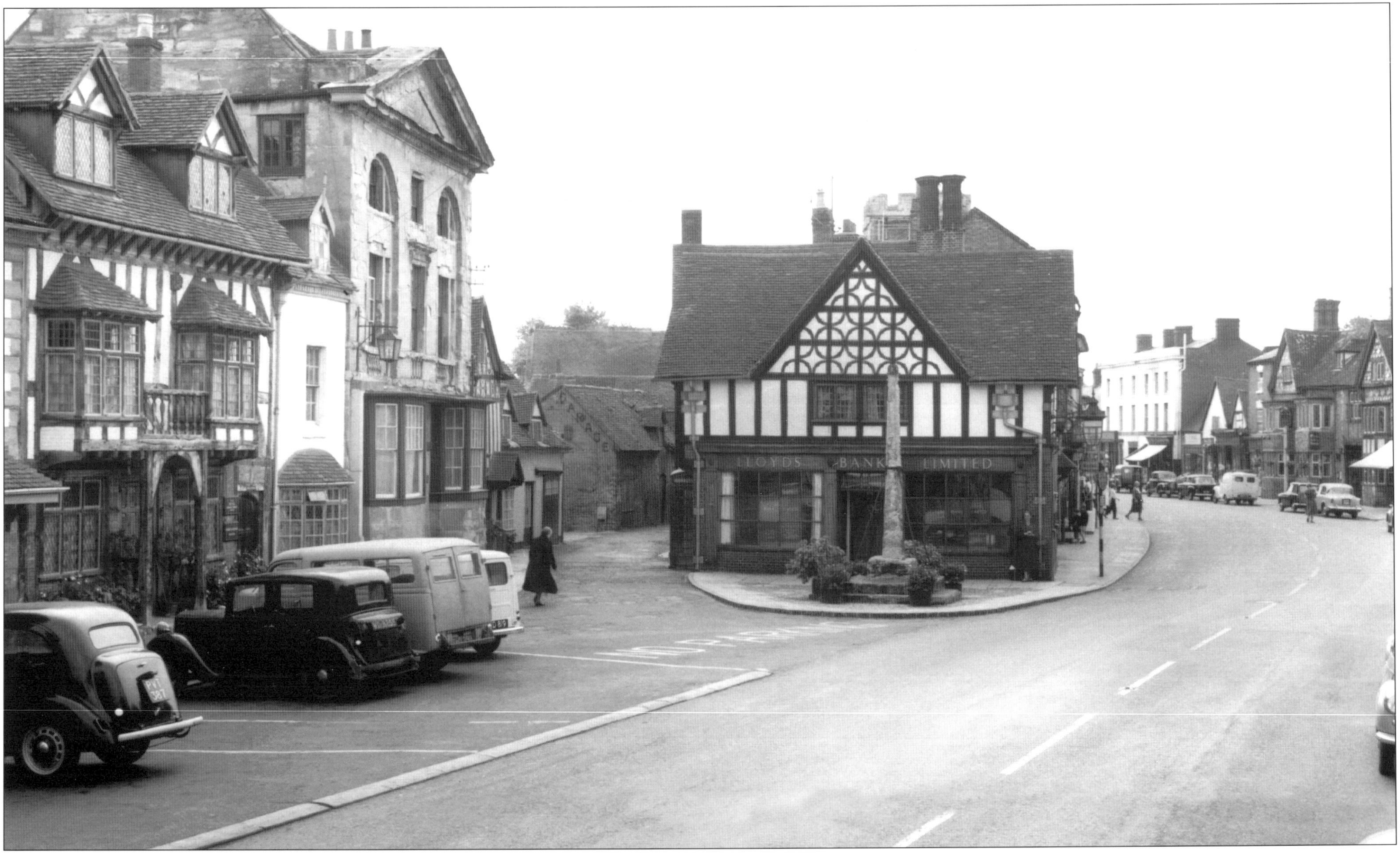

THE MARKET SQUARE, HENLEY-IN-ARDEN, 1955. H414027

The town was once under the control of the powerful de Montfort family. At Evesham on 4 August 1265, Simon de Montfort led the barons against the forces of Henry III. The barons were destroyed, both Simon de Montfort and his son were among the dead. Shortly afterwards Henley was sacked and burnt.

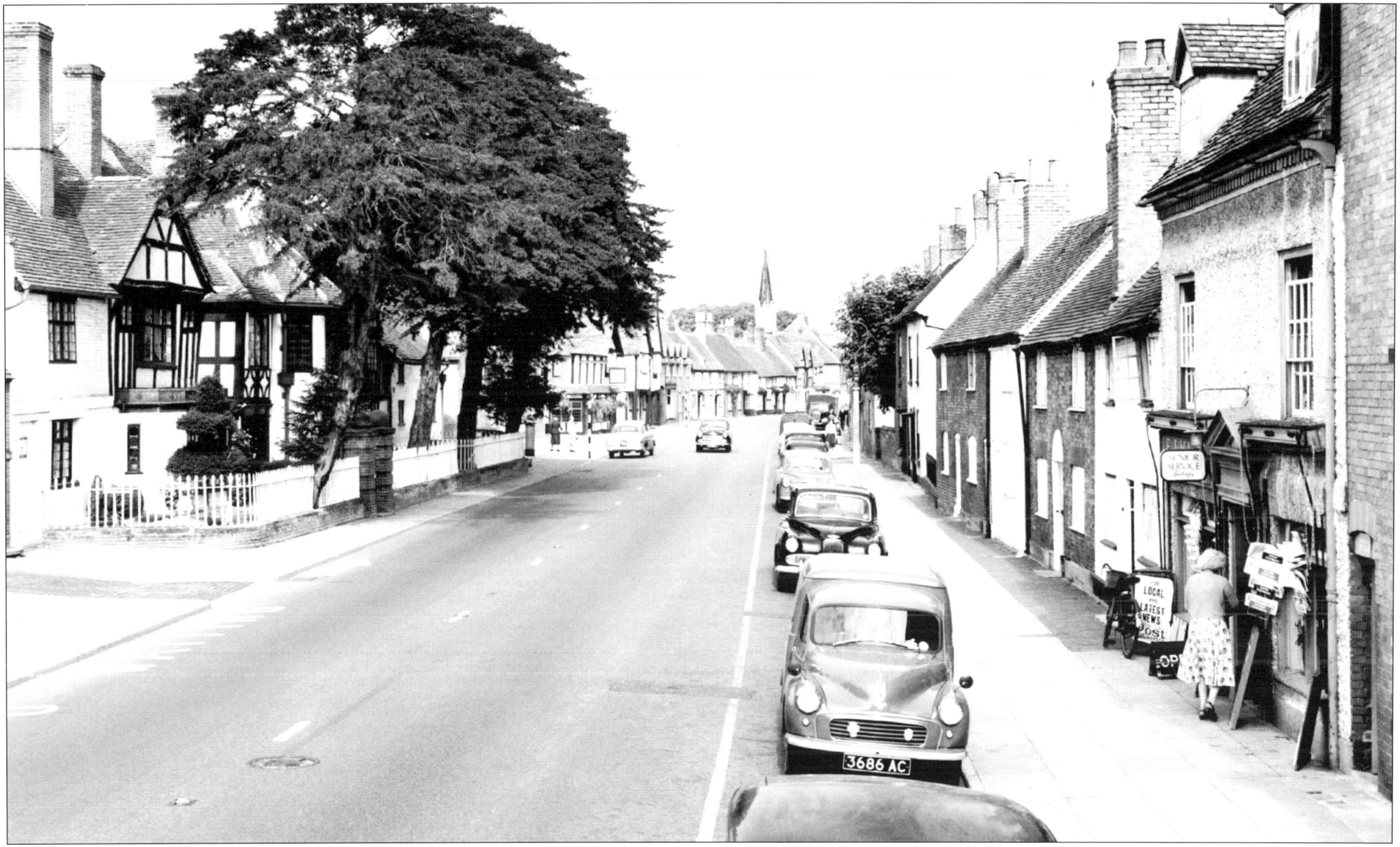

HENLEY-IN-ARDEN, *c*.1955. H414032

The church of St John the Baptist, the Guildhall and parts of the Blue Bell Inn date from the fifteenth century.

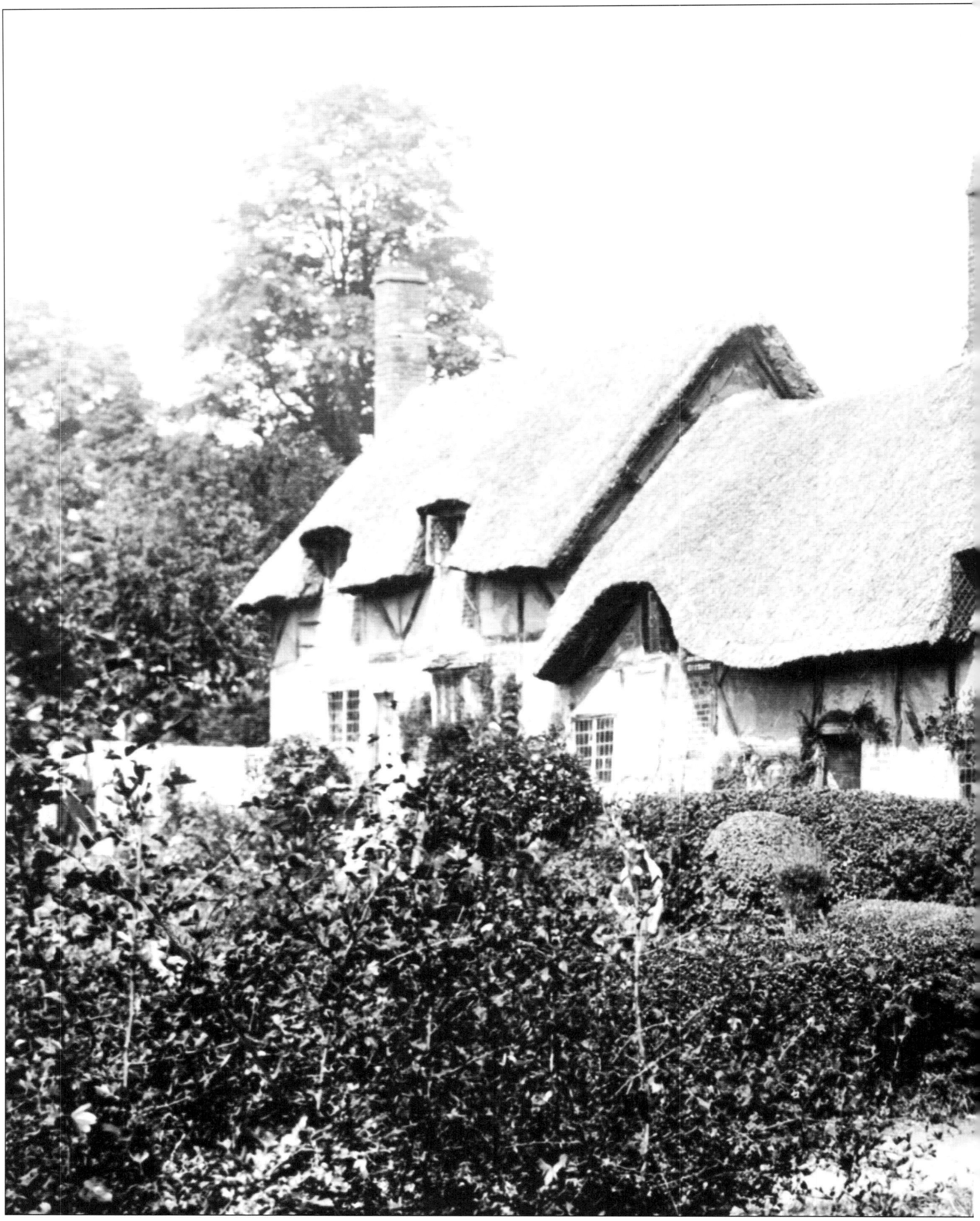

Anne Hathaway's Cottage, Shottery, 1892.
This building is somewhat misnamed. It is not a cottage, it is in fact an Elizabethan farmhouse and Anne Hathaway never owned it.

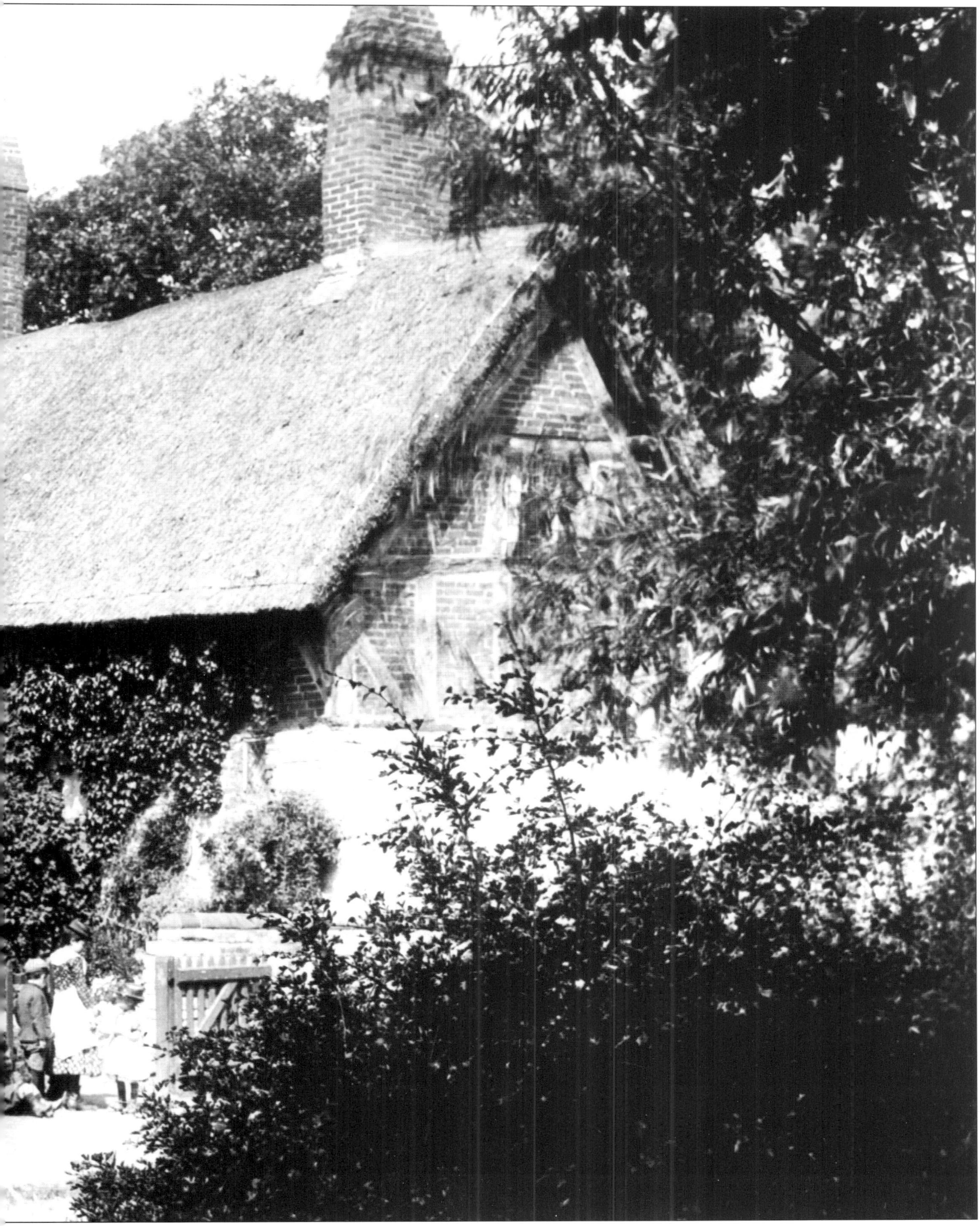

31084

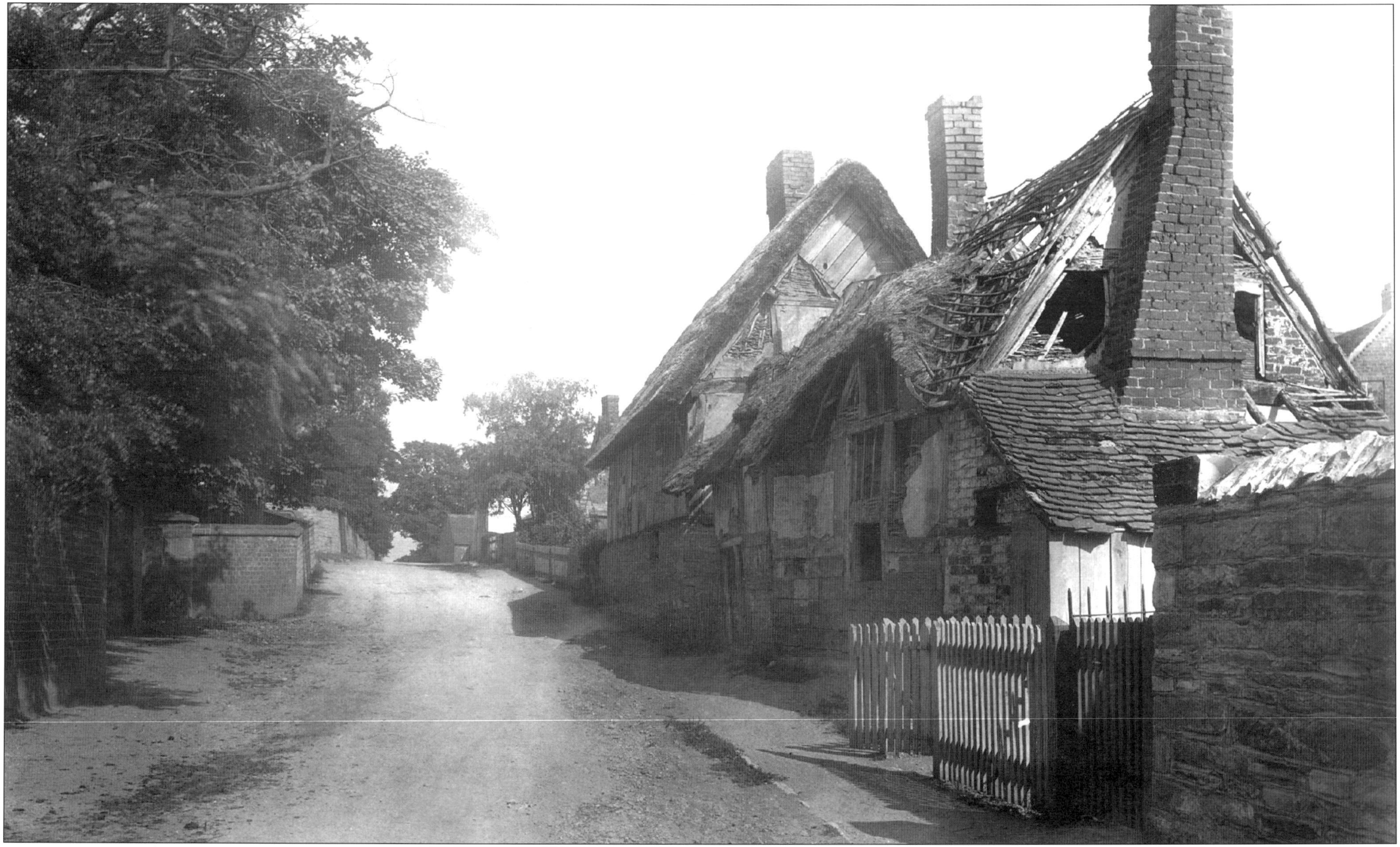

THE VILLAGE, BROOM, 1901. 47346

There were still a number of sixteenth and seventeenth-century half-timbered cottages around, but judging by the state of some of them the village was living up to the 'Beggarly Broom' image given to it by William Shakespeare.

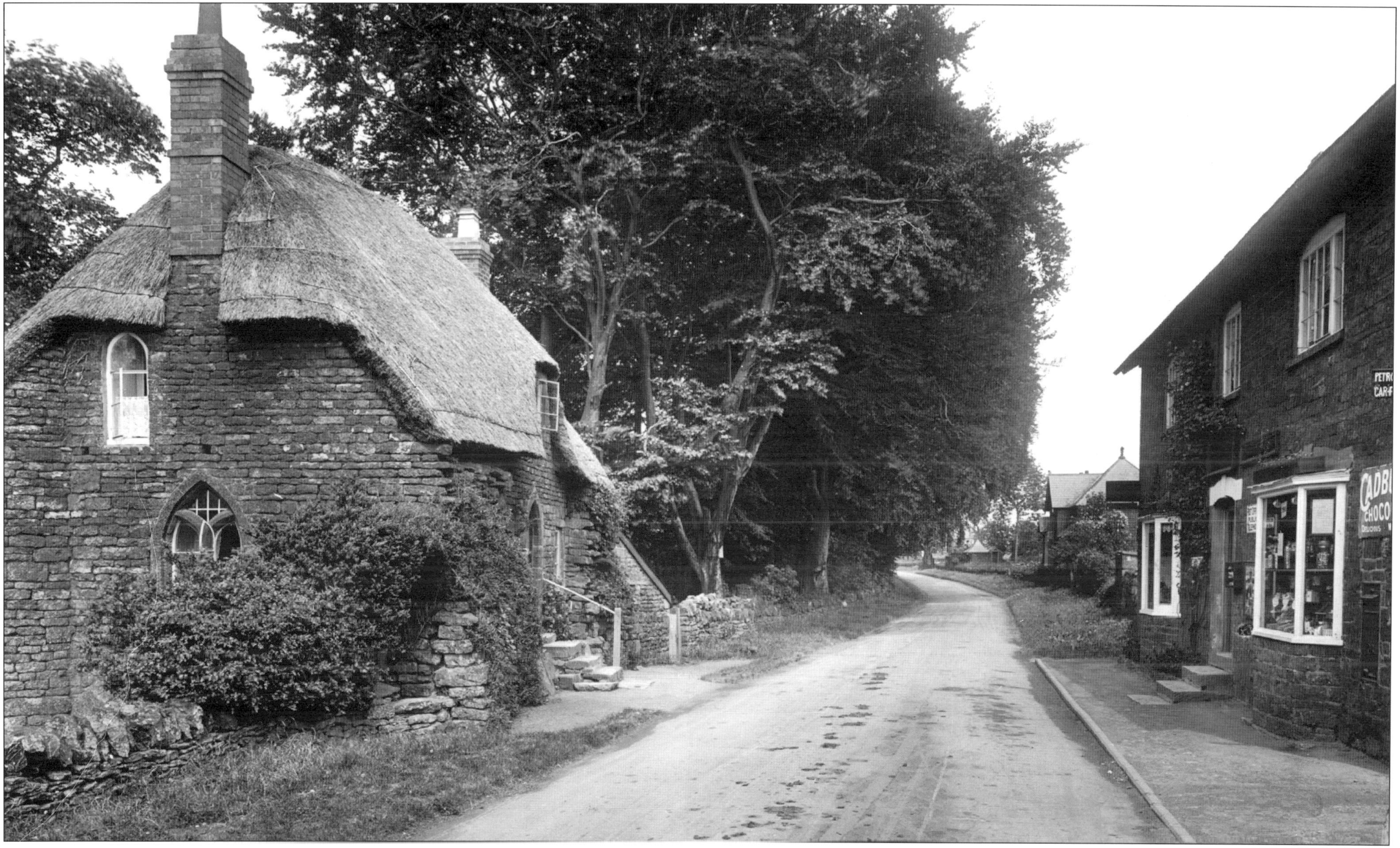

OLD COTTAGES AT EDGE HILL, 1922. 72070

On hearing of the ghostly goings on, Charles I sent a party under Colonel Kirke to investigate. They returned and told the king that they had seen the battle refought and had identified a number of the people taking part, including Sir Edmund Varney and others who had been killed in the original engagement.

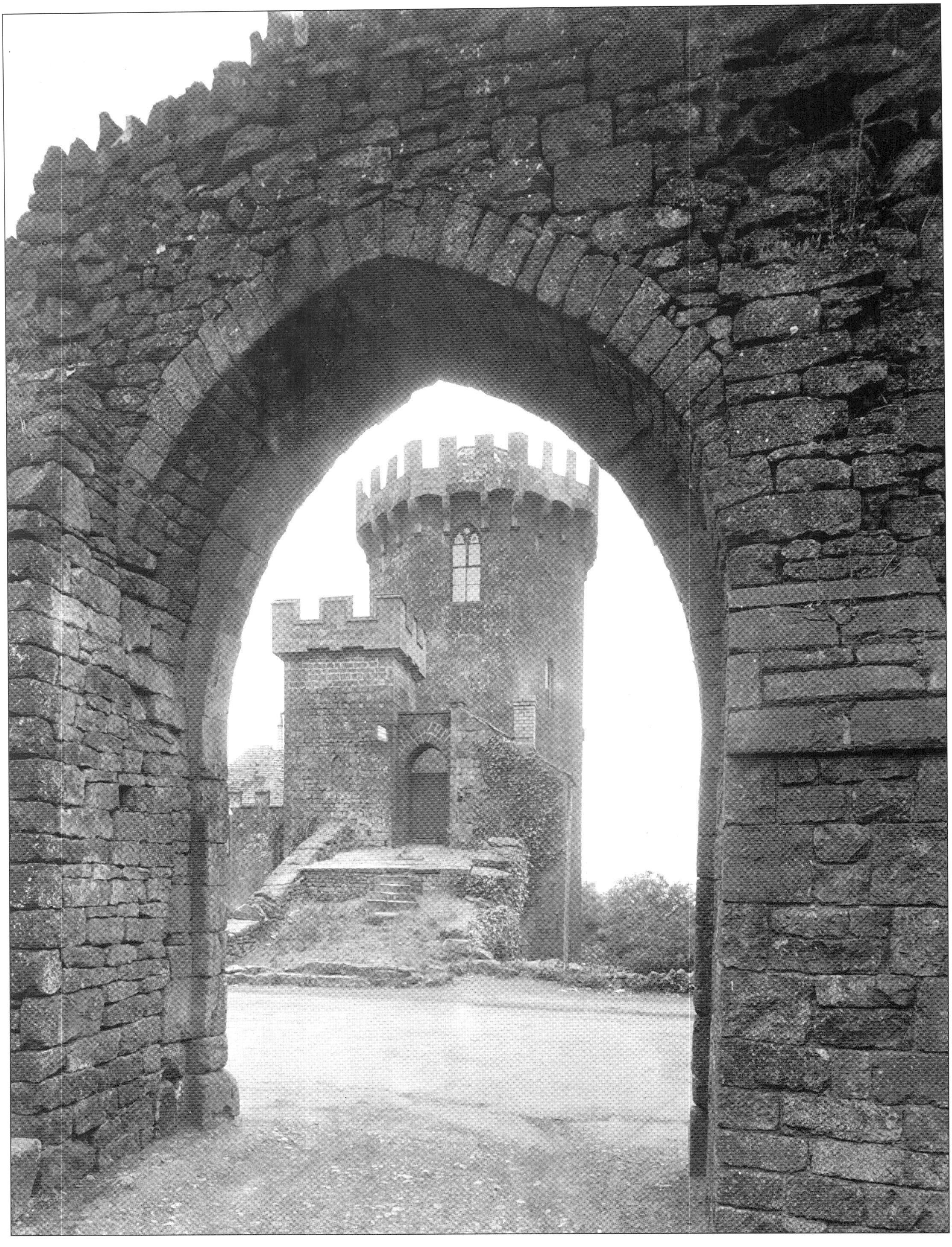

EDGE HILL, 1922. 72073

As early as January 1643 a pamphlet had been published titled *Apparitions and Prodigious Noyses of War and Battels seen on Edge Hill near Keinton in Warwickshire*. This was the first account of ghostly re-enactments of the battle that have been witnessed on countless occasions over the past 350 years.

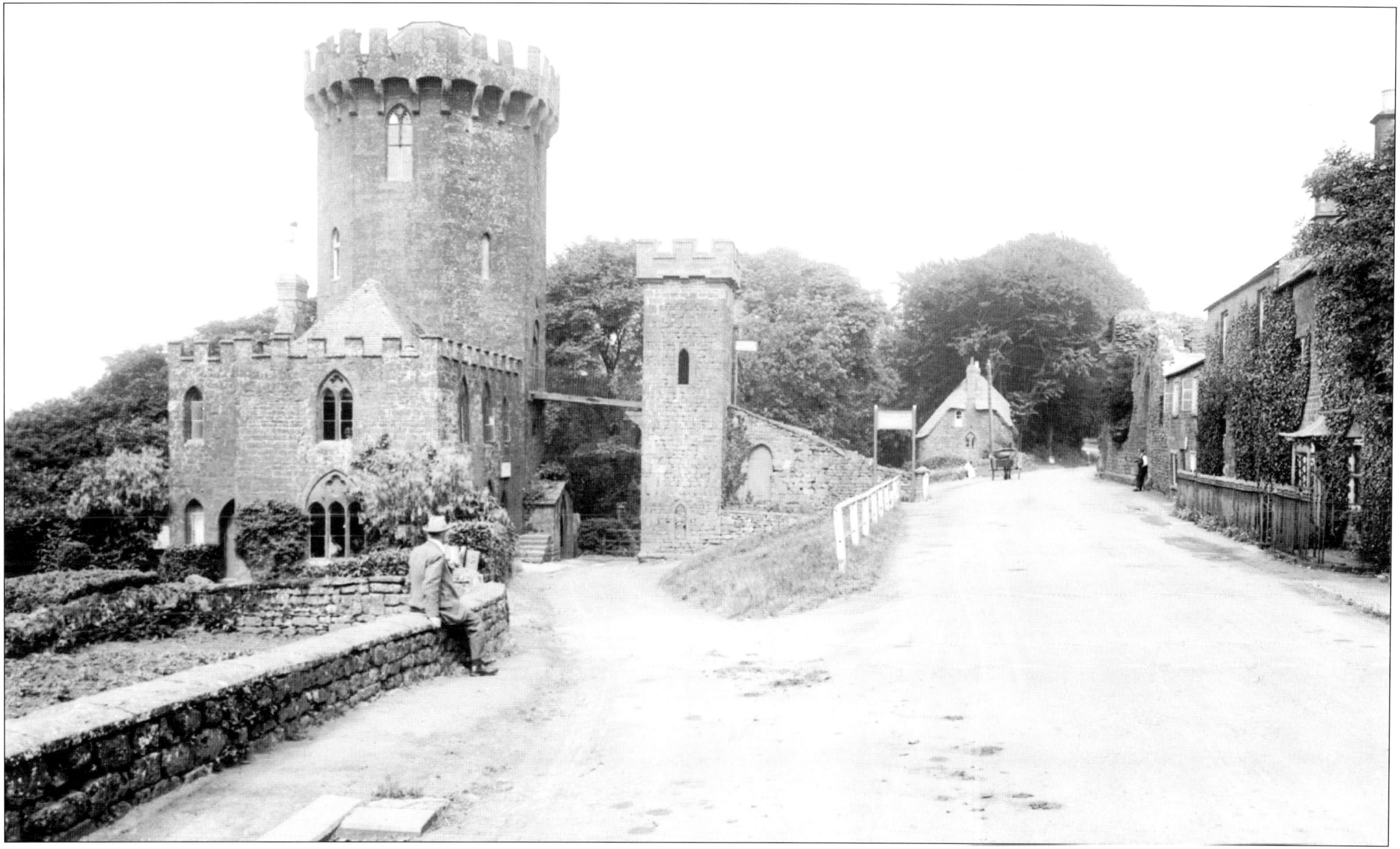

THE ROUND TOWER, EDGE HILL, 1922. 72072

The tower at Edge Hill was built in 1750 to commemorate the battle. The mock-Gothic edifice was later used as an inn.

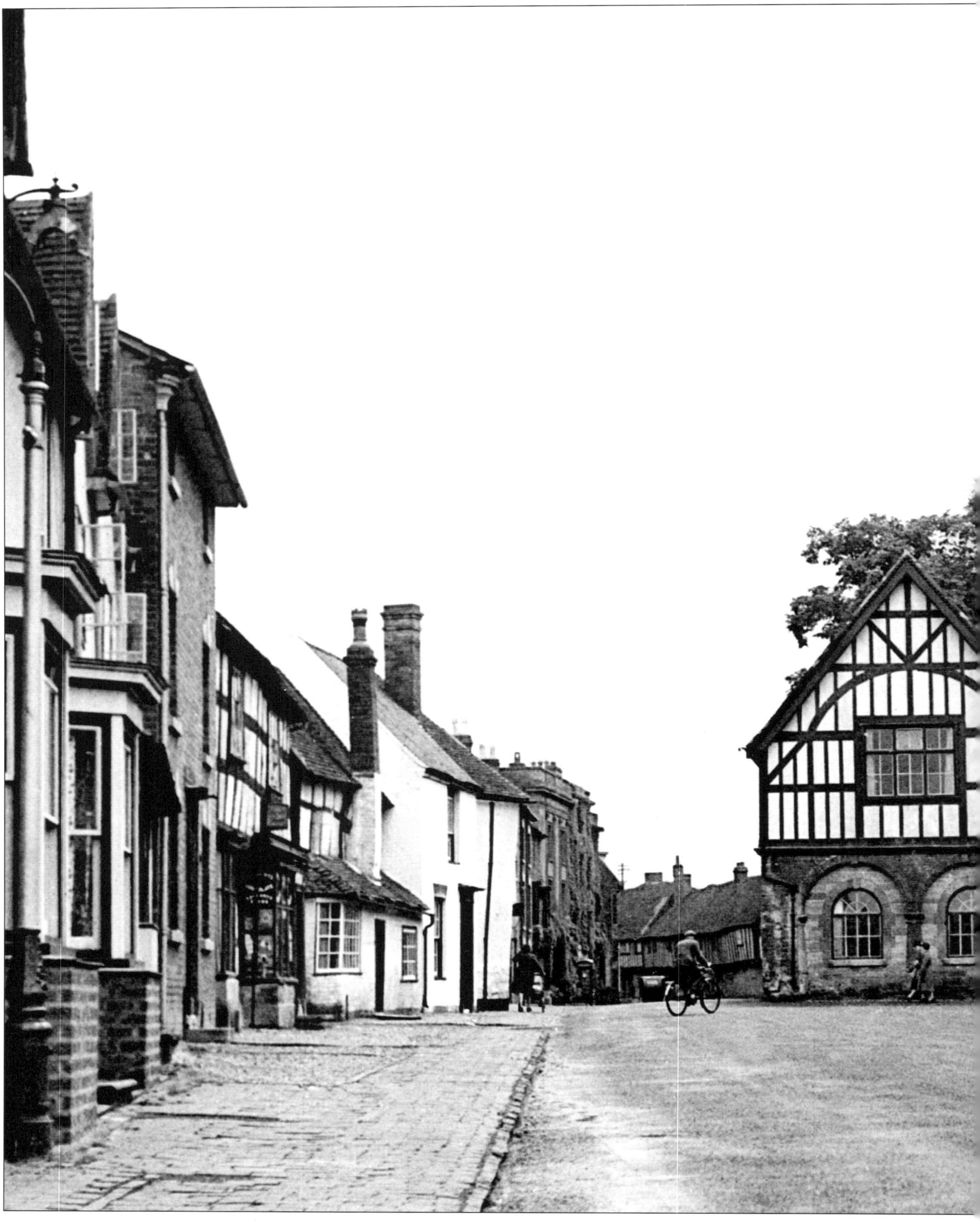

THE OLD TOWN HALL, HENLEY STREET, ALCASTER, *c.*1965.
Built in 1618, the gift of Sir Fulke Greville, first Baron Brooke. Educated at Shrewsbury and Jesus College Cambridge he was a friend of Sir Philip Sidney. Granted a peerage in 1628, he was awarded Warwick Castle, where he was murdered in mysterious circumstances.

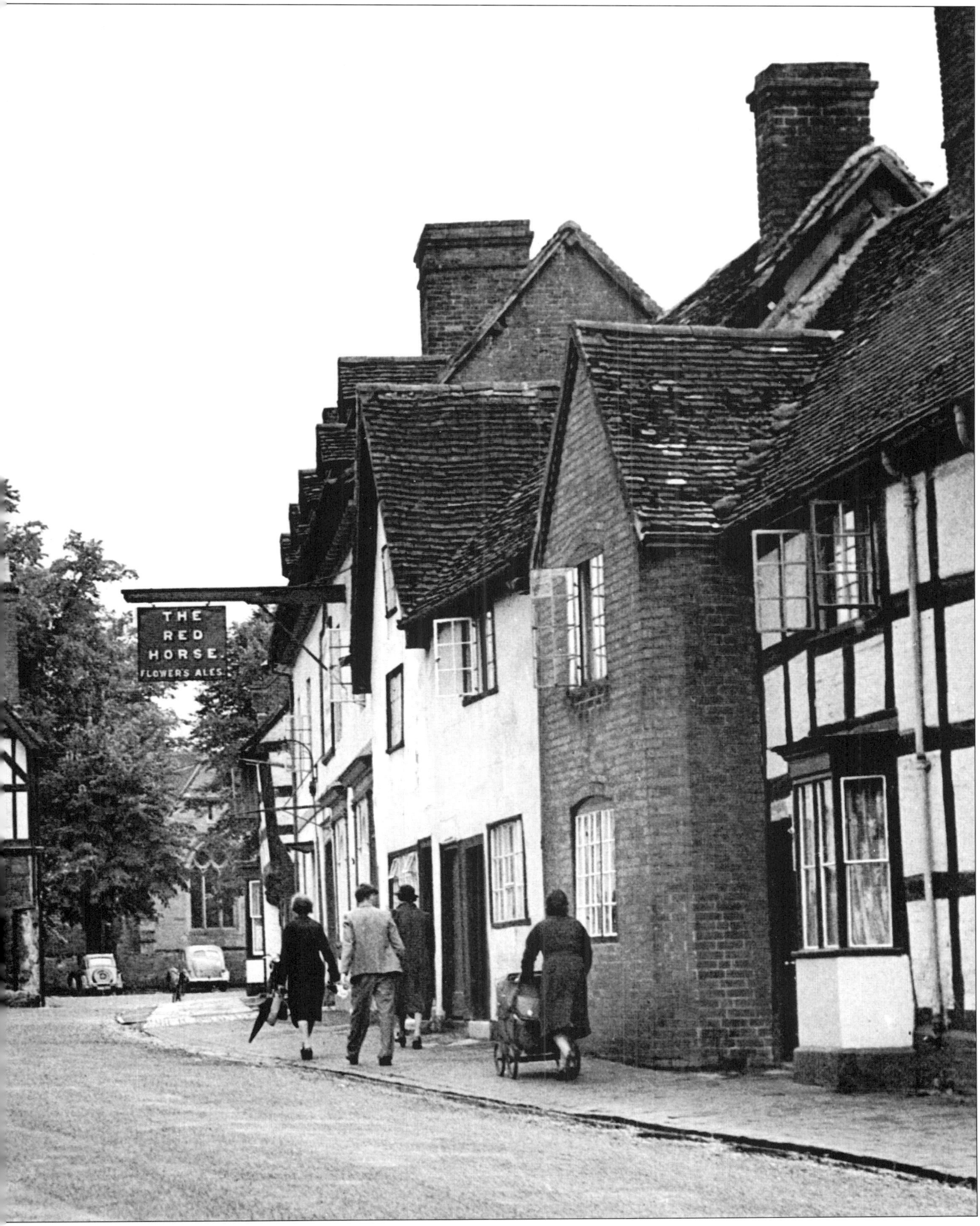

A113016

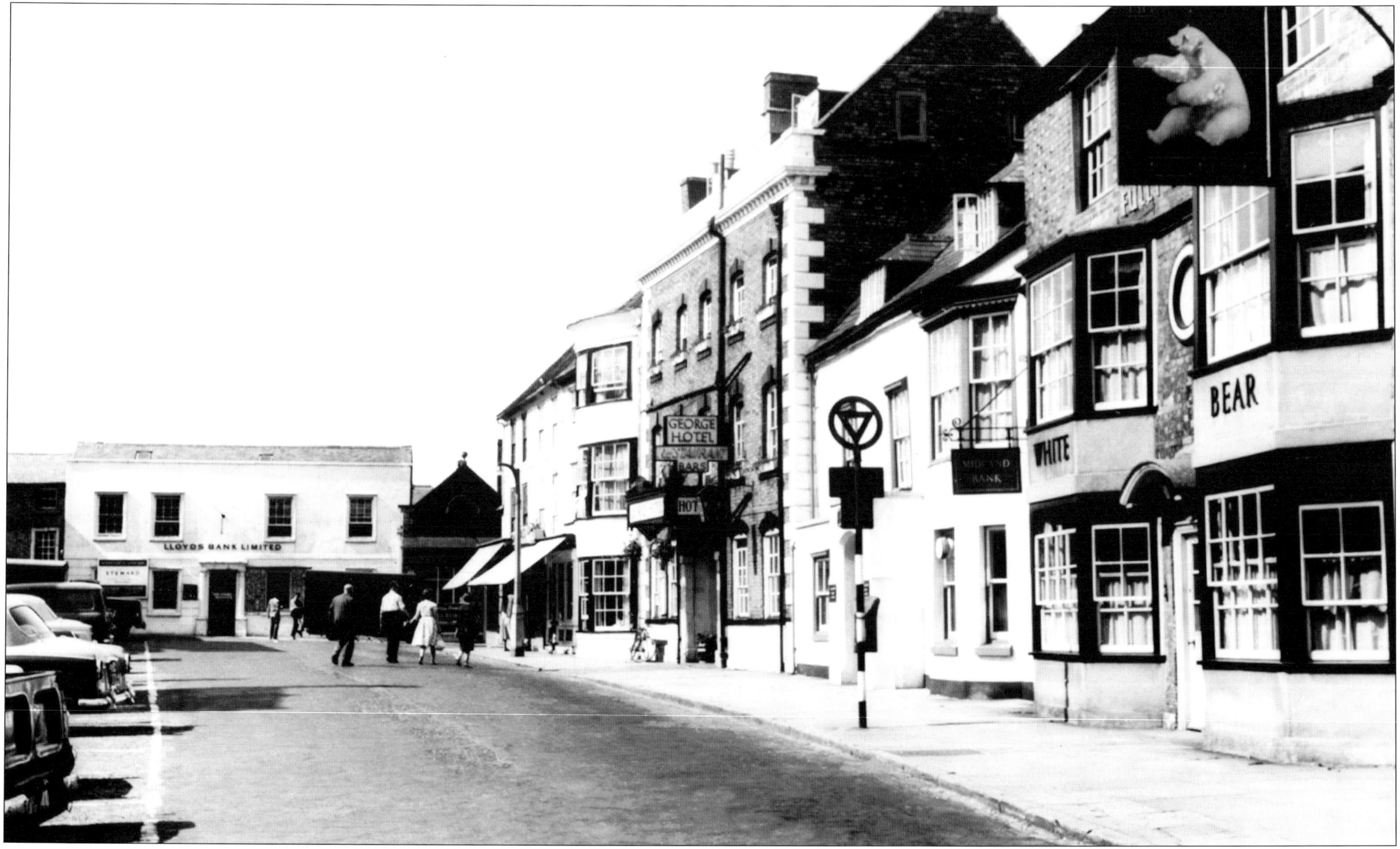

THE HIGH STREET, SHIPSTON-ON-STOUR, *c.*1960. S296016

In the 1920s the Auto Cycle Union (similar to the AA and RAC) recommended both the George Hotel and Ye Olde White Bear as being suitable for its members.

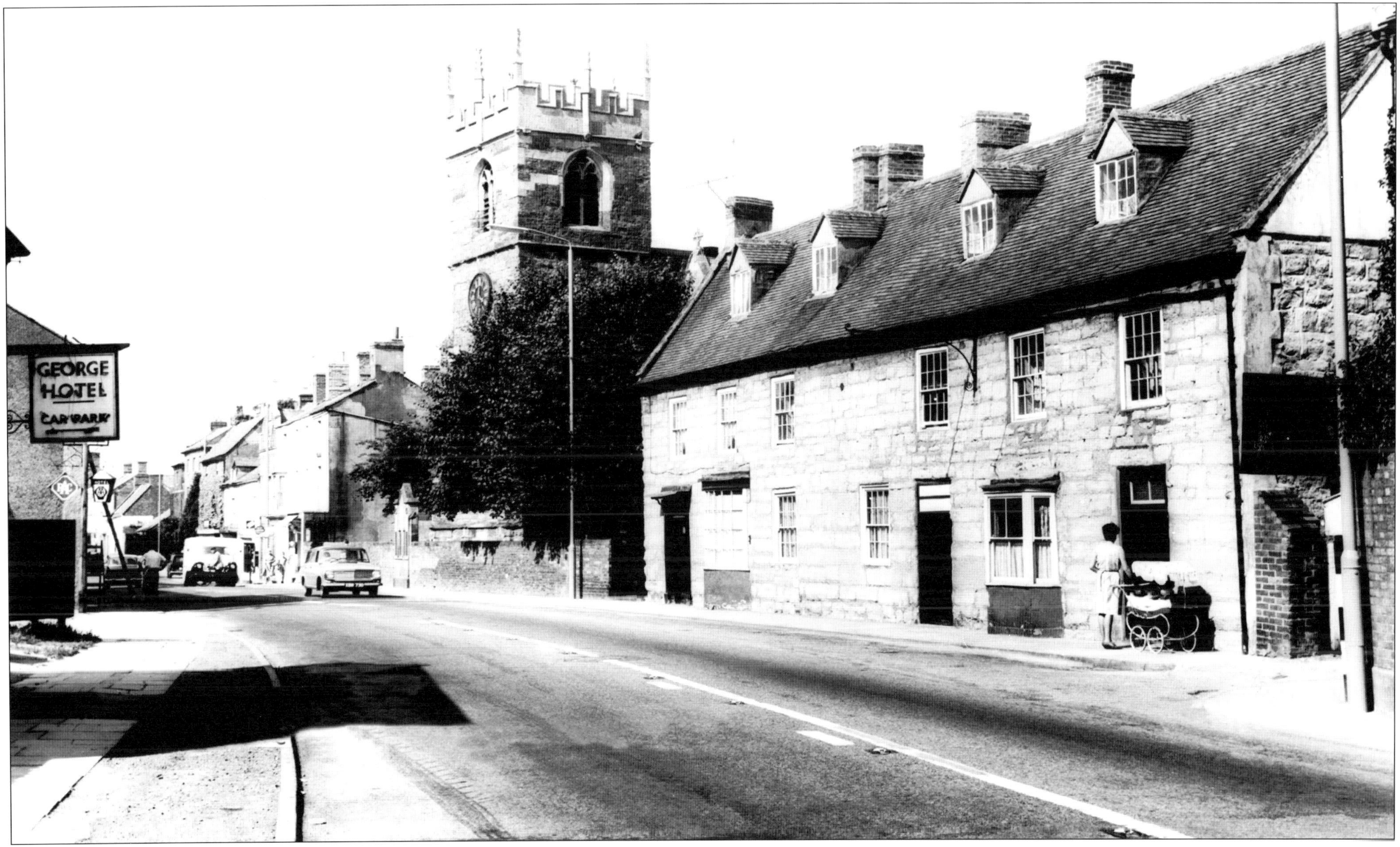

CHURCH STREET, SHIPSTON-ON-STOUR, *c*.1960. S296021

By this date the town had a population of around 2,700. The parish church was designed by G H Street.

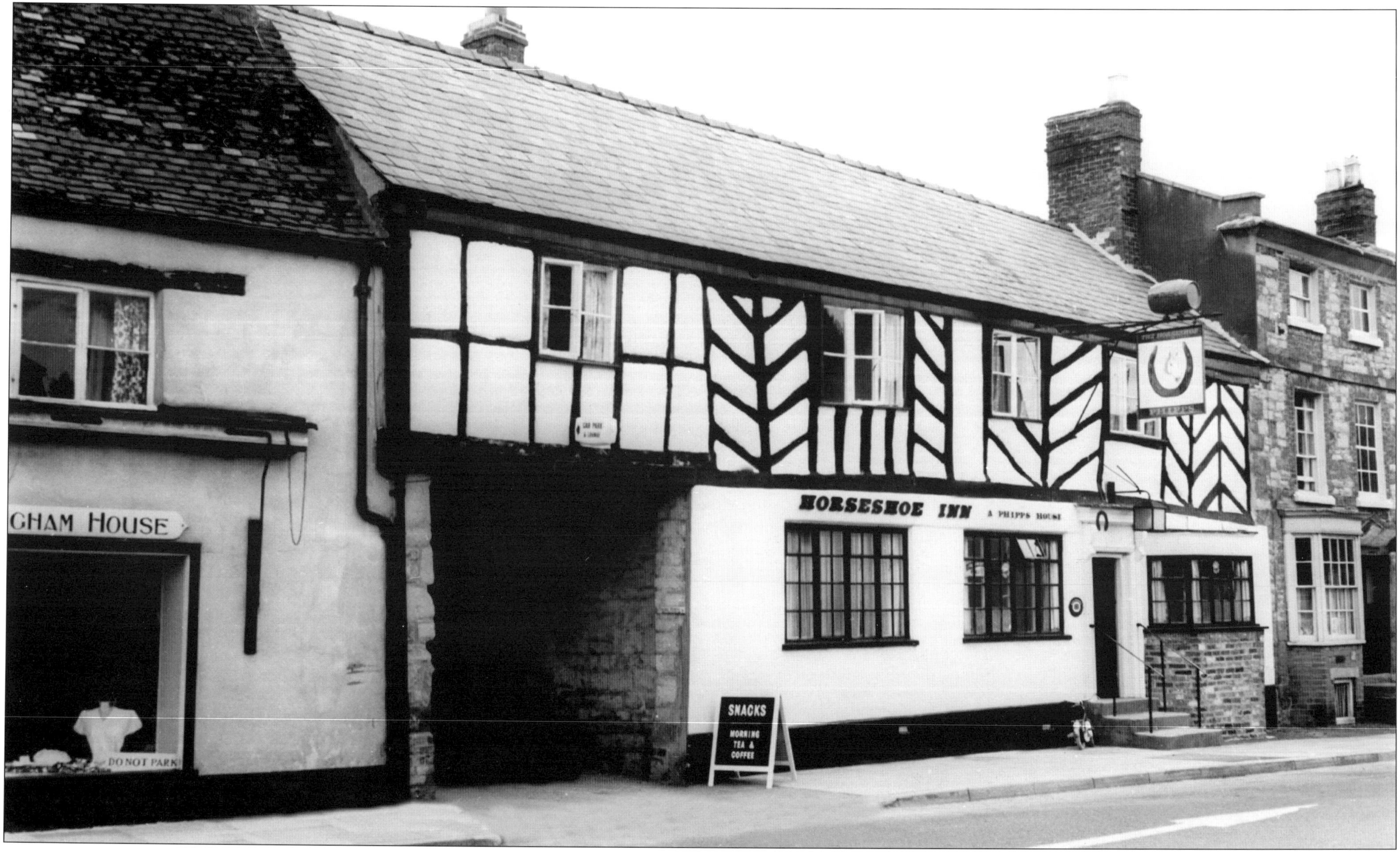

THE HORSESHOE INN, SHIPSTON-ON-STOUR, *c*.1960. S296026

This establishment was one of a number of interesting old hostelries still standing. Another was the thatched-roofed Black Horse.

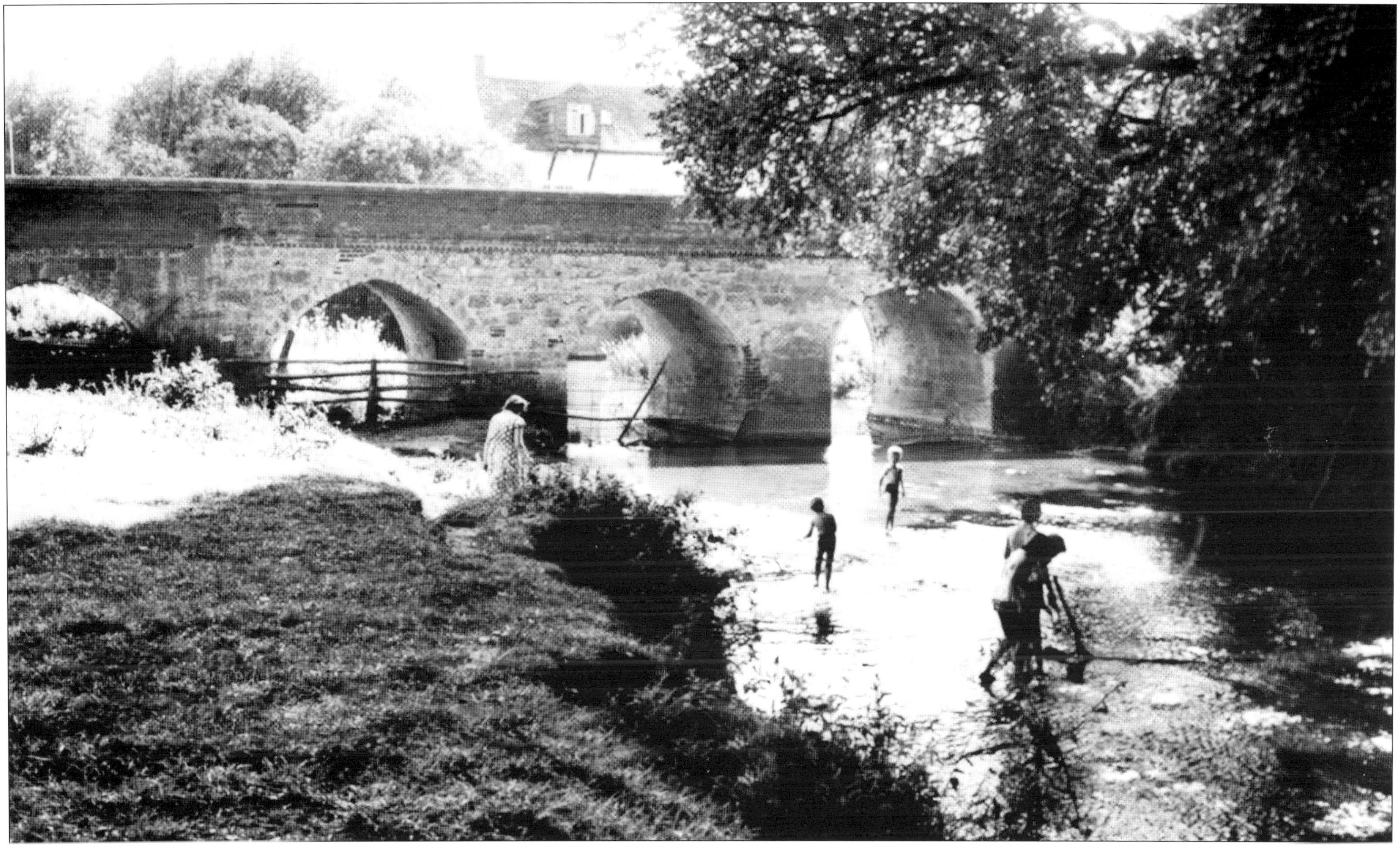

THE BRIDGE OVER THE RIVER, SHIPSTON-ON-STOUR, *c.*1960. S296023

It is many a year since sheep were herded across the bridge to the local market.

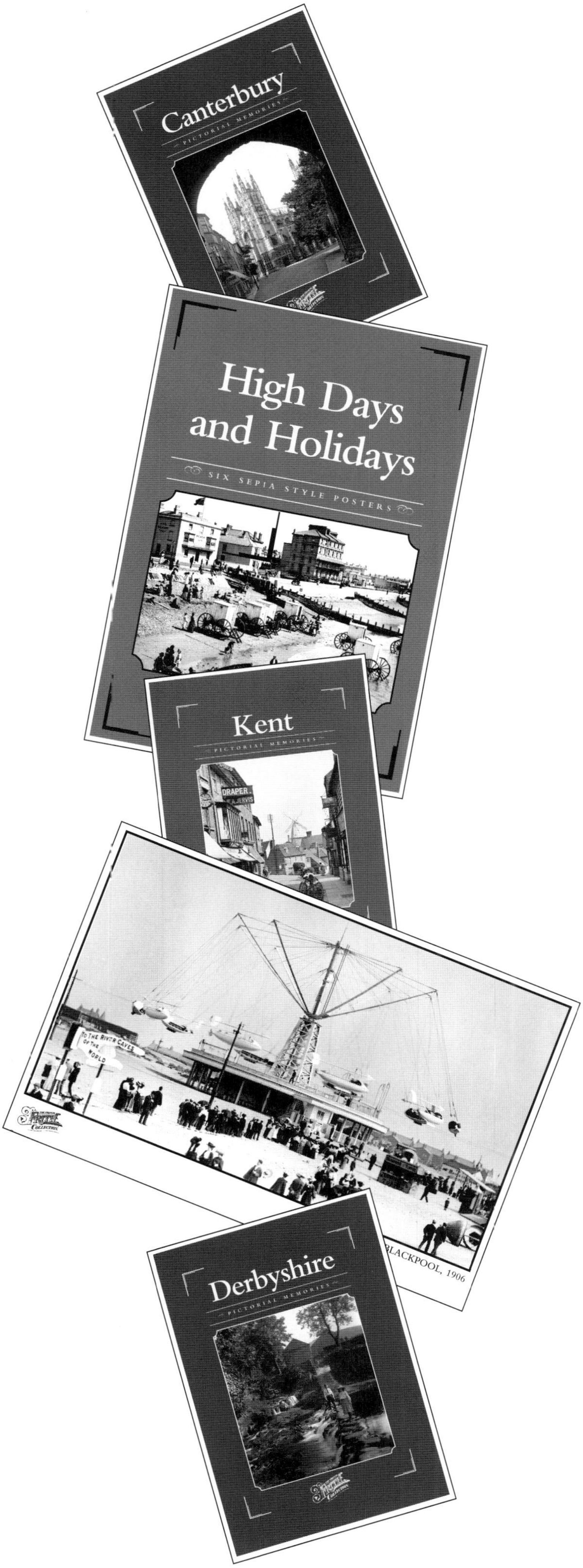
Canterbury
PICTORIAL MEMORIES
High Days and Holidays
SIX SEPIA STYLE POSTERS
Kent
PICTORIAL MEMORIES
DRAPER
BLACKPOOL, 1906
Derbyshire
PICTORIAL MEMORIES